CONTESTED CATEGORIES

Theory, Technology and Society

Series Editor: Ross Abbinnett, University of Birmingham, UK

Theory, Technology and Society presents the latest work in social, cultural and political theory, which considers the impact of new technologies on social, economic and political relationships. Central to the series are the elucidation of new theories of the humanity-technology relationship, the ethical implications of techno-scientific innovation, and the identification of unforeseen effects which are emerging from the techno-scientific organization of society.

With particular interest in questions of gender relations, the body, virtuality, penality, work, aesthetics, urban space, surveillance, governance and the environment, the series encourages work that seeks to determine the nature of the social consequences that have followed the deployment of new technologies, investigate the increasingly complex relationship between 'the human' and 'the technological', or addresses the ethical and political questions arising from the constant transformation and manipulation of humanity.

Contested Categories
Life Sciences in Society

Edited by

SUSANNE BAUER
University of Copenhagen, Denmark

AYO WAHLBERG
London School of Economics and Political Science, UK

ASHGATE

Published by
Ashgate Publishing Limited
Wey Court East
Union Road
Farnham
Surrey, GU9 7PT
England

Ashgate Publishing Company
Suite 420
101 Cherry Street
Burlington
VT 05401-4405
USA

www.ashgate.com

British Library Cataloguing in Publication Data
Contested categories : studies of the life sciences in
  society. -- (Theory, technology and society)
  1. Human body (Philosophy) 2. Categories (Philosophy)
  3. Life sciences--Classification--Social aspects.
  I. Series II. Bauer, Susanne. III. Wahlberg, Ayo.
  570.1'2-dc22

Library of Congress Cataloging-in-Publication Data
Bauer, Susanne.
  Contested categories : life sciences in society / by Susanne Bauer, Ayo Wahlberg.
    p. cm. -- (Series--theory, technology, and society)
  Includes bibliographical references and index.
  ISBN 978-0-7546-7618-8 (hardback) -- ISBN 978-0-7546-9867-8 (ebook)
  1. Social medicine. 2. Medical sciences--Social aspects. 3. Life sciences--Social aspects. I.
Wahlberg, Ayo. II. Title.
  RA418.B38 2009
  362.1--dc22

2009022612

ISBN: 978-0-7546-7618-8 (hbk)
ISBN: 978-0-7546-9867-8 (ebk)

Mixed Sources
Product group from well-managed
forests and other controlled sources
www.fsc.org Cert no. SA-COC-1565
© 1996 Forest Stewardship Council
FSC

Printed and bound in Great Britain by
MPG Books Group, UK

Contents

List of Figures and Tables

Notes on Contributors

Susanne Bauer is a research fellow at Medical Museion, University of Copenhagen (Project: Danish Biomedicine 1955–2005) and at the Department of European Ethnology at Humboldt University Berlin (Project: Imagined Europeans). She holds a Dr of Public Health (University of Bielefeld, Germany) and a MSc in environmental science (TU Berlin). Recent publications include "Mining data, gathering variables, and recombining information: the flexible architecture of epidemiological studies" in *Studies in History and Philosophy of Biological and Biomedical Sciences*, 2008, 39: 415–26 and "Societal and ethical issues in human biomonitoring: a view from science studies" in *Environmental Health*, 2008, 7(Suppl 1): S10.

Andrew S. Balmer is a postgraduate research student based at the Institute for Science and Society at the University of Nottingham. His research is primarily focused on lie detection technology, though more broadly on neuroscience findings and how they are dispersed throughout society, where they find root and how they change their environment.

Adam Bencard is a postdoctoral researcher at Medical Museion, University of Copenhagen, working on philosophical issues relating to the study of bodies in history, as part of the project "Danish biomedicine 1955–2005: Integrating medical museology and historiography in the study of recent biomedicine", funded by the NovoNordisk Foundation. His work is currently focused on issues surrounding the concept of "presence" and its relationship to materiality and objects. He explored these issues in his thesis, entitled *History in the Flesh: Investigating the Historicized Body* (University of Copenhagen, 2007).

Murray Goulden is a research fellow at the Institute for Science and Society, part of the University of Nottingham, UK. He recently completed his PhD in Science and Technology Studies, which is entitled *Excavating Humanness: Palaeoanthropology at the Human-Animal Boundary*. The thesis focuses on the process of constructing humanness in 'missing link' figures, and the interactions that take place between science and non-science knowledge claims over such individuals. During the analysis the boundaries of both human – nonhuman animal, and science – nonscience culture, are explored, with particular interest in the relationship between ambiguity and scientific certainty. The case studies featured in the PhD are Piltdown man, discovered in 1912, and the recent case of Flores Man, the famed 'hobbit'. Publications: "Bringing bones to life: how science made Piltdown man human" in *Science as Culture*, 2007, 16(4): 333–57 and "Boundary-work and the human-animal binary: Piltdown man, science, and the media" in *Public Understanding of Science*, 2009, 18(3): 275–91.

Lene Koch is Professor of Health Policy Analysis at the Institute of Public Health, University of Copenhagen and is currently Head of the Department of Health Services Research. She has done extensive research and published widely on the history of genetics and eugenics and social studies of genetics and reproductive technology and has recently focused on clinical implications of stem cell research. Her doctoral dissertation is published in two books, *Racehygiejne i Danmark 1920–56* on eugenics, and *Tvangssterilisation i Danmark 1924–67* on involuntary sterilization (both Copenhagen, Gyldendal, 2000). Her work has appeared in monographs, edited collections, journals including *Social Science of Medicine* and the *Scandinavian Journal of History*.

Mianna Meskus works as a postdoctoral researcher at the Department of Sociology, University of Helsinki. Her doctoral dissertation book *Elämän tiede: Tutkimus lääketieteellisestä teknologiasta, vanhemmuudesta ja perimän hallinnasta* (Tampere: Vastapaino, 2009) discusses the medical government of human heredity, with specific focus on the history of clinical genetics in Finland, the development of prenatal screening technologies, and their implications for the female body and parenthood. Her previous research work has concerned Finnish abortion policy and power analysis on which she has published several articles in Finnish and one in English: "To exclude or to enclose? Medicalization of abortion in Finland, 1900–1950" in *Scandinavian Journal of History*, 2005, 30(1): 45–60. In addition she has published articles in Finnish on private insurance and the history of risk rationality.

Amrita Mishra is a Postdoctoral Fellow with the Technoscience and Regulation Research Unit of the Department of Bioethics, Dalhousie University, Halifax, Canada. She has been a Research Fellow at the Institute for Advanced Studies in Science, Technology and Society, Graz (2008–2009), working on the sociological aspects of cancer biomarker research. In 2008 she received her PhD from the Jawaharlal Nehru University India. Her doctoral dissertation, grounded in the sociology of scientific knowledge, examined relations of power in an Indian life science laboratory. She has been awarded fellowships by the Indian Council of Medical Research and the University Grants Commission of India. Her post-doctoral research looks at the regulatory challenges and implications of vaccines against oncogenic HPV strains, in the Canadian context, with a focus on Nova Scotia.

Cecily Palmer is based the Institute for Science and Society, The University of Nottingham, UK. She has recently been awarded her PhD thesis in Science and Society. Her research, titled "Humane Collections: exploring ontology and ethos at Human Biological Material (HBM) collections", examines the construction of materials sourced from the human body as both instrumentally and culturally valuable and significant entities, and explores related ideas regarding the ethical and legitimate collection of these materials across a number of UK collection initiatives. Her research involves a comparison of historic teaching and educational HBM collections with contemporary biomedical research collection initiatives in order to explore the ways in which expectations regarding the acceptable collection and use of HBM, produced by diverse constructions of this material, are being negotiated and managed in practice in a modern UK context.

Malin Noem Ravn is an anthropologist, currently working as a postdoctoral researcher at the Department of Interdisciplinary Studies of Culture, Norwegian University of Science and Technology (NTNU), Trondheim. She is studying cultural discourses of twins as part of the project "Perceptions of gender, genes and reproduction", funded by the Norwegian Research Council. Her Dr.polit. thesis was a cultural analysis of contemporary Norwegian discourses of the two bodies of pregnancy; the pregnant woman's and the foetus'. Recent publications include: "A matter of free choice? Some structural and cultural influences on the decision to have or not to have children in Norway", in *Barren States: The Population "Implosion" in Europe*, 2005, edited by C.B. Douglass. Berg Publishers.

Nete Schwennesen is a sociologist, currently working as a postgraduate research student at the Institute of Public Health, University of Copenhagen, where she studies the social implications of prenatal risk assessment. She holds an MA in social science from Copenhagen and Aalborg University, Denmark, and a Master in contemporary sociology from Lancaster University, UK. In 2005 she was a Marie Curie fellow at Science and Technology Studies Unit (SATSU), University of York, UK. Recent publications include: "Practising Informed Choice: Decision Making and Prenatal Risk Assessment - The Danish Experience" in *Disclosure Dilemmas: Ethics of Genetic Prognosis after the 'Right to Know/Not to Know' Debate*, edited by Christoph Rehmann-Sutter and Hansjakob Müller, Ashgate, 2009 and "Beyond informed choice: Prenatal risk assessment, decision-making and trust" in *Nordic Journal of Applied Ethics* 2 (1): 11–31, 2008.

Ayo Wahlberg is a Research Fellow at the BIOS Centre, London School of Economics and Political Science, United Kingdom, working as part of BIONET, an EU-China collaboration on the ethical governance of biomedical research funded by the European Commission's 6th Framework Programme. He holds a PhD in Sociology from the LSE and an MSc in International Development Studies and Social Science from Roskilde University, Denmark. Academic publications include "Above and beyond superstition: western herbal medicine and the decriminalizing of placebo" in *History of the Human Sciences*, 2008, 21(1): 77–101 and "Measuring progress – calculating the life of nations" in *Distinktion: Scandinavian Journal of Social Theory*, 2007, 14: 65–82. Together with Linsey

McGoey he has guest edited a special issue of *BioSocieties* (2007, Vol. 2(1)) on the construction and governance of randomized controlled trials.

Preface and Acknowledgments

The idea for this book came about in close synergy with the Postgraduate Life Sciences and Society Network (PLSSN) which was formed in 2005 by a group of social science researchers grappling with different aspects of life sciences in the United Kingdom and Denmark. The group has met three times over the last four years, in London (2005), Copenhagen (2007) and Helsinki (2008). Participants at the meeting in Copenhagen in January 2007 – which was titled 'Contested Categories' and hosted by Medical Museion, University of Copenhagen with support from BioCampus, University of Copenhagen – decided to bring their papers together in this edited volume.

The editors would like to express their sincere thanks to Hanne Jessen for her engagement and efforts in helping to bring this book project to life. We would also like to thank all participants at the different PLSSN symposiums over the years, as it is through the stimulating debates and discussions held at these events that the ideas for this book have been collectively unfolded. We would in particular like to thank Sarah Franklin, Lene Koch, Nikolas Rose, Uffe Juul Jensen, Thomas Söderqvist, Gísli Pálsson, Ilpo Helén, Herbert Gottweis, Adriana Petryna and Teresa Kuwalik for their contributions and support at the symposiums; we thank Nete Schwennesen, Annette VB Jensen, Megan Clinch, Hanne Jessen, Mikko Jauho and Mianna Meskus for making these workshops happen. For support in editing and proofreading the final manuscript many thanks to Helle Nordberg.

Susanne Bauer would like to thank her colleagues both at Medical Museion, University of Copenhagen and, more recently, at the Department of European Ethnology, Humboldt University Berlin for support and much inspiration on how to study the culture of biomedical sciences.

Ayo Wahlberg would like to thank his colleagues at the BIOS Centre, London School of Economics for providing such a fertile and innovative *milieu* in which to think about life sciences in 21st century societies.

Susanne Bauer and Ayo Wahlberg
Copenhagen

Foreword

Gísli Pálsson

The modern age is characterized by extensive reconfiguration of life itself, a spectacular blurring of categories and a bewildering complexity of biosocial realities and associated technologies. This reconfiguration obviously needs detailed analysis for solid understanding of the late-modern human condition and for informed discussion and decision-making. Focusing on a series of case studies in the Nordic context, the United Kingdom and India, this timely volume draws attention to the practices of bio-technologies – in the literal sense of the crafting and fashioning of life – and their implications for several central issues currently on the agenda. All of these issues relate, directly or indirectly, to one or more of the following themes: emerging notions of personhood, the rethinking of relations of kinship, and debates on human responsibility and the treatment of human bodily material – in laboratories, biomedical institutions, and, of course, in the every-day 'real' world out there which most of us inhabit.

While the social sciences and the humanities have an important role to play on this front, it is by no means self-evident how one should proceed. Overall, it seems, there is tension between, on the one hand, those who seek to provide firm guidance regarding the rules of the game – what *ought* to be done, establishing the *right* way to go with respect to the refashioning and reproduction of bodily material and information – and, on the other hand, those who prefer to focus on 'thick' description, understanding what *is*, how things *really* are. The editors, however, rightly warn that such a distinction may be overly simplistic and detrimental. Surely, good governance demands sensibility to the contours and events of the real world and, likewise, good description needs to attend to moral considerations.

One of the central themes of this book is the categories people apply to living material. Like social discourse, more generally, categories both inform and are informed by the social life in which they are embedded. As speech acts they *do* something apparently more or less on their own, naming the world, not unlike personal names that have fascinated social thinkers for centuries. Drawing upon Lévy-Bruhl's perspective, Bodenhorn and vom Bruck suggest it is 'particularly striking that names have not featured in analyses of the body because they engage all crucial aspects of embodied experience: identification, moral relations, power, the gendering and sexualizing of bodies, and displacement ...' (2006: 20). In a very real sense, the properties of names become embodied in the persons hosting them, through the collective force of the discursive community.

Human bodies are not only cultured through the manipulation and reproduction of bodily material, they also become more and more dependent on technological aids such as artificial limbs and pacemakers, repairing or overcoming the constraints of the body. Increasingly, humans can be described as cyborgs, cybernetic organisms combining both natural and artificial systems. As a result, one can envisage a new discourse on human evolution in the not-so distant future, a discourse similar to, and yet radically different from, the early discourse on the 'missing links' between human and pre-human primates. The category of the human, it seems, will need to be distinguished from, and related to, the post-human as well as the pre-human.

Be that as it may, we are entitled to ask: What are the boundaries of bodies and technologies? Significantly, a leading international company in non-invasive orthopaedics, the Iceland-based Össur, uses the slogan 'life without limits' to advertise its work and products focusing on enhancing the 'natural' body. As new hybrid couplings are created through the crafting of new prostheses upon yet other prostheses, what constitutes the host and what would be the attachment? How do the subjectivities of people with crafted technological aids compare with those of recipients of human and animal organs? With the coupling of artificial intelligence and prosthetics, such questions have become more pressing than before.

One of the central themes addressed in this volume is that of the role of imagery and metaphors in discussions of human bodies and, more generally, life itself. Intensive genetic research over the past decades has revealed what are usually seen as the biologically encoded instructions necessary for constructing and maintaining a living example of an organism. The program theory of genes that suggests genetic information is encoded in DNA prior to development, however, a powerful paradigm in the modern world, is also the result of a particular conceptual and social history, drawing upon a far-reaching Western discourse of codes and messages evident in a diversity of fields including anthropology, linguistics, and biology.

What humans make of life itself is one aspect of what has been referred to as the 'culturing' of life. At the heart of modern science and its take on life is an interesting paradox: it is often acknowledged that the genetic code needs to be taken quite seriously as the bedrock of life, but at the same time it is emphasized that it is not a real code but only a metaphor. Biosemiotics, a growing interdisciplinary science, attempts to remedy the paradox by introducing meaning into biology (Barbieri 2008). According to biosemiotics the cell is a semiotic system complete with signs and signified, much like cultural semiosis. To what extent, we may ask, have the fields of biosemiotics and similar representations on the meaning in, and of, life gained a new boost with the new genetics, what are the benefits and drawbacks, and to what extent do such perspectives need to be qualified by introducing perspectives from epigenetics and developmental systems theory? Might it be argued that biosemiotics offers another way out of the dualistic nature/culture trap, much like, perhaps, the notion of biosociality? Or is it, perhaps, just one more reductionist approach, bypassing the relational and processual dimensions of life. For many social scientists and humanities scholars, the extension of semiotic discourse to life itself is both ethnocentric and misleading.

Several scholars have drawn attention to the parallels between imagery relating to on the one hand, human fetuses and the womb, and, on the other, the celestial world (Pálsson 2009). Duden (1993), for example, explores the path-breaking photographs of Lennart Nilsson documenting 'the beginning of life', published in the *Life* magazine in 1965 and 1990, pointing out that the photographs, the first ones of their kind, and the accompanying text in *Life* repeatedly juxtapose fetuses and astronauts, bodies and space. The 1990 issue elaborates on the first stages of human life by means of celestial language and imagery, starting with a fetus aged two hours:

> Like an eerie planet floating through space, a woman's egg or ovum ... has been ejected by one of her ovaries into a fallopian tube ... The luminous halo around the ovum is a cluster of nutrient cells feeding the hungry egg (quoted in Duden 1993: 13).

Eight days later, *Life* goes on:

> The blastocyst has landed! Like a lunar module, the embryo facilitates its landing on the uterus with leg-like structures composed of sugar molecules on the surface (quoted in Duden 1993: 14).

The fascination with the fetus and outer space underlines human curiosity at the border of the category of the unknown, the urge to extend one's sight by zooming in or out beyond the 'natural' horizon of the human eye. New images and visual horizons, however, sometimes take a life of their own, informing perception and politics. Thus, astronauts tend to speak of a gestalt shift as a result of their voyages into space, when seeing Earth from a distance, a 'Gaia' perspective that seems to facilitate global, environmental concerns. No doubt, images from space, including images from Neil Armstrong's 'giant leap for mankind' when landing on the Moon, have informed public discussions on Earth on several scores. Likewise, the kind of fetal imagery presented by the famous *Life* photographs is likely to have had enormous impact on public discussions of biopolitics, in particular abortion and the rights of women. Duden (1993) addresses the issue with reference to what she calls the 'Nilsson Effect', emphasizing the shift in emphasis as a consequence of Nilsson's photography from the pregnant woman to the fetus and the resultant alteration in power balance between those advocating 'pro choice' and others in favour of 'pro life'.

Some works make similar analogies and connections between fetuses and astronauts, from the vantage point of outer space. Thus, Sofia argues the human fetus operates as a symbol for Earth: 'It is a cosmic symbol. It is not entirely inappropriate that the planet be represented by a signifier of unborn life, for it presently contains all of the possibilities for future life forms. From this perspective, disarmament might be seen as an act to prevent a cosmic abortion' (1984: 56). While Sofia's article is highly playful and speculative, it draws attention to military concerns and the Cold War and their impact for both biopolitics and space exploration.

Given the many ways (and the escalation) of the culturing of life, how should one respond to the simple question Schrödinger addressed early on (Schrödinger 1992 [1944]), namely 'What is Life?' Schrödinger and his contemporaries tended to frame the question mainly within the context of biology. It is important however, to explore how and to what extent the response to Schrödinger's profound question needs to be broader than he could possibly have imagined at the time of writing, prior to the new genetics. Life, indeed, is a contested category. While work in this domain remains heavily theoretical, empirical work adds important reality checks. Collectively, the articles in this volume help chart the space of emerging biosocial realities, theorizing the contested sites and categories involved in their making and ethnographically documenting the pertinent key issues. This is, indeed, one of the important roles of the humanities and the social sciences in current discussions.

References

Barbieri, M. 2008. *Introduction to Biosemiotics: The New Biological Synthesis.* Dordrecht: Springer.

Bodenhorn, B. and vom Bruck, G. 2006. 'Entangled in histories': an introduction to the anthropology of naming, in *The Anthropology of Names and Naming*, edited by G. vom Bruck and B. Bodenhorn. Cambridge, UK: Cambridge University Press, 1–30.

Duden, B. 1993. *Disembodying Women: Perspectives on Pregnancy and the Unborn*, Cambridge: Harvard University Press.

Pálsson, G. 2009. Celestial bodies: Lucy in the sky, in *Humans in Outer Space: Interdisciplinary Odysseys*, edited by L. Codignola and K.-U. Schrogl. New York: Springer, 69–81.

Schrödinger, E. 1992 [1944]. *What is Life?* Cambridge: Cambridge University Press.

Sofia, Z. 1984. Exterminating fetuses: abortion, disarmament, and the sexo-semiotics of extraterrestrialism. *Diacritics*, 14(2), 47–59.

Introduction
Categories of Life

Ayo Wahlberg and Susanne Bauer

Oncomouse, intracytoplasmic sperm injection, foetal scans, gene chips. These have been some of the iconic images used to capture and convey, for some, a sense of rapid advance, progress and hope, while for others, a sense of abomination, fear and anxiety in life sciences research. Whether or not we are about to enter a bio-age, a posthuman future or an era of genetic programming, developments in the 'new' life sciences have come to feature prominently in discussions and debates about humanity's future. It is little wonder then that social scientists have taken to this emerging field and its attendant controversies, scandals, slippery slopes, possibilities, promises and hopes. Yet, the suggestion is that social studies of the life sciences mark a break with philosophical and bioethical engagements with the same. If the latter are concerned with principles of autonomy, authenticity, beneficence, justice and dignity when developing their arguments, the former engage with empirical sites such as laboratories, clinics, biotech companies, patient groups, families and policy making arenas. As always, however, the break is not so neat. Some social scientists have long pointed to injustices and dangers in scientific and medical practice while some philosophers and ethicists have advocated for a more 'grounded' form of empirical or applied bioethics.

As such, when scoping the growing field of life sciences in society studies, it is perhaps more useful to distinguish not so much between philosophic and empirical approaches to engaging with the life sciences, but rather between the hazards and promises that have been attributed to the life sciences as well as the tensions and interactions between them. Developments in the life sciences are seen, on the one hand, as dangerous when leading to eugenic slippery slopes, irresponsible hype, dissolutions of authenticity, clandestine body parts markets and exploitations of desperation. Francis Fukuyama (2002), Jürgen Habermas (2003), Leon Kass (President's Council on Bioethics 2003), Troy Duster (2003) and many others have highlighted concerns about troubling tendencies in biological research. For these writers there is a sense that new technological possibilities for cognitive enhancement, reproductive selection and genetic manipulation are putting our very human nature, dignity and authenticity on the line while also reinforcing social inequities. From a more empirical perspective, Nancy Scheper-Hughes (2002), Kaushik Sunder Rajan (2006), Catherine Waldby (2006) and Adriana Petryna (2006) have highlighted the dark side of bioscience and the taxing toll of globalized organ, gamete, blood and tissue trade, postgenomic research as well as clinical trials especially on socio-economically and/or medically vulnerable human subjects. Still others have warned of alienating and exploitative effects of processes of geneticization, biologization and commodification that the life sciences are seen to have put in motion as well as of distorting and corrupting effects of media-led hyping of life science research (Lippman 1992; Nightingale and Martin 2004; Rose et al. 1984; Shiva 1997). The emphasis in these accounts is again on the social inequities that surround global bioscientific and biomedical practices.

On the other hand, life sciences research is seen as promissory when bringing scientists, clinicians, venture capitalists, patients and families together in a common quest to save and improve lives. Far from approaching developments in advanced life sciences with trepidation, posthumanist and transhumanist theorists have embraced new (future) possibilities for enhancement, immortality, and expansion of human capacities to promote 'personal growth beyond our current biological limitations' (World Transhumanist Association 2002). For these theorists, the promise of bioscience is utopian and arguments are often more hypothetically than empirically informed. At the same time, a number of empirical social studies of the life sciences have also highlighted the promissory nature of bioscience (Brown et al. 2006), albeit against a backdrop of the potentially negative consequences of hype, not to mention potential exploitation of human subjects. These include empirical accounts of how bio-social communities and biological/genetic/pharmaceutical citizens have emerged out of these new configurations of governing life as individuals and groups coalesce around common vital objectives (Ecks 2005; Gibbon and Novas 2007; Heath et al. 2004; Koch and Hoeyer 2006; Rose and Novas 2005). Moreover, ethnographic studies have showed how new reproductive technologies, new genetics and neuroscience can destabilize and transform self understandings and worldviews, while also mobilizing communities and individuals (Franklin 1997; Franklin and Lock 2003; Konrad 2005; Pálsson 2007; Rapp 1999; Vrecko 2006).

Whether hazards or promises are highlighted, there is nonetheless broad agreement that bioscience and biotechnology are impacting on human lives, and in the process, generating new forms of knowledge, subjectivity, capital and value. Some have argued that 'life itself' at the level of tissues, cells, DNA and molecules is being transformed through genetic reprogramming or cellular recapacitation, further troubling any supposed nature/culture divide (Franklin et al. 2000; Rabinow 1996; 1999; Rose 2006). Sarah Franklin says of Dolly, the world's first 'cloned' sheep: 'It is difficult to get to grips with Dolly because she slips out of familiar kinds; her existence does not parse within familiar categories, or, rather, when she is fitted into them, they must twist and change to accommodate her unprecedented existence' (Franklin 2007: 28). Others have stressed the entanglements and simultaneity of nature/culture with the hybrids and heterogeneous assemblages of biocultures, biosociality and citizenship that are found when studying the sciences in society empirically (Latour 1993; Ong and Collier 2005).

It has also been suggested that a bio-economy, complete with new regimes of biocapital (Sunder Rajan 2006) and forms of biovalue (Waldby 2002; Waldby and Mitchell 2006), has emerged as 'vitality can now be decomposed, stabilized, frozen, banked, stored, commoditized, accumulated, exchanged, traded across time, across space, across organs and species, across diverse contexts and enterprises in the service of both health and wealth' (Rose 2007: 3). At the same time, new regimes for the governance of life technologies and science have emerged throughout the world albeit in different national and local forms (Gottweis et al. 2008; Jasanoff 2005). National ethics commissions, participatory consultations, ethical review boards, informed consent procedures, bioethical regulations and codes of conduct have been established in various conglomerations in order to navigate and negotiate the tensions between bioscience's dangers and promises, especially so in a context of scientific uncertainty. Beyond these new forms of capital and regimes of governance, the biosciences have also been shown to alter subjectivities and subject constitution in everyday life, as they are negotiated through a broad range of social practices from healthcare, reproductive technologies and the entry of biotechnologies into everyday lives through pharmaceuticals, GM foods and forms of personalized genetic testing.

Stabilization and contestation

Beyond the concern, fascination and hope that 21st century biosciences have evoked, the collection of studies of life sciences in society found in *Contested Categories* seeks to shift empirical focus from actor-networks, biological citizens, bio-cultures, bio-social communities, bio-economies or bio-governance regimes, to the categories that have both organized and emerged out of life sciences practice. While these former elements certainly feature in the chapters of this book, there is a clear focus on how life science categories come into play in clinical, laboratory, policy, public or personal contexts and in doing so how these can be transformed as well as take on new meanings. The aim is to relocate social inquiry from a domain of hazard-promise to ones of contestation-stabilization and negotiation-reconfiguration.

The chapters present a series of empirical studies that engage with the often shifting and day-to-day realities of life sciences categories as they circulate, inform practice and transform clinics, laboratories, policy arenas as well as public imaginations. Life sciences knowledge is something that is often produced through practice in the restricted sites of laboratories where humans, animals and other non-human actants form complex networks of experiment and data. Yet resulting biomedical categories of embryos, foetuses, genes, human biological materials, serious disease or genetic risk are never 'merely' technical, as they stray, acquire social identities and meanings as well as perform symbolic tasks in public debates, clinical settings or in doctor-patient interactions. Categories and categorization processes in life science research and practice are crucial in the sense that they allow certain objects to be grouped together, certain standards for practice to be formulated, certain limits or boundaries to be proscribed and also certain symbolic understandings to co-circulate among clinicians, patients, scientists and others. Yet, the practical stabilization that routines, regulations, codes of conduct or laboratory protocols afford is never shielded from contestation and negotiation, for example, through clinical encounters, mediated 'public understandings' or informed consent processes.

As such, it is with interlinkages between classifications, concepts, objects, boundaries, practices, understandings and subjects that the chapters in this book engage. Together, these chapters show, from different methodological and theoretical perspectives, how categories of life come to be taken up, contested as well as stabilized in laboratory settings, clinics and public domains. Categories and categorization processes play an important part in boundary-work, classification and taxonomy from bench to bedside, and a key theme emerging from this volume is that of tensions between, on the one hand, the necessity of more or less stable and fixed categories in organizing and guiding laboratory and clinical practice, and on the other, the flexibility and arbitrariness of such categories as they circulate. There is a constant interplay between contestation and stabilization of categories, as these are negotiated and reconfigured in diverse settings.

According to the Oxford English Dictionary, categories, in their most general sense, are terms given to certain *classes* of terms, things, or notions. They invoke similarity, relationship and kindness, while also demarcating, restricting and shielding. They form the parts of whole nomenclatures or taxonomies, i.e. systems of rational ordering, complete with logics and criteria of inclusion and exclusion. For many philosophers they are considered foundational for human experience and social scientists have long pointed to 'the tendency of mankind to classify out the universe' (Tylor 1899 cited in Lévi-Strauss 1969: 13) arguing that 'any classification is superior to chaos and even a classification at the level of sensible properties is a step towards rational ordering' (Lévi-Strauss 1966: 15). For Michel Foucault, this 'order is, at one and the same time, that which is given in things as their inner law, the hidden network that determines the way they confront one another, and also that which has no existence except in the grid created by a glance, an examination, a language; and it is only in the blank spaces of this grid that order manifests itself in depth as though already there, waiting in silence for the moment of its expression' (Foucault 1970: xx). At the same time, these very grids that underpin modern epistemologies and their ordering devices are historically and locally contingent. Different kinds of taxonomies perform different works of categorization; thinking in categories can be both flexible and rigid, imposing rules and boundaries which become negotiable as categories travel beyond localized spheres of practice.

As Bowker and Star (1999) have shown, the building up of ordered systems of classification requires a certain kind of work; they are of course not 'already there'. Instead they depend on infrastructures, technologies of classification, coding charts, indexes, computers, and the like. As they see it, categories 'arise from work and from other kinds of organized activity, including the conflicts over meaning that occur when multiple groups fight over the nature of a classification system and its categories' (Bowker and Star 1999: 285). There are boundaries to be maintained and exclusivities to be protected, yet 'boundary objects' are those that 'inhabit several communities of practices and satisfy the informational requirements of each of them' (ibid.: 297). Analytically scaling those up to the level of society from local and mundane practices leads to descriptions of whole 'boundary infrastructures' which form the grids of modern epistemologies, for perceptions as well as practices. Ubiquitous and infrastructural, categories according to Bowker and Star are something between a thing and an action, and they suggest that *categorical work* consists of 'the juggling of meanings (memberships and naturalizations)' (ibid.: 310). Categories touch things as much as people's lives; they can be extremely powerful yet also ambiguous and negotiable.

When analysing the history of statistical classifications of multiple personality as a disease category, Ian Hacking points to the subdivisions and rearrangements generated by practices of counting, as they create 'new slots [...] in which to fit and enumerate people' as well as 'new ways for people to be' (Hacking 1986: 223). His stories about 'making up people' by categories are always multiple; they can work as labelling from above but also from below as 'numerous kinds of human beings and human acts come into being hand in hand with our invention of the categories labelling them' (ibid.: 236). While it is always humans who do this work of classifying and categorizing, Hacking proposes a, albeit not too rigid, distinction between 'natural kinds' and 'human kinds'. 'It makes no difference to either mud or a mud puddle to call it "mud"' whereas 'classifying people works on people, changes them, and can even change their past' (Hacking 1995: 367, 369). This is Hacking's 'looping effect' whereby classifications of humans changes self-conception and behaviour which in turn demands revisions of classifications and theories, and so forth. His point reminds us that however 'exclusive' the work of classification might be to experts, technocrats and scientists in modern society, the effects of this work as classificatory systems and categories feed back into clinics, laboratories, parliaments, households and other 'human' settings can be personal and intimate.

Medical anthropologists have ventured for some time now that categories and classification systems themselves perform a certain amount of 'work' by providing individuals with ways of relating to, understanding and working upon their selves and others. They can, in a sense, be liberating or empowering when helping patients to 'make sense' of their situation by providing them with metaphors and symbols while also proposing purposive remedial actions (Kleinman 1988). Yet, they can also be divisive, exclusionary, subjugating or stigmatizing if used to compartmentalize certain people as deviant, criminal, poor, sick or apathetic (Becker 1963; Foucault 1967; Goffman 1968). The point being that when categories group together things human (be they social, cultural, biological or economic 'things'), there is a certain reflexive interaction, looping or choreography between categories and persons (their self-understandings, worldviews, lifeworlds, etc.) (Hacking 1986; Rose 2003; Thompson 2005).

Not only do categories and classifications inform grids of intelligibility and 'ways of being', they also inform 'ways of doing' in the form of clinical guidelines, laboratory protocols, good clinical practice criteria as well as more informal norms of practice in particular settings. The relations between ways of knowing and ways of doing have been central to Bachelard's (1984) notion of phenomenotechnology in his studies of what he saw as the 'technical activity' of thought carried out by chemists and physicists in their laboratories, as well as to Canguilhem's (1989) work on the role of biological concepts (e.g. of the normal, the pathological, the reflex or biological regulation) in experimentation and theorization. For Bachelard, realism and rationalism are not to be taken as opposites, rather each scientific experiment has to be approached as both a demonstration and an application so as to reduce 'the gap between explicated reality and applied thought' – 'to the extent that hypotheses have been linked to experiment, they must be considered just as real as the experiments themselves – they are "realized"' (Bachelard 1984: 10, 6). And for Canguilhem, it is the concept that is crucial in the development of methods of objectification for the very practical 'work' that it performs, not just in developing certain codes of observation or conventions of experimentation, but also in making experimentally-observed phenomena intelligible and practicable. It is the logic made possible by the concept that allows for and organizes practices of classification in the laboratory or clinic.

What is more, we have also learned from some four decades of laboratory ethnographies and science and technology studies how scientific facts are made and diseases are enacted through practices of biopsy, bioassay, cell culture, polymerase chain reaction, diagnosis, treatment, counselling and care (Latour 1987; Latour et al. 1986; Lynch 1993; Mol 2003; Pickering 1995; Rabinow 1999). Such studies have shown how inscription devices and 'blackboxing' are indispensable to the stabilization of statements and immutable mobiles in scientific practice. Yet they have also shown how blurred boundaries can create ambiguities, for example, when 'brain death' is diagnosed using apnea or doll's eye tests (Lock 2002), and also how there can be multiple stabilizations at play, for example, when it comes to 'doing disease': 'ontology in medical practice is bound to a specific site and situation. In a single medical building there *are* many different artheroscleroses... [yet] although artherosclerosis in the hospital comes in different versions, these somehow hang together' through a kind of coordination between lab technicians, machines, doctors, nurses, patients and others (Mol 2003: 55, 84). Categories cannot be detached from the mundane practices that they rely on.

Substances, processes and sites

In the chapters that follow, authors explore how life science categories and classifications come to be stabilized, contested, negotiated and reconfigured in a variety of different settings and sites, from museums featuring human tissue collections, oncology laboratories carrying out molecular analysis of cervical tumours, prenatal clinics, medical and scientific journals, popular literature as well as patient pamphlets and parent guides. They show how fixity can be hard to pin down, for example, when negotiating whether a foetus is a person, when maintaining the boundaries of a research site through strict protocols of research supervision or when contesting the classification of particular fossil remains as human. But they also show how necessary such fixity and order are for communication and negotiation through formalized procedures, guidelines and regulations as well as more informal conventions and norms.

All chapters share an empirical concern with how categories of life as well as categorization processes unfold in different contexts and settings. Methodologies and theoretical approaches are, however, not necessarily shared. While some authors have carried out ethnographic research in clinics, laboratories and anatomy and pathology museum collections, others examine and analyse scientific and popular media, patient literature or scientific journals. Some have interviewed patients and 'laypersons', others have interviewed scientists and clinicians and still others have interviewed none. This diversity is intentional, serving to underline the heterogeneity and pervasiveness of categories of life in contemporary society not only in regulations, texts and protocols, but also among people in their everyday lives. While we would not want to limit the breadth and depth of analysis in each chapter, we will point to four themes which consistently crop up, however fleetingly, throughout.

While 'life' is certainly not something exclusive to humanity, the chapters in this book do exclusively examine categories of human life. Indeed, Murray Goulden and Andrew Balmer (this volume) show us how politically contested and charged scientific demarcations of humans from animals can be through their analysis of controversies surrounding the classification of Piltdown man in the 19th century and *homo floriensis* in the 21st. To taxonomize archaeologically discovered remains under the *homo* family, we learn, is more ambiguous than the formalized classification systems that govern such species taxonomies might suggest. In her analysis of the troublesome nature of Human Biological Material (HBM) Cecily Palmer (this volume) shows us how biological material originating from humans (as opposed to from plants or animals) is negotiated as something 'different' or 'special' that begs controversies around dignity and respect, with profound implications for how it is stored, used and/or disposed of. The category of 'human', it seems, is something that needs protecting and shielding from outside incursions perhaps especially because it is seen to bestow certain qualities on biological objects, materials or species. It is a form of respect for human life that is also evident in distinctions between 'red' and 'green' biotechnology, between genetically modified foods/animals and bans on cloning and genetic modification of humans as well as between informed consent and coercion.

A second theme common to a number of chapters are the negotiations that infuse lived or 'lay' experiences with and of biomedical and biological knowledge, materials and substances. Malin Noem Ravn (this volume) revisits bodily substances through an analysis of how a number of pregnant women in Norway think and talk about 'blood' and 'genes' as bodily matter as well as how these categories are seen to influence personal identity. She shows how 'blood' is often viewed in terms of movement, nourishment and intimacy whereas genes are talked about more in terms of fixity, individual core and uniqueness. Yet neither is seen as all-encompassing, leaving scope for individuality and socialization. Through her interviews with tissue collection curators, Cecily Palmer also shows how human biological materials emerge as boundary objects for researchers, oscillating between 'scientific artefact objects' and 'personified human entities'. As she puts it, human materials can become 'unruly' once removed from the body, as they become manipulable and probe-able artefacts yet must still be treated and utilized with respect. Through ethnographic participation and interviews at a prenatal clinic in Denmark, Nete Schwennesen and Lene Koch (this volume) examine the making of foetal life through its visualization, quantification and interpretation in routine prenatal care involving ultrasound scans, risk assessments and consultations, which they argue constitute a process of *matter-ing*. The visual representation of the foetus through ultrasound they argue, building on Karen Barad's theory of agential realism, is made meaningful to involved actors through intra-action between ultrasound technologies, clinicians, quantified risk assessments and expecting couples. Each of these ethnographic studies of life categories (blood, genes, foetus, human biological material), tell us something about how they come to be taken up and negotiated in the everyday contexts of tissue collection curators or expecting couples as biological knowledge, technologies, substances and objects acquire social meanings. However technologized, molecular, detached, numerical or laboratory-based life sciences are today, when human life is the object it seems 'depersonalization' is never complete.

The place of metaphors, concepts, norms and rationalities (grids of intelligibility) in the formation and circulation of categories such as 'at risk pregnancies', the 'body' or 'serious disease' forms a third trope found in a number of chapters. Adam Bencard (this volume) juxtaposes and parallels transformations of conceptual metaphors in the life sciences and in the humanities. He argues that both fields have, until recently, privileged informational metaphors which read the 'body as a text' as seen in the rise of the gene as the 'book of life' on the one hand, and the 'linguistic turn' in historical studies of the body on the other. Yet, in both cases, he suggests, informational models are being challenged through a blurring or complicating of the genetic 'code' by proteomics and systems biology, and a reframing of the body in terms of lived experience rather than discourse and language. From a clinical perspective, Ayo Wahlberg (this volume) also juxtaposes biological norms which emerge out of genetic understandings of conditions such as cystic fibrosis, spinal muscular atrophy and Down's syndrome, with the social norms that he suggests inform estimations of quality of life, severity and suffering. Through an analysis of patient literature and parents' guides aimed at couples who are contemplating or have undergone carrier testing, preimplantation genetic diagnosis or prenatal diagnosis, and drawing on work by Canguilhem and Hacking, he argues that there is nothing in biology that can qualify a disease as serious, moderate or mild, as this latter task relies on negotiations between patients, parents and experts about what it is like 'living with a genetic condition'. From a historical perspective, Mianna Meskus (this volume) describes the institutionalization of prenatal testing and screening in the Finnish healthcare system over the last four decades. By reading Finnish life science journals, health policy documents and popular literature, she charts how rationalities of choice and risk (rather than population health or socio-economic cost reduction) came to organize prenatal screening and testing programmes in Finland with an emphasis on the autonomy and responsibility of pregnant women.

As noted earlier, the study of practices or 'ways of doing' has been a valuable approach when analysing the work of categorization in the life sciences field. A final motif in the empirical studies that follow is that of interlinkages between categories and particular 'ways of doing' scientific research or clinical practice. Through an in depth laboratory ethnography at a tumour genetics research site in India, Amrita Mishra (this volume) shows how laboratory settings are sites of negotiation of space and time regimes. Site access restrictions, spatial ordering within the laboratory, time schedules and virtual communication norms, she argues, all serve to co-produce a reliable and recognisable locale, and to protect it against incursions not only from 'outsiders' but also from possible contamination from within. The 'research laboratory' as a category is indispensable to life sciences work, and Mishra shows how its integrity and purity are constantly at stake. Susanne Bauer's chapter looks at the categorical work of epidemiological research practice. By analysing the levels of analyses and scales of investigation that are used in the science of population health, she shows how the seemingly fixed categories of population and individual, gene and environment, global and local are tied together in the research process, and circulate as deeply entangled or blended categories in society. Just as the social sciences operate through methodological conventions and 'epistemic communities' so too do the life sciences and biomedical practices, and as the chapters in this collection show, methodological innovation, conceptual development and 'discovery' are organized by categories which can become destabilized or reconfigured in the process.

Conclusions: Categories

The promise within the sub-title of this book is that the series of empirical studies found in *Contested Categories* should tell us something about life sciences in society. This is a problematic that, as noted in the opening pages of the introduction, has become both relevant and pressing for social scientists in recent years. We have suggested that, to date, it has been most common to locate life sciences within 21st century societies in terms of the hazards and hopes attributed to it. Life sciences have been seen as both a threat to and a promising opportunity for societies, not only in the affluent 'West' but throughout the world.

The way we have collectively approached the task of examining life sciences in society in this book has been to ask how life science categories (such as 'genes', 'at risk pregnancies', 'laboratory', 'serious disease', 'foetus', 'human', 'human biological material' or 'population') circulate, not only within the restricted confines of laboratories, but also in broader contexts of clinical care, lay understanding, public discussion and academic debate. Where human life is at stake, there is constant interplay, feedback, coordination and choreography between grids of intelligibility, ways of being and forms of practice. And it is in these processes that boundaries, stabilizations and immutable mobiles are formed only to be contested and negotiated as they are taken up in different sites and contexts.

References

Bachelard, G. 1984. *The New Scientific Spirit*. Boston, Mass.: Beacon Press.

Becker, H.S. 1963. *Outsiders: Studies in the Sociology of Deviance*. London: Free Press of Glencoe.

Bowker, G.C. and Star, S.L. 1999. *Sorting Things Out: Classification and Its Consequences*. Cambridge, Mass.: MIT Press.

Brown, N., Kraft, A. and Martin, P. 2006. The promissory pasts of blood stem cells. *BioSocieties*, 1(3), 329–48.

Canguilhem, G. 1989. *The Normal and the Pathological*. New York: Zone Books.

Duster, T. 2003. *Backdoor to Eugenics*. New York: Routledge.

Ecks, S. 2005. Pharmaceutical citizenship: antidepressant marketing and the promise of demarginalization in India. *Anthropology & Medicine*, 12(3), 239–54.

Foucault, M. 1967. *Madness and Civilization: A History of Insanity in the Age of Reason*. London: Tavistock Publications.

Foucault, M. 1970. *The Order of Things: An Archaeology of the Human Sciences*. London: Routledge.

Franklin, S. 1997. *Embodied Progress: A Cultural Account of Assisted Conception*. London: Routledge.

Franklin, S. 2007. *Dolly Mixtures: The Remaking of Genealogy*. Durham: Duke University Press.

Franklin, S. and Lock, M. 2003. *Remaking Life & Death: Toward an Anthropology of the Biosciences*. Oxford: James Currey.

Franklin, S., Stacey, J. and Lury, C. 2000. *Global Nature, Global Culture: Gender, Race and Life Itself*. London: Sage.

Fukuyama, F. 2002. *Our Posthuman Future: Consequences of the Biotechnology Revolution*. New York: Farrar, Straus and Giroux.

Gibbon, S. and Novas, C. 2007. *Biosocialities, Genetics and the Social Sciences: Making Biologies and Identities*. London: Routledge.

Goffman, E. 1968. *Stigma: Notes on the Management of Spoiled Identity*. Harmondsworth: Penguin.

Gottweis, H., Braun, K., Haila, Y., Hajer, M., Loeber, A., Metzler, I., Reynolds, L., Schultz, S. and Szerszynski, B. 2008. Participation and the new governance of life. *BioSocieties*, 3(3), 265–86.

Habermas, J. 2003. *The Future of Human Nature*. Cambridge: Polity.

Hacking, I. 1986. Making up people, in *Reconstructing Individualism: Autonomy, Individuality, and the Self in Western Thought*, edited by T. Heller et al. Stanford: Stanford University Press, 222–36

Hacking, I. 1995. The looping effects of human kinds, in *Causal Cognition: A Multidisciplinary Debate*, edited by D. Sperber et al. Oxford: Clarendon Press, 351–94.

Heath, D., Rapp, R. and Taussig, K.-S. 2004. Genetic citizenship, in *A Companion to the Anthropology of Politics*, edited by D. Nugent and J. Vincent. Malden, Mass.; Blackwell Publishing, 152–67.

Heller, T., Sosna, M. and Wellberry, D. 1986. *Reconstructing Individualism: Autonomy, Individuality, and the Self in Western Thought*. Stanford: Stanford University Press.

Jasanoff, S. 2005. *Designs on Nature: Science and Democracy in Europe and the United States*. Princeton, N.J.: Princeton University Press.

Kleinman, A. 1988. *The Illness Narratives: Suffering, Healing, and the Human Condition*. New York: Basic Books.

Koch, L. and Hoeyer, K. 2006. *Håbets teknologi: Samfundsvidenskabelige perspektiver på stamcelleforskning i Danmark*. Copenhagen: Munksgaard Danmark.

Konrad, M. 2005. *Narrating the New Predictive Genetics: Ethics, Ethnography, and Science*, Cambridge: Cambridge University Press.

Latour, B. 1987. *Science in Action: How to Follow Scientists and Engineers Through Society*. Cambridge, Mass.: Harvard University Press.

Latour, B. 1993. *We Have Never Been Modern*. Hemel Hempstead: Harvester Wheatsheaf.

Latour, B., Woolgar, S. and Salk, J. 1986. *Laboratory Life: The Construction of Scientific Facts*. Princeton, N.J: Princeton University Press.

Lévi-Strauss, C. 1966. *The Savage Mind*. Chicago: University of Chicago Press.

Lévi-Strauss, C. 1969. *Totemism*, Harmondsworth: Penguin.

Lippman, A. 1992. Led (astray) by genetic maps: the cartography of the human genome and health care. *Social Science and Medicine*, 35(12), 1469–76.

Lock, M. 2002. *Twice Dead: Organ Transplants and the Reinvention of Death*. Berkeley: University of California Press.

Lynch, M. 1993. *Scientific Practice and Ordinary Action: Ethnomethodology and Social Studies of Science*. Cambridge: Cambridge University Press.

Mol, A. 2003. *The Body Multiple: Ontology in Medical Practice*. Durham, N.C.: Duke University Press.

Nightingale, P. and Martin, P. 2004. The myth of the biotech revolution. *TRENDS in Biotechnology*, 22(1), 564–69.

Ong, A. and Collier, S.J. 2005. *Global Assemblages: Technology, Politics, and Ethics as Anthropological Problems*. Malden, Mass.: Blackwell Publishing.

Palsson, G. 2007. *Anthropology and the New Genetics*. Cambridge: Cambridge University Press.

Petryna, A., Lakoff, A. and Kleinman, A. 2006. *Global Pharmaceuticals: Ethics, Markets, Practices*. Durham, N.C.: Duke University Press.

Pickering, A. 1995. *The Mangle of Practice: Time, Agency, and Science*. Chicago: University of Chicago Press.

President's Council on Bioethics. 2003. *Beyond Therapy: Biotechnology and the Pursuit of Happiness*. Washington, D.C.: Dana Press.

Rabinow, P. 1996. *Essays on the Anthropology of Reason*. Princeton, N.J: Princeton University Press.

Rabinow, P. 1999. *French DNA: Trouble in Purgatory*. Chicago: University of Chicago Press.

Rapp, R. 1999. *Testing Women, Testing the Fetus: The Social Impact of Amniocentesis in America*. New York: Routledge.

Rose, N. 2003. Neurochemical selves. *Society*, 41(1), 46–59.

Rose, N. 2006. *The Politics of Life Itself: Biomedicine, Power, and Subjectivity in the Twenty-First Century*, Princeton, N.J.: Princeton University Press.

Rose, N. 2007. Molecular biopolitics, somatic ethics and the spirit of biocapital. *Social Theory and Health*, 5(1), 3–29.

Rose, N. and Novas, C. 2005. Biological citizenship, in *Global Assemblages: Technology, Politics, and Ethics as Anthropological Problems*, edited by A. Ong and S. Collier. Oxford: Blackwell, 439–63.

Rose, S.P.R., Kamin, L.J. and Lewontin, R.C. 1984. *Not in Our Genes: Biology, Ideology and Human Nature*. Harmondsworth: Penguin.

Scheper-Hughes, N. and Wacquant, L.J.D. 2002. *Commodifying Bodies*. London: Sage Publications Ltd.

Shiva, V. 1997. *Biopiracy: The Plunder of Nature and Knowledge*. Boston, Mass: South End Press.

Sunder Rajan, K. 2006. *Biocapital: The Constitution of Postgenomic Life*. Durham, N.C.: Duke University Press.

Thompson, C. 2005. *Making Parents: The Ontological Choreography of Reproductive Technologies*. Cambridge, Mass: MIT Press.

Vrecko, S. 2006. Folk neurology and the remaking of identity. *Molecular Interventions*, 6(6), 300–3.

Waldby, C. 2002. Stem cells, tissue cultures and the production of biovalue. *Health: An Interdisciplinary Journal for the Social Study of Health, Illness and Medicine*, 6(3), 305–23.

Waldby, C. and Mitchell, R. 2006. *Tissue Economies: Blood, Organs, and Cell Lines in Late Capitalism*. Durham, N.C.: Duke University Press.

World Transhumanist Association 2002. *The Transhumanist Declaration*. [Online]. Available at: http://www.transhumanism.org/index.php/WTA/declaration/ [accessed on 18 February 2009].

Chapter 1
Human and Object, Subject and Thing: The Troublesome Nature of Human Biological Material (HBM)

Cecily Palmer

This chapter takes as its subject the collected organs, tissues, fluids and fragments of the human body that have been, and continue to be collected and retained as part of scientific and medical practice in the UK. It presents and explores the dual categorization of these entities as both scientific-artefact-objects, and as personified-human-entities using empirical examples of contestation work that has made the duality of these entities visible. Material taken from the human body exists in collections all over the UK. My focus will be on collections that have been amassed and retained in order to function as resources for the production of knowledge in bio-scientific and medical practice. These collections take a variety of forms; from those comprising the iconic glass jars containing recognisable parts of the human body, to those holding small pieces of deep frozen, or paraffin set human tissue, to those in which the human material is fractionated, separated and stored in ever smaller constituent parts.

Collections vary not only in terms of the types of biological material they comprise, but also in terms of the use-value of the materials within. For some it is current as they are used on a day-to-day basis, where as the value of other collections is projected onto the future, the material carefully stored and maintained in readiness for diverse (potential) uses to which they may be put. In some cases historical collections have been revisited with new techno-analytical techniques and thus made to 'reveal themselves' in new ways, contributing to new understanding via the genetic, biochemical or environmental traces left in the biological material within. Collections holding human biological material vary greatly in form and design, but they share an origin and a vision. Firstly, every specimen, sample or fragment has been sourced from a human body at some point in time, and secondly, each of the collections exists because of the usefulness, the instrumental utility, or the potential productivity of human biological material as a material resource for the generation of scientific knowledge. However, materials collected from the human body have not only been defined in terms of instrumental or scientific value. These entities have at times retained an aura of humanness, and have been understood as socially and culturally significant entities associated with individual and collective identities and values. Whilst operating as resources for scientific work, materials removed from the human body may also signify humanness and personhood. This analysis explores the emergence and implication of the 'human' category as a dominant lens through which these entities are understood and interpreted at UK collections of human biological material, and reflects on the possible consequences of 'humanness' as the key defining quality of these entities.

Elements of this analysis have been greatly facilitated by the exploration of 'biotechnological artefacts' developed by Bronwyn Parry and Catherine Gere, who use the term to reflect on 'reworked' preserved and archived human tissues and organs, and their conversion into novel biotechnological forms:

> these artefacts do not suddenly arrive in the world as discreet, fully formed objects, rather they are negotiated into being. Their identities are not fixed, but made and re-made in response to new technologies, new scientific enterprise, public consultation, funding crises, institutional expansion and reform. This engagement alters the constitution of the artefacts themselves, their status and the conditions of their use (2006: 141).

This analysis is particularly pertinent in relation to collections of materials sourced from the human body because it locates these entities within wider institutional, intellectual and cultural networks. It also draws attention to the constitution of these entities, their identities, as dependent on the negotiations that bring them into existence. Further underscoring this analysis are some ideas adopted from Star and Griesemer's paper on cooperation in scientific work in which they develop the analytical concept of the boundary object. A boundary object, most simplistically, is 'an object which lives in multiple social worlds, and which has different identities in each' (1987: 409). This concept was developed to understand cooperation between different social worlds sharing the same territory. 'Social worlds' are defined as collectives of persons with particular audiences and tasks, with differing visions regarding the territory in which they are engaged (1987: 338, 396). In adopting this concept however, I focus not on the facilitation of cooperation attributed to boundary objects as was key to Star and Griesemer's formulation, but rather concentrate instead on the possibility for contestation. Human materials can be 'unruly' entities following removal from the human body, precisely because they exhibit multiple meanings and alternate between classificatory schemes. In so doing they challenge and dispute endeavours to use and manage them. For as Parry and Gere state: 'what a "thing" is – the nature of a "thing" – or at least what that is determined to be – profoundly affects how that thing may subsequently be used' (2006: 139). These scholars pave the way for an understanding of material taken from the human body as ontologically multiple, at times ambiguous entities, negotiated, experienced and manifested differently across contexts and social worlds.

This analysis will use interview data gathered at a number of UK-based collections comprising human biological material in order to consider these collected biological materials firstly as 'scientific objects'; material resources used for scientific work, and secondly as 'human objects'; material entities associated with personhood with associated moral duties and ethical obligations relating to them. At collection sites I conducted interviews with senior scientists, curators, and managers responsible for the establishment, management, care and use of the collections. The following analysis emerged from this empirical material using an iterative thematic approach, which entailed repeated immersion in the data to facilitate the emergence of themes, alongside the use of some *a priori* sensitizing concepts. I explore and reflect on the meanings and values invested in collected human biological material, concluding that material taken from the human body is a useful, valuable, troubling, contentious, and ultimately ontologically volatile entity.

Human materials as scientific objects

At anatomy and pathology collections human specimens are primarily utilized for the teaching and educational use of those in medical training and other heath-care professions, and in some cases the lay-public. Consider the following extract taken from an interview with the senior curator at a non-public teaching collection used by medical and allied health professionals. This informant reflects on the system of classification employed for the pathological human specimens within:

> I have colour coded the specimens in this museum…anything with a red label is a very good example of a common or important condition, blue…is slightly more unusual and is aimed slightly more at clinical medical year students – senior medical students and yellow is the sort of esoteric things we always get stuck with in museums.

This museum was open to medical professionals and other healthcare workers to facilitate their knowledge and understanding of the diseased topography of the body. The pathology collection demonstrates how disease and disorder manifest themselves in or on the human body; through specimens presented as exemplary of already classified and 'known' diseases and afflictions. Within these collections a certain duality of exhibition occurs. The human body exhibits a pathology – that is, some feature, symptom, or quality that is unusual compared to the canvas of the healthy body. This feature is in turn removed from the body and exhibited on the shelves of the pathology museum in order to be seen, and by implication understood, by those learning to work in healthcare or medicine. This curator went on to talk about the relevance of the museum within a global context of disease:

> I've got malaria as a red label, now you don't see malaria in [England] but globally it's killing one person every second, it's a common and an important condition.

Geographer Bronwyn Parry offers an understanding of museums as 'scaled down version[s] of the world that could be surveyed panoptically. By these "extraordinary means" it became possible for collectors to "see" distant places, events and cultures without actually experiencing them firsthand' (2004: 20). In the case of the pathology museum, the collection and display of specimens has been presented as a means to allow users not only to 'see' the effects of disease within the recesses of the body, but also to 'see' the diseases specific to distant locales and cultures at a remove from the persons and the cultures themselves. Although in the talk of the above informant this means of knowing was not an end in itself, but a precursor to dealing with these conditions 'in the flesh', across a potentially diverse range of 'fields'.

At a public history of surgery museum located in the North of the UK the collection manager gave an example of how the specimens could be used in informative and enlightening ways by lay-persons as well as those operating within a clinical-medical pedagogy:

> A woman came round…she said 'could you show me what a cancer looks like?' I said 'yeah of course' – breast cancer. I said 'well can you see the grey circle there? That's the tumour'. She said 'that's great…I'm cured, I'm in remission now, I've been through all the process, I've seen the X-rays, not until you showed me that I actually knew what it was.'

In this particular case of a woman in remission from breast cancer, the specimen exhibiting cancer allows her to 'know' her own illness in a way that other representations or images (such as X-rays) have not. The cancer exhibited by the biological specimen is transposed onto the female viewer's own previously cancerous body – thus enabling her to visualize her own cancer, and in her words to 'know' it. Museum ethnographer Dirk Vom Lehm refers to this construction of understanding as 'reflexive co-realization' (2006: 243), an interpretation that posits an alternating interaction between living body and specimen whereby both bodies are understood by reference to the other.

Human specimens in museum collections are presented and displayed as scientific objects; they are used and interacted with for the education and learning of others. They are informative, providing the opportunity to 'see' and by assumed implication to 'know' the body and its interior and external surfaces and its normal and diseased states. In the case of the above-mentioned specimens, museum collections can be seen as repositories of pathological and anatomical reference. Through their embodiment of already identified and classified disease and disorders, they function to disseminate information and play a role in the acquisition of knowledge and understanding of disease and the body in those who interact with them.

'Making and remaking' human biological material

Utilizing the value of human material as scientific objects is not however as simple as cracking a nut. In fact, in order for collected human biological material to be useful, informational or productive, the material needs to be configured in certain ways. In order for biological material to function in the generation and dissemination of knowledge and information they must first undergo any number of material reconfigurations. The next section of this chapter will therefore explore the labour that goes into this configuration, and offer some reflections on the nature of the 'value' embodied by human biological materials as useful resources.

During a tour at one of the collection sites at which empirical material was generated a technical scientist described the practical aspects of collecting tissue for research purposes while showing me around the laboratory and tissue storage areas. This informant described the material practice involved in making brain tissue into scientifically useful objects. Consider the labour involved in transforming a bodily material into a format in which it may be beneficially used – in this case tissue blocks and slides: following removal from the human body the brain is fixed in formalin to make it firmer, and therefore easier to work with. The brain is then cut into sections, which are placed into plastic cassettes and put into a tissue processor, which sets the tissue in paraffin wax and makes a tissue block. The tissue block is inserted into a microtome, a small machine that shaves very thin slices off the wax block, which are then placed onto a glass slide. The thin wax sections are stained with coloured pigment in order to make particular features of the tissue visible. This is a part description of one variation of a host of procedures which alter the chemical and material composition of human biological material, and which transform the material to an informational resource, via scientific work and established techniques, and the intervention of materials and technologies. The histological techniques described in the above extract are contemporaneously considered something of an archaic technology (Landecker 2002), which while beneficial for deriving information regarding the cellular and structural features of the material in question, do not however facilitate the informational quality of the material in other ways. This difference is articulated in the following extract:

> If I want to study the DNA, the RNA, the proteins of this, as well as the cellular structure and architecture here, I need tissue preserved in a different format from that of the paraffin block, and that's why we need to freeze tissue.

Freezing tissue is an alternative means of preserving biological material so that it can be utilized and drawn upon as and when it is required for research and experiment. Fresh-frozen samples of biological material are deemed to be potentially productive in ways that material in the form of blocks and slides are not, as this manner of preservation may facilitate the material to be informative in ways that other formats of preservation may not allow. These examples reveal the role of technological intervention and intellectual work in the constitution of the collected human material itself. In light of the two means of preservation outlined in the above extracts the material 'making and remaking' of material taken from the human body can be seen. Starting with the same material (the brain) the application of scientific work to preserve and derive the informational potential productivity alters the constitution, indeed *produces* the constitution of the collected biological material in a number of directions and ways. Thus by attention to the laborious interventions worked on collected human biological materials, their 'negotiation into being' (Parry and Gere 2006) as useful and valuable scientific objects also becomes clear.

Human materials, as they exist within the collection, are made to be useful, depending on the preservation technologies available, the scientific agenda of the day and maybe other factors. In light of the technical intervention and labour involved in the collection, preservation and use of human tissue, their artefactual quality becomes apparent. These materials are materially reconfigured and subjected to objectifying and abstracting processes in order to make them useful for the work of science and medicine. Scientific objects are produced from human materials, and these are far from static objects, they are dynamic in that they move and emerge afresh 'with the times'. The instrumental and productive qualities of human materials are consequently variable and contingent, and may emerge in a variety of anticipated, and yet to be anticipated ways.

Indeed, the development and application of new genetic technologies and molecular biological methods to collected human material have made accessible genetic information or minute biological components previously 'unknown' to science, as Parry describes: 'these new technologies ... enabled components that had been previously unknown, inaccessible, or unstable to be efficiently maintained and utilized independently of the organisms in which they were originally produced. These biological derivatives have subsequently come to be constituted as "resources"...' (2004: 48–49). The potential for latent and quiescent properties of collected human biological materials to emerge afresh even from old samples has been used to justify their collection and retention, and casts them not simply in terms of a current utility, but also as unrealized repositories of scientific potential.

Collected human biological material is made to be instrumentally valuable; it is made to produce information that is useful. Older anatomical and pathological collections play a role in the dissemination of established knowledge to professional and lay users, while contemporary research initiatives seek to produce knowledge and understanding regarding health, illness, and the human body; knowledge that is additional and novel, which contributes to and builds on what is already known. In this way they not only transfer knowledge, but generate new knowledge. Furthermore, given the development of new technologies and the role of technology and innovation towards '(re)producing' biological materials so that they or their components may be 'known' in as yet unexploited ways, the utility of older collections is by no means exhausted. The instrumental value of collected human biological materials emerges at the locus of human activity; the application of technology, procedures, protocols and materials, and the biological material itself. As Parry and Gere (2006) emphasize, when studying the biotechnological artefact, it is less a demarcated and clearly defined object, and more an entity that is constantly made and remade in terms of the ways it is used, understood and manipulated. Human materials as scientific objects are highly artefactual entities, ones that are produced and reproduced within the institutionalized spaces in which they are held and utilized, both in established, and yet to be developed ways.

Human materials as 'special' entities

This chapter has so far presented collected human biological materials as artefactual and productive resources, and presented an analysis of these scientific objects as emergent within networks of expertise and in relation to technological interventions. I would now like to consider a further dimension in the 'making and remaking' of these materials and explore the construction of material derived from the human body as socially and culturally significant entities, associated with individual and collective identities and values, and reflect on the implications of this more subjective categorization of materials taken from the human body.

Despite the material reconfiguration worked on biological materials in collections, and despite the work necessary to make them instrumentally valuable resources, the origin of these materials is not so easily erased. Human material has been interpreted as culturally significant precisely because of its status as part of, or derived from the human body (Sharp 2000). Waldby and Mitchell have noted that: 'tissues that move from tissue banks to laboratories to other bodies bring with them variously ontological values around identity, affective values around kinship, aging, and death, belief systems and ethical standards… as well as use values and exchange values' (2006: 34). The 'affective values' and 'belief systems and ethical standards' that emerge in relation to collected materials vary according to the part in question, the circumstances under which it was procured, and the 'type' of body from which it was sourced: 'hearts, blood, brains and eyes…have long seemed more powerful, more central to personhood, or more attuned to spiritual connections than hair, leg muscles, or kidneys [however]…different religious and cultural groups ascribe different hierarchies of values to body parts *and*…these change over time' (Lawrence 1998: 112, original emphasis). Materials taken from the human body may bring with them strong emotional and intuitional significations, such as became clear during the organ retention scandal in the UK from 1999 onwards[1]. The scandal referred to the public knowledge that organs and tissues had routinely been taken and retained during post mortem on deceased children

---

1   See also Liddell, K. and Hall, A. 2005. 'Beyond Bristol and Alder Hey: The Future Regulation of Human Tissue' in *Medical Law Review* 13(2) pp170–223.

without the full knowledge or consent of their parents or guardians[2]. The anger and distress of parents regarding the routine collection and retention of human tissues and organs at post mortem occasioned a major reassessment of the legitimacy and acceptability of such practices, and prompted a legal and ethical overhaul relating to the retention, use and disposal of material from the human body.

Particularly of note in the policy and consultation output is the extent to which materials taken from the human body are categorized as significant and special entities, which thus befit a particular manner in terms of engagement, or interaction with them, and in relation to their use. The Retained Organs Commission, established by the Chief Medical Officer Professor Sir Liam Donaldson in 2001, was the interim authority set up to deal with the return of organs to families affected by retention, and to advise on a new regulatory framework. The following extract emphasizes an understanding of materials removed from the body as significant and meaningful entities:

> Extending beyond the context of organ retention itself, our experience has graphically illustrated that great value remains attached to the bodies of deceased relatives and the need to accord dignity to those who have died. (Retained Organs Commission 2004: 6.4)

Humanness and dignity: Reconciling the past with the future

It is a core idea in Western culture that the human being is entitled to dignity. The assertion of this inherent, non-negotiable quality possessed, or embodied by every human being became a core tenet of Western ideology following the foundation of a series of legal and ethical instruments for the recognition and protection of human rights following the Second World War and the Nuremburg Trials of Nazi War criminals from 1945–1949. Dignity thereafter became enshrined in German law. Article 1 (1) of the German Basic Law of 1949 states that: 'human dignity is inviolable. (Die Würde des Menschen ist unantastbar). As surmized by Beyleveld: 'human dignity signifies that each human has inherent value; each human is worthy of respect; and each human has inalienable rights to the protection of his or her value' (Beyleveld 2001: 15). Dignity is understood as a particular characteristic or quality of the status and constitution embodied by the human being, it is an intrinsic value, a fundamental quality or attribute, or an absolute worth possessed of, and partially constituting, the human being. What is particularly interesting is that in debates surrounding the use and retention of human material in the UK, the expectation that dignity be recognized in the human being has spilled over

---

2   Redfern, M., Keeling J.W., Powell, E. (2001) *The Royal Liverpool Children's Inquiry Report* (London: HMSO) and Kennedy, I (May 2000) *Bristol Royal Infirmary Inquiry: The Inquiry into the Management of Care of Children Receiving Complex Heart Surgery at the British Royal Infirmary*. Interim Report (London: HMSO).

into an expectation that dignity be recognized in the human body and its parts. An understanding of human biological materials as symbolic of the human self or individual from which they came imbues them with a significance which may be understood as a property very similar to that of the dignity possessed by the human being.

When affective or emotional value is invested in human material it is orientated towards the past, and may defy the reificatory processes worked on it in order to make it useful for the work of (future) science and medicine, by identifying the material strongly with its human source and status. In the recommendations of the chief medical officer to the British government, published in 2001, following the publication of the organ retention enquiries, there is a suggestion that where tissues or organs are used for teaching, the family should have the opportunity to prepare a 'life book', which would contain information about the child or adult from whom the material came, to be shown in conjunction with its use:

> The 'life book'…would encourage an attitude of respect and awareness of the fundamental human nature of the tissues and organs being used for teaching and avoid them becoming dehumanised objects. (Chief Medical Officer 2001: 44)

In this recommendation the bodily material, or the body part is allied very strongly with the human subject from whom it came. Indeed the emphasis here is that bodily material *should* signify 'humanness' very strongly. This expressly challenges semantic reification of the body part into an utilisable object, and places the category of 'humanness' centre stage, and with it the moral expectation of 'dignity' and 'respect' in relation to human biological materials. Although the policy and legal overhaul in relation to the retention and use of human material in the UK was sparked in relation to materials taken from the deceased, it is important to note that by the passing of the Human Tissue Act in 2004 it is not human material as the bodies of the deceased which invests these materials with a special status which merits 'dignity', rather, it is the 'humanness' of these entities which is key in terms of their status and significance:

> A key principle on which the Human Tissue Act is based is that all human bodies, body parts and tissue within the Human Tissue Act's scope should be treated with appropriate respect and dignity. (Human Tissue Act 2006: 4)

Contested entities

During interviews with collection managers and curators it became apparent that the construction of human biological materials as significant entities, of a 'distinct status' had had implications for their use as scientific objects and resources. Indeed when collected material signifies the human self from whom it was taken, or is understood as 'human' and therefore significant and special in origin, the categorization of the material as 'scientific object' may be deemed offensive to this more fundamental categorization: that of profound entity with an intense subjectivity.

Particularly with regard to biological material taken from the deceased, diverse understandings of the material may lead to incongruent ideas regarding how it is to be acceptably used or appropriately treated. Perhaps not surprisingly, at times these ideas will not be compatible with one another. In the following extract, taken from an interview with a curator responsible for a teaching collection used by medical professionals, just such a difficulty is illustrated. The informant recounted events following the death of a young woman in the hospital in which s/he was employed:

> Under the law, her next of kin was her father…when [the young woman] died tissue was removed to reach a diagnosis…some of it went for electron microscopy (EM), for EM the size of the tissue that's taken is smaller than a pinpoint, not a pinhead, a pinpoint. Before diagnosis could be reached…the father demanded the return of all his daughters tissue, including EM, and everything was returned to him, and, I think in that instance it was a cremation…two weeks later he came back to the department and said: 'what killed my daughter?' and we said 'sorry we don't know', and he said 'could this have implications for my grandchildren?', and we said 'yes, it could', because…young people do not die unless there is, very often there is a genetic issue underlying, and he was devastated…because his emotional outpouring, his emotional reaction was 'I want everything of my daughter back'…then came 'what killed her, is there going to be implications?' and of course we don't know.

In this narrative two distinct constructions of human material are illustrated; samples were taken in order to function as a source of diagnostic information, however these same samples also signified profoundly as the body of a loved one, and were consequently understood in terms of culturally appropriate behaviour towards the dead – that of laying to rest. In this case the second classification disrupted the first, and consequently denied the role of the retained tissue in the process of information generation permanently, indeed, the emotive and familial associations were privileged over potentially instrumental and informative use. The extract above provides a stark example of contestation regarding biological material held within a scientific institution. In this particular case the source of that contestation was external, and decisive in terms of the trajectory of the material itself. However during data generation within collection settings it was particularly illuminating to find that contestations had also occurred within the collection communities in which human material was stored and managed. Alongside the classification of human biological materials as scientifically utilisable resources, which were answering questions and producing information, there also emerged acknowledgement of the 'humanness' of these entities in the talk of informants. In one interview the human signification elicited by a human biological entity became clear when the informant recollected an outbreak of Legionnaire's disease in the region in which s/he worked:

> One of the first cases in the world was in [this area], not known generally, but he's here actually *(informant gestures to the respiratory section of the collection)*, the gentleman is here in this bay somewhere...

This informant exhibits synecdochism in relation to this particular specimen, as the dissected and mounted lung of the person is described in terms of, indeed equivalent to, the whole; the specimen is here described 'as' the latter, the 'gentleman' from whom it was removed. Similarly, the origin of specimens was alluded to in an interview with a collection manager responsible for the technical upkeep of specimens within a history of surgery museum collection:

> [The specimens] don't look lifelike – no disrespect from this, they look very grey and uninteresting but what makes them exceptional is the fact that these are pieces of someone.

Despite the fact that they 'don't look lifelike' and their drab and unexciting appearance, the origin of the specimens is nevertheless emphasized in this informant's account. Indeed the informant refers to this origin not just as 'human' in a general way, but in a subjectively specific way in terms of personhood as 'pieces of someone', and furthermore within this origin is located the specimen's special, singular, 'exceptional' quality.

The manager at a modern DNA banking initiative, which stored DNA extracted from blood samples donated by healthy participants, also presented the collected material in a way that, far from divesting it from its human source or origin, actually fore-grounded a continuing link between source and sample:

> I think you're just innately mindful that it's not just tubes with solution in them, you're talking about a population of individuals...you need to be mindful that... you are representing that population at some sort of level and not just a resource that can be drawn upon without recourse to thought.

The DNA samples in this DNA collection appeared representative of a living human population not only in a scientifically utilisable way, but also in a symbolic way, and one that carried with it a certain degree of moral responsibility. This informant thinks not of objects ('tubes of solution'), but of individuals. To an extent the participant population 'are' the samples and the samples 'are' the participant population; the DNA extracted from an individual's blood sample is understood as equivalent to the whole, and this in turn affects the way in which the collection is to be used. Regardless of the abstracting processes that have been worked on the collected human blood, and its substantial temporal and material reconfiguration, it nevertheless resists reification. Indeed, across the collection settings at which interviews were undertaken there emerged frequent indications that human biological materials of either deceased or living, child or adult origin, in addition to their scientifically useful status, also signified 'humanness', and were invested with a 'special' status and value.

Institutional contestation

It emerged that the association of parts, tissues or fragments removed from the human body with humanness and personhood had in some cases prompted contestations within the social world of the collection site in terms of departmental and institutional decisions regarding the way in which certain categories of biological material were to be used, treated, and disposed of. During one interview the senior curator at an anatomy and pathology museum based in a large teaching hospital gave an enlightening depiction of the management of a particularly troubling category of material entity – that of the foetal specimen. S/he described the institutional concern that was prompted by the foetal entity and its status under the UK legal framework prior to the passing of the 2004 Human Tissue Act, and how, within the collection setting in which s/he was based, the choice was made to apply an alternative, and morally preferential, categorization of them:

> The law says 24 weeks and above is a viable human, below that it's not viable and there is a difference in the law – one is a person one is a specimen, if you look at a 24 week foetus it is a perfect child…you look at a child of 23 weeks and that under the law is a different thing, that's a specimen, you can do as you will with it…we looked at these and we thought 'how do you make this distinction?...how d'you distinguish between 23 and 24 weeks?' and you can't, and so we said 'ok well 23 week foetuses have got to be treated with respect due to it of course', then you're back to 22 weeks, 21 weeks and so on…we slowly moved further and further back, earlier and earlier gestational age, 'til in the end we felt we could not make a distinction, this is a human being therefore it needs to be treated with respect, so right from week one, all the embryos now and anything above go for cremation with a service.

As described in this extract, the visual comparison of the 24 and 23-week foetal entities did not seem to 'fit' the distinction that had been drawn for them in law. Indeed, despite the fact that these entities were legally defined as 'specimens', and as this informant describes, consequently free of rules or regulation in terms of their subsequent treatment, clearly the categorization of the individuals involved with them defined them otherwise, which led to a change in practice within the collection setting. The categorization of these entities as non-viable and thus 'specimens' was contested and their status as non-persons rejected; instead their human status, and the moral duty due to them on this basis was acknowledged through a revision to disposal practice. At this collection site the disposal practices for 24 week foetuses (cremation) were extended to all foetal and embryonic materials, an action that refuted their categorization as 'things', and instead constructed them as human entities; noteworthy and deserving of respect. It is also significant to add that the institutional recategorization of foetal and embryonic materials as described in the above extract had occurred 16 years before this informant was interviewed in 2006, almost a decade before the Alder Hey and Bristol Royal Infirmary organ retention scandals broke in 1999.

Conclusion: (Re)humanizing biological material – disenabling practice?

This chapter has so far presented human biological materials as 'boundary objects', and 'unruly' ones at that. They defy straightforward classification as either object-specimens or as human-entities, and have the potential to embody a variety of meanings not only across, but also within social worlds – in this case collection settings. In the empirical material generated by interviews at collections holding human biological material it emerged that the 'humanness' of these entities is troubling and has been increasingly emphasized in policy and legal documents as a category that should be morally framed as deserving dignity and respect. The interview extracts included above have demonstrated contestations of the 'specimen-object' categorization of human material in favour of a categorization that foregrounds the intensely subjective, 'special' quality of these entities on account of their human origin and status. Furthermore, contestation occurs within the collection communities that work with collected human material, as well as from sources external to them; as the human material in a number of material forms, and with a variety of genealogies found to signify as more than a freely utilisable scientific resource. The way in which collected human material is categorized has considerable implications for what are considered moral and legitimate ways in which to use and manage it; when human material is conceptualized as an entity around which meaning and significance is constructed in various ways, it is not surprising that claims to the legitimate use of the entity may be problematic with relation to each other. At times these contestations have disrupted totally the use of human specimens or samples as scientifically utilisable resources, at others they have resulted in more subtle changes to working practice, or practical revisions to the treatment and handling of the human biological entities themselves.

Finally I would like to present the argument that categorizing collected human biological materials as subjectively significant, special entities which have until recently been part of individual persons, and casting this heritage as one that entails a moral responsibility to use, treat and understand them in a particular (respectful and dignified) way, may also have 'dis-enabling' consequences. Consider this extract from an interview with a pathologist and policymaker in the area of tissue retention, storage and use. This informant reflected specifically on the 'life book' proposal that has been presented and described previously in this chapter:

[The life book] is not an idea that I would particularly subscribe to on a personal basis, I think there is a need to have information about individuals but personal information is another thing…I mean for example if I'm performing an autopsy on someone I certainly would treat the body with a great respect and would want to follow the wishes of that individual or their relatives, but I don't want to know about them as a person because I would find it very difficult to carry out that job…and I find it easier not to know these various personal bits of information.

This informant describes a certain discomfort with 'knowing' too much about the person, or the 'personal information' relating to person of whom only the body remains. The informant also defends their own ability to interact with bodies in a respectful manner, an ability that s/he goes on to emphasize is not dependent on knowing personal information regarding the body as an individual. This informant raises the intriguing prospect that 'knowing too much' of the person could render the undertaking of work with the deceased body more difficult. Indeed I would like to posit that in some cases the ability to conceptually separate 'bodies' from 'persons' has a vital 'enabling' effect, which may be lost if and when the human biological material as 'person' is brought vividly into the foreground.

The categorization of human biological materials as objects and things, (categorizations which have received criticism), need however to be understood not simply as morally questionable and negative effects resulting from the instrumental use of human derived materials, but perhaps as necessary precursors to the doing of certain work with these materials – which must overcome prevailing intuitions and significations of bodies as 'persons' in order to work with them towards other ends. A dominant categorization of these materials as 'human' and therefore special and profound entities, although designed to address one set of concerns pertaining to the collection, storage and use of human material in the UK, may however have 'dis-enabling' ramifications. The issues of dignity and respect therefore need to be disentangled from the issues of personhood and 'humanness'. Seeing or categorizing human parts, tissues and fragments 'as' objects does not necessarily entail treating them without respect, and further, the demand that these materials be seen or categorized 'as' subjects might make respectful 'use', or indeed any kind of use, more difficult.

Human biological materials have long functioned as scientifically useful objects and resources. A constructivist approach draws attention to the constitution of these scientific objects as dependent on the institutional and intellectual networks in which they are circulated. This approach also allows for reflection on the nature of instrumental value relating to collected biological materials, which emerges at the locus of technology, human activity and the biological entity itself. These entities are thus made and re-made in relation to technological intervention and systems of expertise, and are 'known' in multiple and emerging ways. Additionally however, these entities are also re-made in response to cultural and social pressures, and are 'known' as significant and distinctive entities, and negotiated as such both within and across social worlds. As the above examples have shown, human materials have also been understood as intensely subjective entities with strong connotations of personhood and humanity. Following the organ retention scandal in the UK the 'human' nature of these entities was fore-grounded and presented as a feature that necessitated a moral response. The 'humanness' of these entities was increasingly framed as a profound quality, even bordering on the sacred, and collected human biological materials constructed as a 'special' order of materials, prompting discourse about respectful and dignified collection and use of them.

Categorization of human material as intensely subjective, personified entities has led to contestation and disruption to the ways they are used and managed; at times, the use of human material as scientific object or resource has been deemed incompatible with the affective and socio-cultural significations invested in the entity. At others, working practices have been modified and changed in line with intuitions about the 'nature' of these human entities and the respect due to them. The categorization of human materials as intensely subjective and special entities with significations of an individual person may however, at its extreme, have a dis-enabling effect in terms of the work that is to be done with them. Categorization has implications for what is to be morally, legitimately, and practically done with an entity (Parry and Gere 2006); and as human materials have been 'reclassified' as distinctive entities of a special status, the collections comprising human material have had to deal with these reclassified entities by revisions to procedure and practice. Indeed not doing so may impact on the legality and ethicality of the collection and the practitioners responsible for it. The potential emerges therefore for the impact prompted by contestations and redefinitions of human material entities to be so great that they ultimately lead to an 'erasure' of certain uses of them. The humanness, the personality and the profundity of human material entities, and the imperative to 'do respect' to them as special and distinct entities, could result in a total discontinuation of certain practices or uses of them as their 'special status' appears not to be manageable in any other way. Human biological materials are troublesome objects both within and across communities: the objectified specimen-object may exist at the same time as the personified human-subject, emanating an ontological instability which will continue to provoke negotiations and revisions in the use and management of these entities.

References

Beyleveld, D. and Brownsword, R. 2001. *Human Dignity in Bioethics and Biolaw.* Oxford: Oxford University Press.

Chief Medical Officer. 2001. *The Removal, Retention and Use of Human Organs and Tissue from Post Mortem Examination: Advice from the Chief Medical Officer.* London: Department of Health.

Human Tissue Authority. 2006. *Guidance: Public Display.* London: Department of Health.

Landecker, H. 2002. New times for biology: nerve cultures and the advent of cellular life in vitro. *Studies in History and Philosophy of Biological and Biomedical Sciences*, 33(4), 667–94.

Lawrence, S.C. 1998. Beyond the grave – the use and meaning of human body parts: a historical introduction, in *Stored Tissue Samples: Ethical, Legal and Public Policy Implications*, edited by R. Weir. Iowa City: University of Iowa Press, 111–42.

Leigh Star, S. and Griesemer, J. 1989. Institutional ecology, translations and boundary objects: amateurs and professionals in Berkeley's Museum of Vertebrate Zoology, 1907–1939. *Social Studies of Science*, 19(3), 387–420.

Parry, B. 2004. *Trading the Genome: Investigating the Commodification of Bio-Information*. New York: Columbia University Press.

Parry, B. and Gere, C. 2006. Contested bodies: property models and the commodification of human biological artefacts, *Science as Culture*, 15(2), 139–58.

Retained Organs Commission. 2004. *Remembering the Past, Looking to the Future. The Final Report of the Retained Organs Commission*. London: Department of Health.

Sharp, L. 2000. The commodification of the body and its parts. *Annual Review of Anthropology,* 29: 287–328.

Vom Lehm, D. 2006. The body as interactive display: examining bodies in a public exhibition. *Sociology of Health and Illness*, 28(2), 223–51.

Waldby, C. and Mitchell, R. 2006. *Tissue Economies: Blood, Organs and Cell Lines in Late Capitalism*. Durham, N.C.: Duke University Press.

Chapter 2

Substances of the Body:
Blood, Genes, and Personhood

Malin Noem Ravn

Our 'material' is given from the start. And that material must be our genes, or what else could it be?

Quote from interview with Carla

How do we understand our bodily substances, and what significance are we willing to ascribe to them in making us 'who we are'? In this chapter I set out to explore how the bodily substances of 'blood' and 'genes' inform notions of personhood among lay people in Norway. Through the text I illustrate how diverse meanings are ascribed to the concepts of blood and genes as both constituents of bodies and as mediating substances between bodies. I examine how connections are produced between the bodily substances and esteemed cultural values, such as individuality, uniqueness, relatedness and heredity, thus making these values stand out with an almost nature-given quality.

Blood and genes are categories of the body, and as such closely associated with the concept of the 'natural'. That which is understood as 'natural' is often also understood as 'given', which is one of the reasons for the gene to have gained fame and/or notoriety as a truly contested category. I set out to explore how lay people themselves interpret, negotiate and contest this influence from 'nature' in their lives, investigating the tensions between the limitations and possibilities presented in understanding oneself through such categories of the body. In exploring the differences between perceptions of genes and perceptions of blood we get an indication of how bodily categories can slide between the given and the made – and implicitly shed light on cultural notions of the relationships between nature, culture and personhood.

The text is based on material from two research projects: the first was an interview-based investigation of how pregnant women perceived the pregnant body and the foetus' body. Here I draw upon my exploration of what the pregnant women regarded as decisive for them to see the foetus as a 'person'. The other project focused on the intersection of gender, genes and reproduction, where I interviewed among others twins and parents of twins on subjects such as biotechnologies, genetic technologies, and concepts of similarity and difference. In the present context I have highlighted how the interviewees reflected over the concepts of biological identity and kinship.

In the following section I prepare my exploration of blood, genes and personhood by briefly discussing the concept of the person as it is used in anthropological debates.

On persons, bodies and substances

In the tradition from Marcel Mauss' (1985 [1938]), the person is a significant anthropological analytical category. Mauss argues that what for Euro-Americans appear as obvious and innate categories – our conceptions of the *person* and the *self* – better should be understood as historically produced cultural constructs. He shows us how concepts of the person vary with 'systems of law, religion, customs, social structures and mentality' (1985 [1938]: 3). This idea of a culturally formed conception of the person implies that there are fundamental and radical cultural differences in how people understand themselves as social and moral actors, how people understand themselves as related to other people and to nature, how people see themselves in relation to society, and in how people understand and perceive themselves as bodies.

To specify what the concept of the person implies as an analytical category, it is useful to make a distinction between *person* and *individual*. With *individual* I here understand a single member of humanity, an observable physical entity. A *person*, on the other hand, is the meaningful social unit which Morris (1994) classifies as a 'cultural category'. The philosopher McCall (1990) indicates a one-to-one relationship between the individual and the person, where the person is understood as the social meanings we ascribe to the physical individual. The formulation of this kind of one-to-one relationship between individual and person implies that *all* human individuals are ascribed social meaning as persons, and it indicates that *only* human individuals can be regarded as persons. As such, it is a definition that may cover what has traditionally been held to be the Euro-American understanding of the person, even though it does not include the ethnographic variation in the conception of the person. Let us now take a closer look at the specificities of the Euro-American concept of personhood.

Characteristics of the Euro-American concept of the person

La Fontaine writes that the distinction I introduced above between the individual and the person is hard to make for Western Europeans (1985: 125). This conflation of the concepts of individual and person is a central characteristic of the Western cultural complex' individualistic conception of the person; what is often called Euro-American individualism. In the Euro-American individualism *all* humans are in principle ascribed status as persons, through an idea of an inclusive and universal humanity. The Norwegian anthropologist Tord Larsen writes: 'The idea of an inclusive humanity presupposes that we can imagine an identity as a "human", pure and simple, and disregard the social identities this human may carry'. It is the *individual qua individual* which is ascribed rights (Larsen 1996: 123, my translation). That is; an abstracted and emptied formalized individual, detached from concrete contexts.

This concept of the person as an autonomous, bounded individual can be extracted from for instance legally defined, medical and theological discourses in the Western world, and in this definition, social differences between individuals are made insignificant in a conception of a universal equality between people. Several anthropologists, among them Janet Carsten, have made an effort to nuance the anthropological notion of Euro-American personhood. Carsten writes:

> While fully acknowledging the importance of the value of individualism in the West, and its prominent expression in many legal, medical, philosophical, and religious discourses, it is important to recognize that Western notions of the person express other values too. These are present in very familiar and everyday contexts, and they also evoke qualities similar to those that anthropologists have been accustomed to attribute to persons in non-Western cultures (2004: 97).

Carsten deducts from her empirical material that close kinship ties are perceived of as intrinsic to personhood, and the specific argument she thus makes is that relationality is an important but analytically neglected aspect of Euro-American constructions of the category of the person (Carsten 2004). This corresponds with Melhuus' contention that discourses of identity are biologized in the sense that biogenetic connectedness is perceived as a core element of identity. Knowing your biogenetic origin is tantamount to 'knowing who you are' (Melhuus 2007: 43, 53). Following this I include the concept of relationality, in the form of kinship, in my analysis. Furthermore, in everyday Euro-American constructions of personhood, not only that which makes us similar to each other is valued: The characteristics that make people different from each other are also emphasized; the qualities that particularize the individual and constitute it as someone we can learn to know as a concrete other, as a distinct and unique personality.

To sum up so far: *Individuality*, *uniqueness* and *kinship* are core elements of Euro-American personhood. We gain identity and value through being autonomous and distinguishable from other people, but we also gain identity through being connected to certain other people in certain ways. The question to follow is: How are these three prominent aspects of personhood associated with and mirrored in our perception of the human body?

The individual body and its constituents

The Euro-American concept of personhood is culturally co-constructed with – and inextricable from – the concept of the body. With the autonomous indivisible individual as the prime social entity to carry meaning, the individual body is also a prime locus for significance. The body is, parallel to the person, individualized (Giddens 1991). The understanding that the boundaries of the person coincide with the boundaries of the physical body is an idea that is supported by biomedicine's understanding of the human body. Traditionally the body is understood as indivisible and secluded, with a clear border between the inner and the outer; one person in one body. The individual body symbolizes the person, is the person, and is the person's property (Elias 1978 [1939]: 253; Larsen 1998).

The body is perceived as both given and made – understood to be an inseparable mix of natural and social processes. It is incorporated into lay knowledge that we to a certain degree socially shape our bodies, and make them meaningful to our selves through culture, through for instance how we adorn our bodies, what we eat, drink, how we move etc. The body's constituents, though – its flesh, its liquids, its organs, and its cells – are to a greater degree understood as 'pure' nature. In the dominant Euro-American epistemologies the natural processes are thought to be best known through the natural sciences. Genetics, medicine and biology are posed as providers of hegemonic knowledge about the body's constituents, and hence, about our bodies and about ourselves. In this way, categories of nature and biomedical categories have the potential to gain immense power of influence over our self-understanding. But the categories do not move unchanged from the spheres of the natural sciences to people's everyday life. Lay people interpret, negotiate and contest the knowledge and the biomedical categories in diverse ways, making them meaningful vehicles for self-understanding in their everyday lives.

In this text I mainly focus on the categories of genes and blood. Genes have become an obvious choice in this context as they are increasingly considered to be the body substance most fundamental to Western personhood (Conklin and Morgan 1996, Nelkin and Lindee 1995). In this text I use 'genes' as an emic concept. This means that I use 'genes' not as scientifically defined, but in the same fluid fashion that my interviewees use the concept. Judith Roof (2007: 2) argues that the notion of DNA inevitably is confused or conflated with the 'gene' by the public, and I discovered the same tendency in my material, which can be illustrated by this excerpt from an interview:

> There is this spiral figure that is pictured a lot of places you know, or is that DNA? Oh – no – this is awkward –genes, is that … is that the same as DNA? DNA is a molecule, but if there is a difference between DNA and genes … I don't know. Are genes in *addition* to the DNA molecule or are genes *part* of the DNA-molecule? I really don't know. Do you?

This obscurity of the relation between genes and DNA emerged in the narratives of most of my respondents, as they regularly mixed and mingled the two concepts, not necessarily reflecting on any difference between them. 'Genes' was the word they used most, and thus I follow this practice in my text.

In this text I refer to blood and genes (and sperm and egg cells) as bodily *substances*. This is to be understood as an analytical strategy rather than a descriptive categorization. The concept of substance has been an important analytic tool to anthropologists of kinship and personhood, and the utility of the concept is largely due to its breadth of possible meanings, Janet Carsten argues. In anthropology, the concept of substance is used to trace the symbolic transformations of for instance food, blood, sexual fluids, sweat, and saliva, and to analyze how these constitute personhood and are passed from person to person in diverse ways. The concept makes it possible to link thematic clusters such as procreation, feeding, bodies, gender, personhood, and relations between kin, with a focus on the phenomena's processual character (Carsten 2004: 109, 132).

Although I regard genes as a self-evident bodily substance to discuss when it comes to personhood, I have found it stimulating to juxtapose the focus on genes with a focus on blood. The reason for the juxtaposition of the two substances lies in the movement from blood to genes as a substance of kinship in Euro-American thought. David M. Schneider, a pioneer in anthropological studies of Euro-American kinship, argued that 'relatives' by Americans were defined by 'blood' and that: 'The blood relationship is [...] a relationship of substance, of shared [concrete] biogenetic material' (1968: 25). This understanding of kinship is in a state of dependence on science, Schneider claims, where science is given the power of definition over what kinship 'is'. In Schneider's text, and in much of the subsequent literature on contemporary Euro-American kinship, concepts such as 'blood', 'biogenetic substance', and 'biological ties' are used interchangeably, without further discussion. Janet Carsten has pointed out that both 'blood' and 'biogenetic substance' remain unexplored as symbols in Schneider's text, and that it would be useful to focus both on the concepts separately and on how they are in relation to each other (Carsten 2004). Inspired by Carsten, this text is an initial dig into my material to see how the concepts of blood and genes differ from each other for my informants – whether and how blood and genes belong to different chains of meaning. In the next section I investigate how the interviewees talk about 'blood' and 'genes' as bodily matter, and how they regard the two substances' influence on personal identity.

Blood, genes and personal identity

When confronted with questions such as 'what is blood' and 'what are genes', the interviewees answered in rather similar manners. Their descriptions of blood were offered (more or less) confidently and often embodied rather specific elaborations both on what they thought to be the components of blood[1] and on the functions of blood.[2] The functions of blood were furthermore associated with experiences of blood in everyday life, and their understandings of how everyday life and life style choices could influence the blood system (through eating, drinking, exercise, stress etc). Blood was contextualized as a substance that was highly important in

---

1   Such as blood platelets, blood vessels, white and red blood corpuscles, and plasma.
2   Such as transporting oxygen throughout the body.

the daily workings of the body; and a substance with which they had had concrete experiences: They had bled, they had seen, felt, smelled, and touched blood.

Genes, on the other hand, were more of a challenge to describe. The answers were more hesitating and vague, and most used well known phrases such as 'material of inheritance', 'programmes', 'building blocks of the body', or even offered me to read up on the subject in an encyclopaedia. Genes emerged as a complex and rather abstract subject, which primarily belonged to the world of advanced science, sliding into the sphere of the mysterious and incomprehensible through descriptions such as 'something tiny and mystical inside us'.

Despite the rather vague understanding of what genes 'are', the interviewees were in no doubt when it came to the question of the importance of genes. 'Genes do a whole lot, a whole lot. They determine who we are both as a species and as persons,' one of them stated. Another said 'I believe that genes contribute to everything that is me', and he specified 'My qualities as a leader, my understanding of mathematics, my skills to play and communicate with children, my musicality – or rather lack thereof – my sense of humour; I believe that genes contribute to determine all of this.'

This sounds overwhelmingly deterministic, but it is important to note that all of the interviewees also emphasized genes as being a sort of basis, or potentiality, that life worked on, and so none of them rendered life experiences as unimportant in shaping them as persons. As such, they were much in tune with modern genomics that state the genes/environment relationship as extremely complex. The persuasion, though, that the genes defined the 'framework' that they could develop within is worth noting. Carla, an identical twin who at the time was pregnant with twins, put it like this:

> I think our basic personality is in the genes. I really do not know, but I think so. Our attitude towards life, our basic mentality, for instance. We are of course influenced throughout life, and shaped by our experiences, but our 'material' is given from the start. And that material must be our genes, or what else could it be?

Carla's contention is based in her experience of differences and similarities between her twin sister and herself. She thinks that they are different 'on the surface', and that these differences have come from them leading different lives, but that they are totally similar in what she calls their basic constitutions. From this experience of similarity she draws the conclusion that the 'basic constitution' of personality is effected by genes.

In comparison to the power with which this image of genes as influencing personal identity recurs in many of the interviewees' narratives, blood is made more or less irrelevant. The following argument about blood and identity was offered by an interviewee who was a blood donor:

You can give blood, and you can receive blood, and that does not change your identity in any way. If it was an identity-giving substance, then donating blood, and blood transfusion certainly, would be a much more controversial issue. But it is not. There are not many varieties of blood, only four I think, and then some sub-grouping of rhesus negative or positive. And there are not only four sorts of people in the world, are there? So blood can not matter that much. Whereas there is an indefinite number of gene combinations.

Being a unique personality is a crucial element in the conception of Euro-American personhood. Blood can not in the understanding of this interviewee be identity giving because then there would only be 'four sorts of people in the world', while the endless variation of possible gene combinations match the expectation that all human beings are unique. In reality there might not be any causality between uniqueness in personality and uniqueness in genes, but in the strong cultural anticipation of uniqueness, the relation between genetic uniqueness and uniqueness in personality seems here to be understood as a causal link rather than as a correlation. Every human individual's unique set of genes is believed to vouch for a unique personality.

The cultural indication of a causal link between genetic uniqueness and uniqueness in personality was perceived as both faulty and potentially threatening to another of the interviewees; Eva, the mother of presumably identical twin boys. The reason for her discomfort was that if an individual's set of genes determines the individual's personality, then her boys would be seen as two versions of the same person, which, she strongly emphasized, they were *not*. She maintained that the boys were both quite unique, and very different from each other, even if they might happen to have similar sets of genes. She says that she had her own little 'research project' going in observing her boys, and she had come to the conclusion that physical things, like looks and build, were genetic, while psychological traits and personality were less influenced by genes. Her boys resembled each other a lot, but, as she said, 'they are completely different persons.' Her understanding of the work of genes was that there is a germ to personality there at conception (in the genes), but from then on it develops in tango with the circumstances, through life in the womb and after birth. And she was very definite about personality primarily being formed through social experiences in life. 'Otherwise life wouldn't matter!' she stated. In her upbringing of her sons, her main goal seemed to be to ensure that they developed distinct personalities. 'We are very attentive to the differences between the boys', she said, 'When we spot differences, we try to strengthen them through our feedback. We *cultivate* the differences, so to speak!'

Prainsack and Spector (2006) have argued that identical twins are more positive to the thought of human reproductive cloning than the rest of the population. Their contention is that identical twins have real life experience with having identical sets of genes, and as such not being genetically unique, but still feeling and knowing that they are unique individuals. Therefore, they do not fear 'replication' of identity through cloning, as they do not ascribe the genes the ultimate power of making people unique as persons. Identical twins are two distinct persons, and therefore one can assume that clones also would become two distinct persons goes the argument. Viewed from this perspective, fear of human reproductive cloning is an argument based in genetic reductionism and determinism.

Eva explicitly states a similar view when she says that it reduces her boys if she were to believe that genes determined them as persons. 'I believe that life experiences themselves are more influential than genes in all the important aspects of personality', she stated, and continued 'and having identical genes does not mean that you are "identical"'. Noting her refusal to give genes a definitive importance, I thought it was quite interesting that she was very eager to have her boys DNA-tested to see if they really were identical. I therefore asked her what difference the DNA-test would make for her. She stated that the tests would do a lot of difference in her everyday life with the boys:

> If the tests show that the boys are identical twins, we will keep up the work we are doing [in cultivating differences], but if the tests show that the boys are fraternal twins, then we can relax a bit more, because then we know that they *are* different also by nature.

What I read out of this is that despite her declaration that genes mean less than nurture, and that genes do not determine personality, she does not rest assured that this is the case. Also, the boys just being very similar to each other *without* having the same set of genes (as would be the case if the twins turn out to be fraternal), is not perceived by Eva to threaten the boys' individuality and uniqueness. It seems to me that it is not similarity in itself that challenges the individuality of the boys in Eva's perception, but rather what *causes* their similarity. Similarity by 'social life' or accident is less threatening than similarity by nature.

Now, to investigate further how genes are envisaged as part of our constitution given by nature, I will take one step back and take a look at how we imagine what happens at 'the start of life'. Concepts of personhood are co-produced with the social meanings given to bodies – and to the substances of the body – and this is particularly evident in the local views of *emerging* bodies, as they are seen to come into being through the processes of procreation, reproduction and foetal development (Conklin and Morgan 1996: 657). The guiding question in the following section is thus how the bodily substances in Euro-American procreation theories and embryology correlate with the core elements of our conception of 'the person'.

The making of a foetus

Informed by biomedicine, the Euro-American popular view of conception is that it primarily involves two bodily substances: The egg cell from the female and the sperm cell from the male. These cells each contribute half of the genetic substance to the embryo, so that the genetrix[3] and the genitor each contribute equally to their baby-to-be's genome. This means that the genetrix and genitor are both equally 'related' to the foetus, in line with the Euro-American bilateral kinship system. In this context, egg cells and sperm cells gain their primary importance by being carriers of genes.

The sperm and egg melt together, and the new being's DNA is formed. The fertilized egg is perceived to be of another order than the cells it originated from, which is the basis for one of the dominant (although highly contested) Euro-American notions of when a person begins; that a new human being gains moral value at conception. This point of view is for one thing based on the argument that the fertilized egg's DNA is a unique composition, and that the fertilized egg hence is something different from the maternal body it resides in. This is, of course, a controversial matter. Euro-Americans do not agree on when to ascribe human value in the developmental course of new life, and this controversy is well documented in for instance the public debates on abortion and stem cell research. Suggestions to when 'a person' begins range from at conception; via at the 'primitive streak'[4]; when the foetus can be said to develop consciousness; when the foetus is viable outside the womb; and to at birth. The arguments vary, but we can detect what may be a culture-specific commonality in the tendency to seek fixed, structural, and most often *biological* markers of when the fertilized egg/embryo/foetus could be said to become an individual (Conklin and Morgan 1996: 660). This gives biology the power of definition of a socially constructed category, giving it the impression of being a category given by nature.[5]

Debates about human value/personhood are most often based on points of view in principle and are primarily led in the discursive spheres of politics, law, medicine and theology, where 'an embryo' or 'a foetus' are abstract and generalized entities. In the following section I will see the foetus through pregnant women's eyes, to see what happens when we move from the generalized 'an embryo'/'a foetus' to the specificity of 'my embryo'/'my foetus'. I will illustrate how pregnant women present blood and genes as relevant to their comprehension of the foetuses they carry, in the question of whether and how they perceive of the foetus as a person.

---

3   In anthropological kinship theory, the concepts of 'pater' and 'genitor' have been used to distinguish between the man who is socially recognized as father (pater) and the man who is believed to be the physiological parent (genitor). The concepts of 'mater' and 'genetrix' have similarly been used to distinguish between the woman socially recognized as mother (mater) and the woman believed to be the physiological parent (genetrix).

4   Ca 14 days after conception.

5   Alternative *socially* defined ways of ascribing personhood could be for instance the first time a baby was nursed, or at ritual occasions such as a name giving ceremony, where it would be a social action that indicated the moment of entry into personhood, and not the autonomous biological development of the physical body in itself.

The foetus as a person

Most of the pregnant women in my material said that they perceived of the foetus as a 'person', especially through the last stages of pregnancy.[6] And although there were several stages on the path to seeing the foetus as a person, most of the women viewed the foetus' genetic composition as one of the *basics* for being a person. The women I interviewed read a lot about pregnancy, especially early on in pregnancy. Referring to the literature, they regarded the foetus' genetic composition as influential on 'what' and 'who' they felt it (had the potential) to be. A booklet[7] that several of the interviewees referred to states: 'Much is already determined the moment the sperm and the egg-cell melt together. (…) The tiny cell contains 23 pairs of chromosomes – half from each of the parents. These contain the genes that decide many of the child's personality traits' (*Svangerskapsboken* 2000: 17, my translation).

The pregnant women expressed the notion that already the fertilized egg was an entity that was 'something in itself', ascribing it a basic individuality. The foetuses' inherent kinship was also noted upon: That the foetus already was related, through it's genes, both with the pregnant woman herself, but even more important, it seemed, with persons other than the pregnant woman. One of the women told me that she had revealed the secret of the pregnancy to her mother by saying 'You have a little grandchild in my tummy!', and another woman said that she was awed and touched by the thought that what was growing within her was a 'mix' of her and her husband: 'It is so beautiful, that we unite and make something completely new, that is part of both of us' she said. Genes thus were understood to produce direct kinship links between the foetus and a complete web of relatives.

Most of the women talked about the developing embryo as an entity with important innate qualities, but the knowledge that the embryo contained genes from the very start was presented as not emotionally 'revealing' in itself. Rather, the women used this knowledge to frame the concrete sense impressions later on during the course of pregnancy. It was when they could *sense* the foetus that it definitely started to *make* sense as a concrete person to them. Thus the perception of the foetus as a 'person' grew throughout pregnancy.

Talk about the foetus' genes were more prevalent in the later stages of pregnancy, when the women saw birth to be within reach, and when they eagerly imagined what the baby would be like, as in this quote from Greta, 30 weeks pregnant: 'We wonder about what personality the baby will have. Because it isn't quite me nor quite my husband, even if it has genes from both of us. It is a completely new and different being. And that will be exciting, to see *who* it is'. Here we see that genes are taken as the substance of both kinship and uniqueness, and Greta establishes an implicit

---

6   There was of course considerable variations, and one of the women also stated that she did not perceive of the foetus as a person at all, but rather as a part of herself.

7   In the geographical area I did my research this booklet was handed out to all pregnant women through the maternity clinic check-ups.

causal link between genetic equipment and personality. Such a link was the object of much discussion and reflection amongst the informants. Several of the women struggled with my questions of where the foetus' personality came from. They all thought that it to some extent had to be inborn, even though all emphasized that both life in the womb and life itself had a strong impact on personality. '*Something* has to be there from the start' was the recurring phrase. 'Start' here not meaning birth, but conception. Not knowing where else personality *could* come from, rendering for instance religious explanations such as 'ensoulment' inadequate, most of the women, on a scale from quite reluctant to more convinced, after some reflection answered that personality probably had a basis in biology, and more specifically, in genes. For what else was there from the start?

The foetus' basic constitution then, was believed to come from the genes. The further development of the foetus was perceived as an autonomous, uncontrollable biological process in principle independent of social action, and which the pregnant woman could not influence much herself. The understanding was that 'the body does it itself'. Maria, one of the pregnant women, said:

> When the sperm has managed to fertilize the ovum and all that, (…) you don't have control at all. It is a bit weird, actually, that in the beginning it is the body that fixes everything. You can't do anything with it. Well, you can help, of course, with being careful with what you eat and what you drink. No cigarettes and no alcohol and all that. But it doesn't really change the development itself.

It is the body or biology that actually *makes* the foetus develop, but as Maria states, the pregnant women can 'help'. This brings me to the role of blood in 'helping' the foetus develop properly, which I will follow in the next section of the text.

Through the blood: 'Mothering' a foetus

Whereas genes played the lead role in the *constitution* of the foetus in the pregnant women's narratives, blood in important ways played a leading role in *nurturing* the foetus. The foetus' life in the womb has increasingly come to be regarded as a part of a person's biography, both in a medical sense and in an emotional sense. For instance the health care services in Norway (especially nurse-midwifes) encourage pregnant women to think of their foetuses as 'babies' early in pregnancy, probably to ensure that the pregnant women act accordingly; that they follow the recommended behaviour, and act as 'responsible' pregnant women. Not only through renunciation (dietary restrictions, to abstain from alcohol and nicotine), but also through following firm recommendations of emotional actions, such as caressing the stomach, talking and singing to the foetus (the belief being that one through these actions establishes emotional bonds to the foetus/child to be). In this way, a pregnant woman is coerced into a mother, bringing out both her responsibilities as a mother and her motherly love at a rather early stage (Ravn 2004).

In this 'mothering' of a foetus, the blood plays an important role. The whole idea of the necessity to abstain from, for instance, alcohol and nicotine is based on the notion that the foetus shares the pregnant woman's blood system. In this system, every 'bad' substance will travel from the pregnant woman's blood stream into the foetus. All of the pregnant women I talked to mentioned this at some point; that the foetus took part in their daily lives through what they ate, drank, etc, mediated through the blood. Several also interpreted emotions to be transported through the blood, from pregnant woman to foetus; that for instance feelings such as joy, fear and stress were made into chemicals and hormones in the maternal body, and then passed on through the blood stream to the foetus. It was partly through the blood that the pregnant woman's actions and emotions could influence the foetus. In this context blood becomes the substance of love, caring and protection (or in the reverse case, the dangerous substance of neglect, abuse and pollution). In these stories, then, blood becomes a mediator between mother and child, actually doing part of the work of the mother-child bond. Somehow blood becomes a mix between nature and nurture.

The nature/nurture debate can be traced back to Sir Francis Galton, who in 1874 wrote 'Nature is all that a man brings with himself into the world; nurture is every influence that affects him after his birth.' In Galton's days the question of whether pregnancy was nature or nurture was of no – or only theoretical – concern. The new reproductive technologies have brought new questions concerning the status of pregnancy: Gestation has become a 'cultural ambiguity' (Strathern 1992, 27). This contestation is formulated to the point in the case of surrogate motherhood.

Surrogacy is prohibited by law in Norway. This has, however, led to the practice that Norwegian couples in need of this assistance seek help abroad on their own initiative, most often in the United States. The Norwegian anthropologist Kristin Spilker (2008) discusses the story of a male homosexual couple who has travelled to California to have twins by gestational surrogacy. In gestational surrogacy there is a distinction between the woman providing the egg and the woman carrying the foetus through pregnancy, thus making two biological mothers, one 'genetic' and one 'gestational'. The couple in question prefers gestational surrogacy even though this is more expensive and a more complicated procedure, mainly because they want to keep egg donor and surrogate mother separate and as such 'escape' the power of motherhood's cultural and symbolic value. Spilker shows how the couple perceives of the symbolic position of the gestational mother as less threatening than that of the egg-donor. The egg-donor has a genetic tie to the child which is irrefutable, and which seems to be more identity-giving to the child than the tie made through nine months of bodily symbiotic life with the gestational mother. The actual sharing of all of the blood, being part of the same blood system, is thus perceived to be less identity giving than sharing of half of the genes. The gestational mother is by the couple described as important through her nurturing abilities, as a 'nanny', as they express it. In this, the couple equates gestation through pregnancy with caretaking and upbringing of a born child.

In the context of 'emerging life', both genes and blood represent the realm of nature, but in slightly different ways. Whereas genes becomes biology or nature in a deterministic sense, vouching for the 'given' in both the child's individuality and it's basic kin relations, blood becomes nature as part of upbringing or nurture; a substance that the mother herself to a certain degree can influence through life style choices, and through which she can act out her relationship with the child. The quality of the 'nature' she provides becomes an achievement, an action, thus slightly blurring the division of nature and nurture.

In discussing perceptions of the conception and foetal development, I have stated that the basic kinship bonds are present in the foetus already from the very start. In the next section I will take a closer look at the specificities of how the interviewees talk about blood and genes as connective substances.

Genes as a connective substance: Kinship and inheritance

Blood has long been the symbol of kinship in the Western world, shown in phrases such as 'blood relatives', and 'our own flesh and blood', demarcating groups of belonging such as 'blood-lineages' after specific social rules. In earlier times, the idea of blood as the substance of kinship was founded in the belief that conception itself was the mixing of male and female fluids, where the fluids were understood to be purified blood.[8] Furthermore, blood was also seen to be directly involved in inheritance, in that physical traits, illnesses etc were transmitted through the generations via the blood itself (Jones 1996). Charles Darwin, for instance, believed that specific traits were inherited through the blood, transmitted from parents to children, while Gregor Mendel was the first to suggest that inheritance does not reside in the blood, but as units of information passed on through sperm and egg (Keller 2000).

Blood as a symbol of kinship is still relevant and the phrases above are still used actively in several languages[9]. Even so, people do not understand blood to be the 'actual' substance of kinship or inheritance. Blood has been replaced by genes as the general substance of kinship, and as the specific substance of inheritance. In his studies of lay notions of inheritability in Great Britain, Richards (1997) argues that his interviewees knew that blood played no part in conception, as they could describe the specifics of sexual relations and conception, but that they did not link the concept of inheritability to this knowledge. His interviewees made a conceptual divide between 'sexual intercourse and conception on the one hand, and with the transmission of inherited characteristics on the other' (Richards 1997). Richards contends that his informants do not have any notion of a specific 'genetic'

---

8   Pythagoras and Aristotle in Jones (1996: 11).

9   Norwegian examples include 'blodsslektning' (relative by blood), 'blodsbånd' (blood ties), 'ens eget kjøtt og blod' (one's own flesh and blood), and 'blod er tykkere enn vann' (blood is thicker than water).

material of inheritance. Most of my interviewees, on the other hand, do make these connections explicitly, and actively refer back to conception and the 'mixing of genetic material' when they are to describe both kinship and inheritability.

One of my informants used the phrase 'related by blood' in an interview, and I asked him to specify what he meant by it. He stated: 'When I say that we are related by blood, it is just a metaphor for us being genetically related'. In this way, 'blood – talk' is understood as the symbolic language for the reality of genes. In Strathern's words: '[W]hile 'flesh and blood' might be a symbol, it is a symbol for what Euro-Americans take to be literally true: that those joined by substance are kin, and it is the act of procreation that accomplishes the joining' (Strathern 1995: 349). Genetic ties can be traced and technologically tested, and as such they become a concrete tracking device, and the *evidence* of a particular kinship bond (as in DNA-testing for paternity). Genes as a connective substance are not only understood to be fundamentally including (you cannot undo or deny a genetic bond), they are also understood to be fundamentally excluding (you cannot socially 'make' a genetic bond). Even so it is not obvious what we make out of these genetic connections: Genetic relations do not automatically lead to social relations.

In some ways, counting relatives or biological connections through blood or through genes amounts to more or less the same. After recounting his perception of what happens at conception, when the egg and the sperm merge, one of my male informants went on to talk about 'degrees' of genetic relations. 'Siblings share 50% of the genetic material' he stated 'and also 50% with our parents and our children. That means we have 25% the same genes as our grandparents and future grandchildren, and then so on goes the math.' The degree of biogenetic relatedness can be accurately figured out, and different 'percentages' of shared genes coincides with different fixed positions in the web of kin relations. A specific kinship relation corresponds to a specific 'amount' of common genes.

This way of counting 'relevant' relatives through genes could easily have been done by using the image of blood as the substance of kinship instead. The kinship group is vaguely delineated through reference to a relevant but unspecified amount of biogenetic substance, and a relevant amount of social and emotional significance ascribed to the person in question. A difference between blood and genes as substances of kinship emerged, though, when the informants talked about the specificities of *inheritance*, and the understanding of particular similarities between kin.

Genes were readily associated with the concept of inheritance by all of the informants. Although inherited qualities are understood to be diverse, the two types of inherited qualities that all informants mentioned were physical traits and disorders/illnesses. Several interviewees referred to typical family traits that they themselves could observe in specific relatives in different generations. They linked such physical traits of similarity to the work of genes. This can be illustrated by one of the women I interviewed, who after the birth of her son described him to me: 'He has the Hansen nose, which he inherited from my grandfather, who in turn got it from his paternal aunt. And one of my cousin's children has got it as well. It must be a dominant gene, it seems impossible to get rid of!' In this way, what is interpreted as physical family traits were presented to me as concrete evidence of the inheritability of specific genes, where the work of these specific genes was manifested in individual bodies.

In this context genes were seen as small entities that travelled through the generations, and nuanced the image of an 'amount' of unspecified genetic relatedness. The percentage of shared genes is coupled with the question of *which specific genes* that are shared. In this way, one-to-one links were made between individuals who were thought to 'have' or 'share' certain genes. Furthermore, some of the informants talked about genes that were 'activated' or not, as one male interviewee that with a burst of laughter said: 'I don't think *any* of my mother's genes have ticked in – we are almost completely different species!'

In this way, genes as a substance of kinship work in a more particularizing way than does blood. Genes become more of a concrete tracking device for connections than blood is, and represents a potentiality of making specific connections between specific individuals, no matter the 'amount' of genetic relatedness. Specific one-to-one kinship bonds can be singled out, and have the potential of being made socially relevant. In Strathern's words: While blood could be seen as a symbol of a communicative event, genes are the bits of information themselves (Strathern 1992: 178). Whereas blood inevitably will be diluted, genes travel through the generations unchanged, criss-crossing the downward stream of time and life that the image of blood lines indicated.

Conclusion: Personhood and categories of nature

Both blood and genes are categories of the body, but the chains of meaning they are embedded in are quite different. Genes are associated to the language of science, technology and imaginations of the future, while blood belongs to the context of everyday life, concrete reality and old times past. Genes give incontestable, static contributions to identity, while blood is perceived as more in movement, more processual; blood does *work*. Work within bodies, and work between people. One way of seeing it is that while genes belong only to nature and become undeniably important for the givens of identity, blood – moving between nature and nurture, between biology and social life – becomes important for sociality, for the enactment of and for the quality of social bonds.

Euro-American concepts of personhood demarcate the individual as a social and moral actor, and emphasize individual qualities, such as uniqueness as core values. The concept of personhood and the cultural values it mirrors precede the era of the gene, but the concept of the gene, as it is presented in popular science and as it seems to be interpreted by lay people, is moulded in such a way that it can fit in perfectly as a device for self-understanding. Genes not only can verify that every individual is unique, but in so doing they also anchor the social value of uniqueness in nature. In our bodies we can read who we belong to, quite specifically, through the genes. Not only who we share a certain amount of kinship with, but who we are similar to, in different ways. Genetic kinship is given by nature, it is definitively excluding and definitively including. Genes individualize us, connect us to each other, make us unique; genes give each individual a 'core' that society and social life can mould further.

In a double act of meaning production we inscribe our bodily substances with meaning, and then we interpret ourselves through these substances. This co-production of substances and selves to a certain degree consolidates our cultural values as bodily, and hence as natural givens. And the way in which genes are seen to be the guarantor of the core elements of personhood, makes the concept of personhood itself stand out with a nature-given quality.

But even though few of the people I have interviewed have contested the importance of genes in making us who we are as individuals, genes do not necessarily come out as all-important entities in everyday life or in emotional life. Pregnant women describe the knowledge of the foetus' unique genes as a way for them to intellectually acknowledge or imagine it as a separate entity. This knowledge, though, is not emotionally revealing for them, it does not lift the foetus out of the abstract and into their concrete worlds. Genes are an abstract and somehow distant entity – depersonalized, one might say. Whereas blood, even though also a bodily category belonging to nature, represents intimacy and closeness and the actual *enactment* of a relationship. And, when it comes to kinship, the existence of a genetic bond does not imply the enactment of a social bond. Genes are rather a basis, a structure, which we evolve within, representing both limitations and possibilities.

Believing in nature, as that which is given, seems in certain contexts to represent assurance for my informants. All of the interviewees expressed a belief in a complex interplay between nature and culture in making us 'who we are', and all of them held on to the thought that 'something' had to be there from the start. In this thought, the concept of genes fit in with what they already believed to know about themselves and about humanity, and as such represented a passable explanation –sometimes in lack of other explanations. As Carla said: 'Our "material" is given from the start. And that material must be our genes, or what else could it be?'

References

Bagge, S. 1998. *Det europeiske menneske: individoppfatninger fra middelalderen til i dag.* Oslo: ad Notam Gyldendal.

Carrithers, L., Collins, S. and Lukes S. 1985. *The Category of the Person: Anthropology, Philosophy, History.* Cambridge: Cambridge University Press.

Carsten, J. 2004. *After Kinship.* Cambridge: Cambridge University Press.

Clarke, A. and Parsons, E. 1997. *Culture, Kinship and Genes: Towards Cross-Cultural Genetics.* Basingstoke: Macmillan.

Conklin, B. and Morgan, L.M. 1996. Babies, bodies and the production of personhood in North America and a Native Amazonian society. *Ethos*, 24: 657–94.

Elias, N. 1978. *The Civilizing Process: The History of Manners*. Oxford: Basil Blackwell.

Galton, F. 1874. *English Men of Science: Their Nature and Nurture*. London: MacMillan and Co.

Giddens, A. 1991. *Modernity and Self-Identity: Self and Society in the Late Modern Age*. Stanford: Stanford University Press.

Ginsberg, F. and Rapp, R. 1995. *Conceiving the New World Order: The Global Politics of Reproduction*. Berkeley: University of California Press.

Jones, S. 1996. *In the Blood: God, Genes and Destiny*. London: Harper Collins Publishers.

Keller, E.F. 2000. *The Century of the Gene*. Cambridge: Harvard University Press.

La Fontaine, J.S. 1985. Person and individual: some anthropological reflections, in *The Category of the Person: Anthropology, Philosophy, History*, edited by L. Carrithers et al. Cambridge: Cambridge University Press, 123–40.

Larsen, T. 1998. I begynnelsen var Amerika: den amerikanske indianer, kontraktteorien og den vitenskapelige revolusjon, in *Det europeiske menneske: individoppfatninger fra middelalderen til i dag*, edited by S. Bagge. Oslo: ad Notam Gyldendal, 174–226.

Mauss, M. 1985. A category of the human mind: the notion of person; the notion of self, in *The Category of the Person: Anthropology, Philosophy, History*, edited by L. Carrithers et al. Cambridge: Cambridge University Press, 1–24.

McCall, C. 1990. *Concepts of Person: An Analysis of Concepts of Person, Self and Human Being*. Aldershot: Avebury.

Melhuus, M. 2007. Procreative imaginations: when experts disagree on the meaning of kinship, in *Holding Worlds Together: Ethnographies of Knowing and Belonging*, edited by M.E. Lien and M. Melhuus. Oxford: Berghahn Books, 37–56.

Morris, B. 1994. *Anthropology of the Self: The Individual in Cultural Perspective*. London: Pluto Press.

Nelkin, D. and Lindee M.S. 1995. *The DNA Mystique: The Gene as a Cultural Icon*. Ann Arbor: University of Michigan Press.

Prainsack, B. and Spector, T.D. 2006. Twins: a cloning experience. *Social Science and Medicine*, 63: 2739–52.

Ravn, M.N. 2004. *En kropp, to liv: svangerskapet, fosteret og den gravide kroppen – en antropologisk analyse*. PhD dissertation, Department of Social Anthropology. Norwegian University of Science and Technology (NTNU), 2004:72.

Richards, M. 1997. It runs in the family: lay knowledge about inheritance, in *Culture, Kinship and Genes: Towards Cross-Cultural Genetics*, edited by A. Clarke and E. Parsons. Basingstoke: Macmillan, 175–94.

Roof, J. 2007. *The Poetics of DNA*. Minneapolis: University of Minnesota Press.

Schneider, D.M. 1968. *American Kinship: a Cultural Account.* Englewood Cliffs, N.J.: Prentice Hall.

Spilker, K. 2008. Eggcellens representasjoner: vitenskap og kultur, in *Vitenskap som dialog, kunnskap i bevegelse: tverrfaglighet og kunnskapskulturer i endring*, edited by K.H. Sørensen et.al. Trondheim: Tapir.

Strathern, M. 1992. *After Nature: English Kinship in the Late Twentieth Century*. Cambridge: Cambridge University Press.

Strathern, M. 1995. Displacing knowledge: technology and the consequences for kinship, in *Conceiving the New World Order: The Global Politics of Reproduction*, edited by F. Ginsburg and R. Rapp. Berkeley: University of California Press, 346–64.

Svangerskapsboken 2000. Second edition, 7th reprint. Stavanger: Sandvik.

Sørensen, K.H., Amdahl, E., Gansmo, H.J., and Lagesen, V. 2008. *Vitenskap som dialog, kunnskap i bevegelse. Tverrfaglighet og kunnskapskulturer i endring*. Trondheim: Tapir.

Chapter 3

Governing Risk Through Informed Choice: Prenatal Testing in Welfarist Maternity Care

Mianna Meskus

In the beginning of the 1990s, the maternity care system in Finland experienced a change that had far-reaching consequences for general practitioners and nurses as well as for pregnant mothers. A new prenatal screening test called the maternal serum screen or trisomy risk screening test, was taken into nation-wide use over a very short period. Based on the biochemical analysis of levels of alphafetoprotein (AFP) and human chorionic gonadotrophin (hCG), it was a test aimed at detecting chromosomal disorders, in particular Down's syndrome. Since medical geneticists considered it safe, easy and cheap, by 1995 two-thirds of the Finnish municipalities were offering the test in public health maternity care free of charge. A majority of hospital districts began offering it to all pregnant mothers, regardless of age (see Santalahti and Hemminki 1998; Asmala 1995).

As serum screening was being widely introduced in Finland, medical geneticists in the neighbouring country Sweden took a critical stance to prenatal screening altogether. In its general terms of reference on prenatal diagnosis, released in 1993, the ethical committee of the Swedish Society of Medicine stated that prenatal diagnosis should be offered to risk groups only and that it should not be carried out as screening. All parents should be given information on prenatal diagnosis. However, the diagnostic test should only be offered to mothers and partners who specifically asked for it. The idea behind the policy formulation was to guarantee parents' informed choice. The Swedish Parliament ratified the ethical committee's general terms in 1995 (Prenatal diagnostik... 1993: 2232–6, Kammarens protokoll 1994: 102, Wahlström 1998: 1273). This meant that Swedish parents chose whether they wanted to ask for prenatal testing or not. Finnish parents' choices were meanwhile linked to taking part in the screening; whether to participate or to opt out from the test that was offered to all pregnant women as a matter of routine.

Amongst the Nordic countries, prenatal screening for chromosomal disorders via blood serum tests was taken into generalized use only in Finland (Santalahti and Hemminki 1995: 6). It is the medical rationale underlying this national particularity that is the object of my study. The Finnish case is indicative of how new medico–technical interventions into parenthood – in the form of prenatal diagnosis and screening – are introduced, legitimated and institutionalized within public health maternity care services. A contextual feature that likewise makes the Finnish case interesting is the combination of internationally state-of-the-art research into genetic medicine and molecular biology, a welfarist health care system described as being typically 'Nordic', and relatively liberal regulation of biomedical research when it comes to, for example, the use of personal data (cf. Tupasela 2008: 27–28).

This chapter discusses three 'translations' in medical rationalizations, related to discussions and practical implementations of prenatal testing from the beginning of 1980s until the first years of the twenty first century. These translations concern, first, the expansion of the 'at risk' category to eventually include all women; second, the shift from public health objectives and disease prevention towards an emphasis on choice for women; and third, the problem of educating the public about genetics and hereditary diseases without generating excessive expectations towards the medical government of inborn or genetic anomalies. Analysis of these themes brings forth two notions that are of particular interest here due to their contested nature. One is the category of *risk* as referred to in definitions of 'risk pregnancies'. The other is the category of *choice* as referred to in the idea of 'informed choice'. I will show how the contestedness of risk and choice reveal an elementary ambivalence in medical understanding about the purpose of prenatal testing; how it indicates the difficulties medical geneticists have in, on the one hand, respecting parents' autonomy and, on the other hand, in promoting health policy aims.

My analytical interest in these two contested categories is connected to discussions about the conditions of possibility of risk governance, subjectivity and freedom in modern societies. The question of personal freedom as an object of practices of government has been both theoretisized and analysed empirically in numerous studies (e.g. Barry et al. 1996, Burchell et al. 1991, Dean 1999, 2002a, 2002b, Petersen and Bunton 1997, Rose 1989, 1999), some particularly in view of the implications of the new genetics (*e.g.* Conrad and Gabe 1999, Hallowell 1999, Helén 2002, 2004, Petersen and Bunton 2002, Koch and Svendsen 2005, Rose and Novas 2005). I use an 'analytics of government' framework to focus my study in the multiple relationships between national health policy, prenatal testing, institutionalization of the field of medical genetics and pregnant mothers' and their families' choices and experiences within maternity care. While more extensive methodological elaborations on the approach can be found, for example, in Mitchell Dean's *Governmentality* (1999) or in Nikolas Rose's *Powers of Freedom* (1999), here I take up only the following general points: An analytics of government is a way of analysing those regimes of practices that try to direct, with a certain degree of deliberation, the conduct of others and oneself. The approach gains critical purchase on regimes of practices by making clear the forms of thought implicated in them (Dean 1999: 21, 40).

This means that an analytics of government strives to examine the conditions under which regimes of practices come into being, are maintained and become transformed. The inspiration for studies on government comes from Michel Foucault's work on the characteristics of political reason in the 'modern' West (see e.g. Foucault 1991). In this chapter the focus is on the birth and development of certain practices of medical government and their modes of reasoning in the Finnish welfare society.[1] The underlying idea has been to disengage from the notion of state-centricity when studying 'Nordic' welfare practices. Instead, my aim has been to analyse arrangements of government of life that in concrete, material ways concern people's happiness and ways of living and being (Helén et al. 2001).

The data used for this chapter is a combination of expert discussions amongst professionals and expert addresses to lay people. It includes articles published in Finnish *medical journals and compilations* from the 1970s until the first years of the twenty first century, the authors being mainly medical genetics pioneers and experts. In addition, I analyse certain *health care documents*: national recommendations to municipal maternity care personnel concerning the organization of maternity care, as well as written information for parents on prenatal screening. Furthermore, the data includes *popular articles* on prenatal testing aimed at the general public: articles published in health magazines including medical geneticists' interviews, and an instructive book on genetics and family planning written by a prominent Finnish doctor in medical genetics. The material is mainly in Finnish and English translations of the quotes are my own. I have tried to be faithful to the vocabulary and expressions used in the documents, sometimes at the cost of their fluency in English.

In the following, I will first briefly shed light on certain relevant technological and political arrangements concerning prenatal testing in Finland. An analysis of the introduction of prenatal diagnosis and screening within Finnish maternity care follows. After this I turn to look at how parents have been informed about and offered prenatal screening, following which is an analysis of expert debate on how Finnish parents have adopted forms of risk thinking promoted by medical geneticists.

The techno-political setting

Biomedical research into the technical aspects of prenatal screening methods has been intensive in Finland since the beginning of the 1970s. The interconnection between basic research and clinical applications has been especially intense in the field of medical genetics. This has reinforced the close relationship between medical science and public health care. For over two decades, the technology to screen and diagnose foetuses for possible congenital diseases and abnormalities has been an elementary part of medical care offered to pregnant women. Typical

---

1   The chapter is based on my work on the history of hereditary thinking in Finland from the eugenic politics of the 1940s, through the institutionalization of medical genetics and its applications in maternity care, to the turn of the millennium discussion on molecular medicine and genetic testing. The text corpus analysed here is a part of the systematically collected data of the research, ranging from 1940 until 2003 (see Meskus 2009).

to the Finnish case, prenatal screening tests were introduced into maternity care as soon as they had become technically available and applicable (Norio 1991: 329, Santalahti and Hemminki 1998: 12, Helén 2004: 32).

Ultrasound screening was first introduced in Finland in the 1970s, simultaneously with the chromosomal analysis of cultured amniotic fluid (amniocentesis). Amniocentesis was by the 1980s transformed from a diagnostic test into a screening test for foetal chromosomal abnormalities offered to the part of population defined as 'aged mothers'. Chorionic villus sampling (the analysis of placental tissue) was also initiated in the 1980s to achieve prenatal diagnosis. More extensive prenatal screening started, as indicated in the introduction, in the beginning of the 1990s through the introduction of serum screening (Santalahti and Hemminki 1998: 8–13, Asmala 1995: 2585–8). Since then, a majority of pregnant mothers have been offered some form of prenatal testing. The latest turn in screening practice was the Decree on Screening, passed by the Council of State in 2006, which obligates all municipalities to offer pregnant mothers under 40 years a first-trimester screen that combines a serum screening test with the measurement of nuchal translucency via ultrasound in order to detect chromosomal disorders (Decree 1339/2006).

The institutionalization of prenatal screening during the past thirty years has been doctor–driven. In developing as well as in promoting foetal diagnostic and screening techniques, medical geneticists have been key actors, writing extensively about the Finnish maternity care system and the organization of pregnancy follow-up. It has been, in particular, the wish of medical genetics professionals that screening activities be increased and made accessible throughout the country. Noteworthy is the fact that expert discussions have been disease-oriented and mainly concerned with medical facts. They have focused on medical, technical and infrastructural conditions of foetal diagnosis and screening, whereas social, ethical or regulatory issues have been given less attention (Laurén et al. 2001: 19, 25, Santalahti and Hemminki 1998: 12, see also Meskus 2009).

Although prenatal diagnosis and screening have since the 1980s been occasionally questioned by disability activists and critical physicians or parents, this has neither amounted to a wider public debate nor to any general opposition towards the screening techniques and practices. There have been two distinctive peaks in the public debate on screening during the last two decades: the first one concerned selective abortion and took place in the mid-1980s, and the second one broke out in the mid-1990s as a reaction to the introduction of the above-mentioned serum screening programme. The debates were carried out mainly in the *Letters to the Editor* sections of daily newspapers as well as in the main Finnish disability activism bulletin. These critical outbursts were short and did not lead to any major changes in maternity care practices. Policy makers have emphasized that there has never been a big public outcry on the screening issue in Finland, mainly because there is a remarkable trust – unlike in many other countries – in the public health system, including tests offered in maternity care. Municipal maternity care centres are attended by 99% of pregnant women (Ettorre 2001: 69, Aro and Jallinoja 2001: 143, Laurén et al. 2001: 31–2, Jallinoja 2002: 32). As a consequence, by the 1990s, no extensive discussions of the prerequisites, costs, benefits, effects or ethics of prenatal screening tests had been held at the health policy level. Also, no national public body had planned or analysed prenatal screening practices in depth (Santalahti and Hemminki 1998: 13, see also Norio 1994: 642). Prenatal testing had become part of general maternity care through the local professional and political influence of medical geneticists and other doctors.

How was prenatal screening initiated in practice? Medical research on the techniques of foetal diagnosis and screening was most often carried out in university central hospitals of which Finland has five. The offering of prenatal screening to mothers attending maternity care was initiated through a co-operation between university hospital medical geneticists and maternity care doctors in municipalities located within the area of the particular university hospital. Likewise, political decision-making on whether to introduce a new diagnostic or screening test and how to define target groups has been decentralized until the beginning of the present century. In municipalities, policy decisions concerning health services have been made by politically elected local health committees which lean on expert advice (Norio 1991: 337–8, Santalahti and Hemminki 1998: 12–13, Wrede 2001: 199, 203). However, the state has aimed to guide local practices through national guidelines and recommendations. Prenatal diagnosis and screening were taken up in guidelines from 1988, 1995 and 1999. I will take a closer look into the 1995 guidelines later on.

Detecting risk pregnancies

When prenatal diagnosis was first taken into clinical use in Finland in the 1970s, the enthusiasm of the medical profession lay in nascent technological possibilities of detecting severe developmental disorders. The testing technology first taken into use in prenatal diagnosis was amniocentesis, developed through international collaboration between biomedical researchers. By studying cultured cells derived from a sample of amniotic fluid from the pregnant mother's womb, clinical geneticists could construct the 'karyotype' or the 'chromosome map' of the expected baby and look for chromosomal alterations on it (Aula et al. 1971: 1375–6, Santalahti 1998: 9–10, see also Rapp 2000: 27–30). Amniocentesis was introduced by pioneer clinical geneticists as being beneficial on two levels. On the individual and family level, the doctors said, prenatal screening *offered parents a choice*; amniocentesis opened up a possibility of preventing the birth of a disabled child through selective abortion. Testing produced knowledge of the foetuses' chromosomes and gave parents a choice of deciding whether to have the baby or not (Chapelle 1972: 441–3, Aula et al. 1975: 1064, Norio 1975: 504, Aula 1978: 19–20). The other benefit was regarded to be the possibility of *preventing inborn disorders at the population level*. This was a public health question. Clinical geneticists emphasized that prenatal testing would offer possibilities to 'reduce considerably' chromosomal anomaly cases 'in the population' (Aula et al. 1975: 1064). Furthermore, Finnish pioneers linked population-level benefits to the question of *reducing the economic costs of disability*. If the prevalence of disability, understood mostly as Down's syndrome, could be decreased this would according to genetics experts have significant economic implications (Norio 1970: 475, Chapelle 1972: 443, Aula et al. 1975: 1071–2).

At first, doctors and scientists offered amniocentesis as a diagnostic test to pregnant women with a known family history of or risk factor for foetal disorder. By the beginning of the 1980s, however, diagnostic testing was transformed into a screening test. This meant that prenatal testing was directed to 'symptomless' mothers with a 'normal' pregnancy but who were considered to be at 'increased risk' of chromosomal disorder due to their age (Santalahti 1998: 9–10, Seulontatutkimukset 1999: 39–40). The early prenatal screening practice was built upon the widely accepted fact that 'aged mothers' had the highest risk of giving birth to a baby with a chromosomal disorder called trisomy, the most common of which was Down's syndrome. But how should the target group of aged mothers be determined? The central problem in consolidating prenatal screening as a maternity care practice became how to define the age limit.

This debate about the age limit depicts the elementary contestedness and flexibility of the risk pregnancy category as a medical indication for offering prenatal screening. Initially the age limit was set at 39 years but this was 'for economical reasons'. Doctors noted that people had started to have children later in their lives indicated by the fact that the number of pregnant mothers belonging to the age group of 35–9 years had started to increase. This posed challenges to an effective prenatal screening practice – to optimizing the possibilities of detecting and preventing chromosomal disorders. Doctors hoped that the age limit for a screening test would be lowered to 37–8 years. They also pointed out that in international recommendations the minimum age for prenatal diagnosis was 35 years. Under this age the miscarriage risk caused by amniocentesis would be greater then the risk of having a chromosomal disorder. Hence to lower the age limit below 35 was not considered appropriate (Aula and Chapelle 1980: 1877, Norio 1983: 295). The views of medical experts were heard, and by the end of the 1980s the National Board of Health recommended that all mothers above 35 years would be offered an amniocentesis or a chorionic villus sampling test (Santalahti 1998: 11).

According to medical genetics experts, foetal diagnosis and screening were well-grounded additions to the already established system of prenatal care and maternity services offered free of charge to all pregnant women. It was considered an ideal situation that as many parents as possible could be offered the choice of testing their expected baby's chromosomes, and that this could be done through maternity care (Autio 1982: 4, 1989: 3005, Norio 1989: 1872–5, Salonen 1989: 121). The screening technology that ultimately enabled the expansion of the object of testing was serum screening. This meant that the reference point of the 'at risk' category shifted from aged mothers to any pregnant mother. Age as a prime risk indicator of the statistical probability of a Down's syndrome was bypassed and testing was offered to all pregnant women regardless of age. The medical practice became focused on revealing increased risks in all age cohorts. The Finnish medical profession emphasized that the use of serum screening was justified because 'risk mothers can be found more in number and more extensively than before'. Screening for Down's syndrome could be extended 'also to young mothers' (Asmala 1995: 2585–8, Santalahti and Hemminki 1998: 8–13).

Risk in its multiplying configurations (O'Malley 2000) has become a means of governing citizens, a tool to conduct the conduct of individuals regarded as free and autonomous. Prenatal screening has been one thread in these processes of developing risk governance and governance through risks. The Finnish medical profession's rationalizations on prenatal technology and its practical applications indicate the continuously expanding, even all-encompassing, nature of risk as regards pregnancy. Lealle Ruhl (1999: 108) has observed that nowadays there is no such thing as a 'no risk' pregnancy. Constructions of risk in pregnancy derive from highly medicalized discourses, statistical sampling of data, and probability calculations which portray pregnancy as a state requiring careful and detailed risk prevention. One crucial outcome of this is that many pregnant women have learned to identify themselves and their anxieties in relation to their given specific risk figures. The responsibilization of pregnant women is conducted *through the notion of risk* which, as we have seen, is a continuously re-formulated, re-negotiated category (see Rothman 1994, Browner and Press 1995, Rapp 1995a).

Informing about choice

I will next turn to the question of choice and its conditions of possibility within foetal testing offered through Finnish maternity care. Medical genetics has leaned on the principle that choice – freedom of choice or informed choice – is the primary legitimation of prenatal diagnosis and screening (Meskus 2009, cf. Rapp 2000a: 37, Petersen and Bunton 2002: 57). In Finland, genetics experts have since the 1980s wanted to define the screening practice as a service which first and foremost answers parents' needs and demands. According to professionals' shared understanding, testing is best legitimated if attending is self-motivated as an individual or family-based act of informed choice (Meskus 2009).

In the following, I analyse informed choice from the perspective of screening information given to parents. I look at a national recommendation book titled *Screening Tests in Maternity Care* (Seulontatutkimukset... 1995), which was directed at maternity care personnel in all municipalities and which included two model leaflets of screening information to pregnant women and their partners. The guidelines were published during the time serum screening was being introduced in maternity care across the country. I consider the information material to be crucial in forming the conditions of pregnant women's and their partners' choices. I am interested in how the objects of choice and the purposes of screening were presented to parents attending maternity care. How was the risk of a development disorder explained? As I will show, mothers' and parents' choices become a highly contested category from the perspective of this material.

Concerning prenatal screening, the national recommendations from 1995 stated that 'during the first visit to a maternity care centre, parents should be given written information about which screening tests can be taken in Finland and what can be detected by them' (Seulontatutkimukset...1995: 31). Maternity care personnel were hence advised to inform parents about the techniques used and medical abnormalities screened for. No explicit stance was taken on how the information should be formulated or how the purpose of prenatal screening should be explained. However, there were two sample leaflets attached to the book that were used at the time in two Finnish hospital districts to inform parents about prenatal screening (Seulontatutkimukset...1995: 59–61). Since these two documents were attached to the national recommendations, I assume the maternity care expert team in charge of the recommendations considered them as model examples of parental informing on the issue.

The first model example was called *Developmental Disorder Screening Leaflet of the County of Central Finland* (DSL leaflet in the following).[2] It was a one-page fact sheet signed by the deputy chief physician of the hospital maternity clinic. The information was given in a listing manner, presenting the medical 'facts' and explaining the screening practice as briefly as possible. Percentages concerning miscarriage risks and the sensitivity of the test offered were presented to parents. The other example leaflet, used by Tampere university central hospital, was titled *Screening of Fetal Developmental Disorder: A Guide for Mothers* (below titled the AGM leaflet).[3] In this four-page long guide the information was presented as answers to frequently asked questions. Aspects of the screening process, particularly the meanings of test results, were presented more thoroughly than in the DSL leaflet. Both, however, centred on medical facts: who were being screened, what could be found and what were the brief medical descriptions of the conditions screened for.

The leaflets explained that the purpose of screening was first and foremost to detect the most common developmental disorder, Down's syndrome. Via serum screening, the bulletins stated, mothers below 40 years got to know, whether their foetus had an increased risk of Down's syndrome. Both introduced the syndrome very briefly. The nature of Down's syndrome was explained by referring to concepts of chromosome disorder and severe developmental disorder. The AGM bulletin defined it and its prevalence as follows:

> Down's syndrome is the most common of chromosome diseases that lead to severe mental disability and congenital malformations. It is found in approximately one

---

2   In Finnish: Tiedote kehityshäiriöiden seulontatutkimuksesta Keski–Suomen läänin alueella.

3   In Finnish: Sikiön kehityshäiriöiden seulonta: opas äideille.

in 600 newborns annually. Down's syndrome is caused by an extra chromosome 21 or 21-trisomy.

The DSL leaflet used the expression 'defect based on a chromosome disorder'. Rayna Rapp (1995b: 70–1) has called the vocabulary of genetics powerful and universalizing. According to her, it easily tempts us to assume that, for example, the biomedical definition of Down's syndrome requires no further particularizing interpretation before the technologies with which it is associated can be beneficially applied. Furthermore, routinized public health screening has made Down's syndrome the iconic condition of prenatal testing, described by geneticists and genetic counsellors when explaining diagnostic technologies to potential patients (Rapp 2000b: 184–5). Although Rapp has studied the social impact of amniocentesis in America, many of her points are relevant also in the Finnish context, especially her finding that Down's syndrome is in the limelight of medical practice. The Finnish serum screening leaflets for mothers mentioned several times that the serum test could *also* reveal the risk of congenital nephrosis and neural tube defects. However, these conditions were not defined further and their difference to chromosome disorders was not explained. The screening procedure was explained mainly with reference to chromosome disorders and especially Down's syndrome.

The testing was designed to screen and eventually, if so chosen by the expecting mother, to diagnose foetuses with atypical chromosomes. However, at the same time, the information sheets gave a picture that prenatal screening tests offered parents reassurance that the expected baby *did not* have Down's syndrome. Both bulletins explained that eventually only very few mothers would be found to carry a foetus with a chromosomal anomaly. The AGM bulletin announced twice that a majority of the children that fell into the risk group following screening were born healthy. The link between screening ('the risk') and diagnostic test ('the final certainty') was thus depicted as a possibility of being reassured of the baby's normality. The aspect of reassurance has come up also in Rapp's studies on genetic counselling in that counsellors have explicitly described the goal of prenatal diagnosis as giving reassurance to mothers concerning their risk status (Rapp 1995a: 180).

The voluntariness of the screening procedure was taken up already in the first sentences of both information leaflets. The contexts in which the voluntariness-statements were made are noteworthy. The AGM bulletin began by explaining that 'the follow-up of pregnancies and prenatal testing are part of Finnish maternity care' after which it announced that 'now mothers can participate in voluntary screening that searches for severe foetal developmental disorders'. The DSL leaflet stated that 'the test is done in maternity care centres during the 15th gestational week and all expecting mothers can take part in it if they want to. Participation is hence fully voluntary.' In both leaflets voluntariness was connected to a statement that all expecting mothers could take part in the screening if they wanted. Thus they began by defining serum screening as both a voluntary and a 'normal' or 'routine' maternity care practice offered to all mothers. This indicates the paradoxical aspect of prenatal screening: On the one hand, screening has become a normalized part of maternity care, a 'service' offered to all mothers. On the other hand, routine-like uptake of prenatal screening has been considered its most severe problem as it undermines the legitimacy of the practice, since parents should make reflexive decisions about participating in screening in order to act out their autonomy (Santalahti 1995: 43–44, 1998: 61, Meskus 2009).

Reading through the leaflets, the picture of informed choice becomes more complicated. In the DSL fact sheet it was advised that parents should consider their choices before attending the screening. Parents were advised to think about their stance to abortion and the miscarriage risk caused by amniocentesis in advance. The leaflet did not mention that parents could change their mind during the process or that they had the right to interrupt it. Nor was it explained that parents would not have to take the diagnostic test, even if the screening test turned out to be positive, i.e. indicating a risk of foetal chromosomal anomaly.

The AGM leaflet, on the contrary, stated that 'the mother has a right to change her mind about participating at any stage of the screening'. It also emphasized that taking part both in the screening and possible diagnostic tests was voluntary. However, the contradictory nature of this leaflet arises from the fact that while mothers' voluntariness and right to change their mind were mentioned, in a section titled *What do screening results mean?* it also stated that 'positive screening result means that the foetus has an increased risk of serious developmental disorder. In this case further testing is warranted.' Hence if something alarming was found in the screening test, mothers had the *right* to get a free diagnostic test. Yet again, it could also be read as indicating that it would be *advisable* to attend the diagnostic test.

The analysis above opens up a situated micro-level view to the question of informed choice, the formal principle of prenatal screening. Several researchers have pointed out that the language of risk, on which medical judgements are based and which is characterized by negative definitions of disability and deviance, marks the situations of choice (Rothman 1994: 14, Rapp 1995b: 73–74, Ruhl 1999: 104, Petersen and Bunton 2002: 197, 201). Studies have shown that the voluntariness of testing for health risks can be experienced by mothers as merely theoretical due to fears of being regarded as irresponsible by health care personnel (Chadwick 1999: 297, Lippman 1999: 288). On the other hand, for many women prenatal screening has, according to Petschesky (1987: 279, 282) and Rapp (2000a: 124–6), given positive experiences of greater control regarding their pregnancy. Predicting the expected baby's health and normality has become self-empowering for many western, especially middle–class mothers and parents. My point here is simply to highlight the fact that choices concerning the health and life of one's expected baby are made within situations in which conditions are significantly founded in medical and health care rationales – infused for example in information material handed out to parents. This brings us to the inbuilt contradiction of Finnish foetal testing practices; namely that medical genetics experts have wanted to constantly expand medical risk control and detect more Down-foetuses, but in the name of parents' choice rather than in the name of public health and economical justifications, although these have been crucial in institutionalizing the practice from the very beginning. The above analysed maternity care material indicates the difficulties medical and health care expertise have had with simultaneously respecting parents' autonomy and promoting medical and public health aims which lay by definition behind all population screening (Meskus 2009).[4]

Risk-consciousness and excessive expectations

Foucault-inspired studies on modern forms of power have indicated that projects aiming at making citizens responsible for the government of their own lives have become fused with individuals' projects for themselves – and have moulded into personal desires and needs (see Rose 1999: 88). Prenatal testing can be analysed as one practice through which expecting mothers have been made the subjects of their own life and health and through which they have learned to understand risk calculations concerning the foetus in their womb. However, my data indicates an interesting albeit not unexpected *looping effect* (cf. Hacking 2002) between expert knowledge and people's self-understanding. I will illustrate this in the following discussion on citizen education about genetic issues and parents' excessive expectations of medical risk control. This section shows that what began as medical aims of risk control and disease prevention have also become part of citizens' demands directed back at medical practice and health care.

During the 1990s, Finnish experts' concerns about citizens' knowledge on genetic issues became a central topic in their writings. The molecular turn in biological research and the incorporation of molecular biology within medical genetics had brought, among other changes, DNA-analysis and gene tests to the forefront of clinical genetics. These novelties were described in professional medical journals as marking a 'new epoch in biomedical research' and promising a 'gene era' in the whole field of medicine (Kääriäinen 1998: 2461, Peltonen-Palotie 2001: 939). In their view, a new level of research and knowledge had opened up in the prevention of genetic diseases. This, in turn, gave medical geneticists a reason to believe that genetic knowledge about human health and illness would have consequences throughout the health care system. It would transform the care and counselling given to citizens and affect numerous people throughout their whole life (e.g. Aula and Palotie 1991, Palotie 1993, Palotie and Ranki-Pesonen 1994, Peltonen-Palotie 2001).

---

4   It was included into the Public Health Act of 1972 that municipalities were obliged to organize population screenings when the early detecting of a disease could be considered generally beneficial (KOM 1969: A3, 37).

In medical thinking, the question of informed choice and voluntariness was becoming ever more urgent. The development of genetic testing and screening had to be based on the same principles that were the foundation of testing and screening of inborn developmental disorders in maternity care: the respect of mothers' and parents' autonomy (e.g. Kääriäinen 1994, 2000, 2002a). This, in turn, could only be ensured by appropriate knowledge. It was emphasized that citizens should be prepared to confront genetic knowledge that concerned themselves as well as their children and relatives. The Head of Department of Clinical Genetics at Oulu University Central Hospital noted at a celebratory medical genetics seminar in the beginning of 1990s that the general public already seemed to know a lot about prenatal diagnosis and even something about hereditary diseases as well as genetic counselling services. He concluded, however, that much still needed to be done by way of enhancing people's readiness for genetic knowledge: 'We should educate people, the population as well as professional staff, so that they will understand if they have a genetic problem that needs to be solved' (Leisti 1992: 33).

Doctors wished that people would receive information on genetics as early in their life as possible. Medical genetics experts took up student and school health care as well as a possibility of including basic knowledge on genetic testing in school health education. Through such initiatives citizens could be reached already before they had started a family and had children (Sipponen et al. 1999: 24, Kääriäinen 1994: 761, 2000: 909–13, Hiilesmaa and Salonen 2000: 880–6). Early education was legitimated by parental choice: Future parents would be given the chance to decide 'whether they wanted to find out, with the help of advanced medical means, about the health of the foetus during pregnancy'. It would also enable them to consider in advance their personal stance towards selective abortion (Ryynänen et al. 1990: 1434).

Medical and health care professionals expressed the need to enhance people's capacities to choose freely for themselves regarding knowledge about their own or their potential child's genetic status. At the same time, however, another theme arose concerning citizens' relations to genetic issues. It was the problem of parents' expectations about the possibility to predict and control their expected baby's health – according to doctors these expectations were becoming unrealistic. Medical geneticists and genetic counsellors were professionals who in their practical work came across such expectations. Some of them took up the question in public. In a popular health magazine *Good Health* (Hyvä Terveys) which offered its readers medical information about disease prevention and care as well as guidance for a healthy life, the issue came up in the latter part of 1990s. In an article titled *Foetal testing does not guarantee a healthy baby* a medical specialist from the prenatal diagnosis unit at Helsinki University Central Hospital stated that 'most parents want that their carefully planned children are healthy. I see daily in my work mothers who would want to know about their future child much more than it is possible to examine' (Sipponen 1995: 51). In another article the clinical geneticist of the *Family Federation of Finland* (a non-governmental organization specialized amongst other services in genetic counselling) stated that she came across situations she characterized as 'child quality control'. There were people who wanted to know about the probability of their family's good characteristics being inherited by their future children. She also noted that 'sometimes parents have brought to my reception a child with a fairly harmless deformation. I have then been asked how this could happen with the gene tests taken and everything. One must then once again repeat that no test gives absolute certainty about the expected child' (Helasti 1997: 21).

Some years later established Finnish medical geneticist Helena Kääriäinen published a book called *Your Genes and Mine* (2002) in order to inform couples planning to have children about current genetic knowledge and the practical possibilities of genetic counselling and genetic diagnosis.[5] The book offered support and understanding for parents' worries and hopes concerning their future children. However, excessive expectations were also addressed. In chapters titled *For those who want to know everything possible in advance* and *One cannot choose one's baby* readers were explained that there exists no all-embracing gene test with which one could ensure that a child was healthy. Kääriäinen wrote that although the media gave a picture that new genetics opened up various prospects and although the knowledge of hereditary conditions had increased considerably, it should be understood that it was impossible to choose a child according to characteristics desired by parents. She noted that 'maybe part of the beauty of life is indeed due to its uncertainty and limitedness' and advised parents to learn to live with life's uncertainties. All parents worry about the future of their children, but, the author concluded, parents 'should not get caught up in just fearing for diseases' (Kääriäinen 2002: 9, 45, 90–2, 104–6).

What do these discussions implicate? The Finnish data demonstrates that prenatal testing in maternity care has been understood as a means of acting out autonomy and freedom to choose. Parents' need to know about the expected baby's health and their desire to choose between risks have been seen by experts as 'natural' conditions of parenting when legitimating the use of medical genetics to control risk pregnancies. In a sense, mothers and parents have been expected to want the possibility of choice whether they themselves realize it or not. At the same time medical professionals have found the capacities of these autonomous parents lacking. They have been thought of as lacking adequate information on genetic issues and on the possibilities of detecting hereditary or congenital deviance and disease (Meskus 2009). Ways to enhance parents' autonomy and freedom have been sought after, civic education in genetic issues being the main one of them. This means that choice as an expression of personal autonomy has been regarded both as an *essential or ideal condition* of parenthood and an issue that needs *nurturing and support* from medical experts (cf. Hindess 1996). To add to this paradox, parents' alleged excessive desires and wants concerning the health of their expected baby has emerged as a theme in medical discussion. The category of choice has become contested from a new perspective: parents have

---

5   In Finnish: Sinun geenit ja minun.

started to demand for unrealistically broad risk control in view of their expected baby. Pregnant women and their partners have taken the objective of medical pregnancy control outside its 'rational' limits.

Conclusion: Ambiguities of risk and choice

In this chapter I have used medical articles on prenatal testing and civic education as well as information material directed at parents as paths to analyse the case of prenatal diagnosis and screening in the context of Finnish maternity care. The welfarist 'service' of prenatal screening is taken as a techno-medical practice that aims to 'conduct the conduct' of pregnant women and their partners towards more extensive awareness of their expected child's inborn or genetic risks, as well as towards choices opened up by risk information. My aim has been to outline those forms of medical thought, or modes of medical rationalization, that have marked the Finnish testing system.

Two key categories, risk and choice, have emerged from the analysis, and their contested nature has been the prime focus. As the analysis shows, in the process of institutionalizing prenatal screening the interlinked notions of 'at risk' and 'risk pregnancy' have become flexible categories in that they have constantly been expanded to include ever more pregnant women. The contestedness of risk becomes highlighted likewise in medical professionals' understanding of the need to educate citizens on genetic risks while simultaneously trying to manage parents' excessive demands of medical risk prevention. Risks should be acknowledged but only to the extent medical experts consider reasonable and realistic.

Meanwhile the notion of choice – informed, autonomous choice – for pregnant women and their partners regarding whether to participate in foetal testing becomes contested due to an inbuilt contradiction in screening practices. The contradiction has its roots in medical aims to both detect risk pregnancies for public health disease prevention and to enable free parental choice in prenatal testing. What is noteworthy is that, at least in the Finnish context, the problematization of choice as it comes to new biomedical techniques and practices is in no way fading out but is instead becoming ever more urgent. Choice and patient autonomy are seen as primary principles in biotechnological research as well as in clinical applications of molecular genetics with its promises of 'personalized' medical care. The present day welfare system with its tendency to view citizens as clients and consumers of health care enforces the principle of personal freedom and responsibility (Helén 2008: 8–9). This gives rise to a paradoxical situation: Technological possibilities to intervene in 'biological' bodily processes have multiplied and pressures of cost-effective preventive health care have increased, but health care authorities cannot oblige or publicly encourage individuals or families to attend testing. The reason for this is that the principle of patient autonomy and freedom of choice is regarded as politically and ethically unquestionable (Meskus 2009).

The tension between techno-medical possibilities of intervention and the unquestionability of patients' autonomy helps understand another paradoxical characteristic of the prenatal testing service. This arises from the tendency of the health care system and health care actors to withdraw to a position in which their responsibility is regarded as purely technical: to expose pregnancies with a risk of a chromosome disorder through cost-efficient and accurate methods. Meanwhile the ethical responsibility of the risk management falls on the pregnant woman (Helén 2002: 126). This means that foundational questions concerning 'life itself' become increasingly redefined as individual problems and issues. It also indicates that collective political decisions become reduced to technical matters, which 'depoliticizes' many aspects of life and presents medical technology as value neutral, unproblematic and even inevitable (Petersen and Bunton 2002: 68, 71).

Hence prenatal screening is often defined as a neutral technology whose purpose it is to offer individual mothers and families the possibility to choose. However, it is too much a politically produced practice to be pure technology. Likewise, it is too much a techno-scientific creation to be purely political. Emphasizing parents' freedom to choose in the name of personal risk management helps control the enmeshing of science and politics in this particular form of medical care. Furthermore, although applications of new genetics cannot be held as alone liable for present day parents' needs and desires to ensure the health and normality of their offspring, medical genetics is not 'outside' this development either – a point I have wanted to make in this chapter. Medical conceptions of normality, deviance, illness and health as well as of technological possibilities to govern these 'conditions' have shaped the frames within which we can experience parenthood today and perceive the future of our potential children.

I thank Susanne Bauer, Hanne Jessen and Ayo Wahlberg, as well as Turo-Kimmo Lehtonen, for their useful criticisms and suggestions in the writing and re-writing of this chapter.

References

Aro, A.R. and Jallinoja, P. 2001. Prenatal genetic screening: The Finnish experience, in *Before Birth: Understanding Prenatal Screening*, edited by E. Ettorre. Aldershot: Ashgate, 143–55.

Asmala, K. 1995. Downin oireyhtymän seulonta Suomessa [Screening of Down's syndrome in Finland]. *Terveydenhuolto*, 25: 2585–88.

Aula, P. 1978. Periytyvien tautien ja kromosomihäiriöiden raskaudenaikainen toteaminen [Diagnosis of hereditary diseases and chromosomal disorders during pregnancy]. *Ketju*, 1: 19–23.

Aula, P., Karjalainen, O. and Leisti, J. 1971. Intrauteriinisesti diagnosoitu kromosomitranslokaatiotapaus [Intrauterine diagnosis of a case of chromosome translocation]. *Duodecim*, 20: 1374–7.

Aula, P., Karjalainen, O. and Seppälä, M. 1975. Lapsivesitutkimus sikiön kehityshäiriöiden varhaisdiagnostiikassa [Amniocentesis in the early diagnosis of foetal developmental disorders]. *Duodecim*, 18: 1064–76.

Aula, P. and Palotie, L. 1991. Geneettiset seulonnat – osa huomispäivän lääketiedettä [Genetic screenings – part of tomorrow's medicine]. *Duodecim*, 107: 1961–63.

Autio, S. 1982. Vammaisuuden ehkäisy: eettisistä perusteista [Prevention of disability: ethical principles]. *CP–lehti*, 8: 4–5.

Autio, S. 1989. Sikiödiagnostiikka 2: sikiödiagnostiikan päämäärät [Prenatal diagnosis 2. The objectives of prenatal diagnosis]. *Suomen lääkärilehti*, 30: 3005–9.

Barry, A., Osborne, T., and Rose, N. 1996. *Foucault and Political Reason: Liberalism, Neo-Liberalism and Rationalities of Government*. London: UCL Press Limited.

Browner, C.H. and Press, N.A. 1995. The normalization of prenatal diagnostic screening, in *Conceiving the New World Order: The Global Politics of Reproduction*, edited by F.D. Ginsburg and R. Rapp. Berkeley: University of California Press, 307–22.

Burchell, G., Gordon, C. and Miller, P. 1991. *The Foucault Effect: Studies in Governmentality*. Chicago: University of Chicago Press.

Chadwick, R. 1999. Genetics, choice and responsibility. *Health, Risk & Society*, 1(3), 293–300.

Chapelle, A. 1972. Prenatal diagnostik [Prenatal diagnosis]. *Kätilölehti*, 10: 441–7.

Conrad, P. and Gabe, J. 1999. *Sociological Perspectives on the New Genetics*. Oxford: Blackwell Publishers.

Dean, M. 1999. *Governmentality*. London: SAGE.

Dean, M. 2002a. Powers of life and death beyond governmentality. *Cultural Values*, 6(1&2), 119–38.

Dean, M. 2002b. Liberal government and authoritarianism. *Economy and Society*, 31(1), 37–61.

Decree 1339/2006. *Decree of Council of State on Screening*. [Online]. Available at: http: www.finlex.fi/fi/laki/alkup/2006/20061339 [accessed 9 December 2008].

Ettorre, E. 2001. Experts' views on prenatal screening and diagnosis in Greece, The Netherlands, England and Finland, in *Before Birth: Understanding Prenatal Screening*, edited by E. Ettorre. Aldershot: Ashgate.

Foucault, M. 1991. Governmentality, in *The Foucault Effect: Studies in Governmentality*, edited by G. Burchell et al. Chicago: University of Chicago Press, 73–86.

Hacking, I. 2002, Inaugural lecture: Chair of Philosophy and History of Scientific Concepts at the Collège de France, 16 January 2001. *Economy and Society*, 31(1), 1–14.

Hallowell, N. 1999. Advising on the management of genetic risk: offering choice or prescribing action? *Health, Risk & Society*, 1(3), 267–80.

Helasti, P. 1997. Perinnöllisyysneuvoja torjuu pelkoja [Genetic counsellor wards off fears]. *Hyvä Terveys*, 7: 20–1.

Helén, I. 2002. Risk and anxiety: polyvalence of ethics in high-tech antenatal care. *Critical Public Health*, 12(2), 119–37.

Helén, I. 2004. Technics over life: risk, ethics and the existential condition in high–tech antenatal care. *Economy and Society* 33(1), 28–51.

Helén, I. 2007. The new public health, governance and health citizenship. Paper presented at 18th Nordic Conference in Social Medicine and Public Health, Helsinki, October 2007.

Helén, I. et al. 2001. *The Ethos of Nordic Welfare*. Unpublished research proposal.

Hiilesmaa, V. and Salonen, R. 2000. Äitiyshuollon seulonnan mahdollisuudet ja ongelmat [The possibilities and problems of screening in maternity care]. *Duodecim*, 8: 880–6.

Hindess, B. 1996. Liberalism, socialism and democracy: variations on a governmental theme, in *Foucault and Political Reason: Liberalism, Neoliberalism and Rationalities of Government*, edited by A. Barry et al. London: UCL Press Limited, 65–80.

Jallinoja, P. 2002. *Genetics, Negotiated Ethics and the Ambiguities of Moral Choices*. Publications of the National Public Health Institute, A2, Helsinki.

Kammarens protokoll. Riksdagens snabbprotokoll. Protokoll 1994/95:102. [Parliament minute] Available at: www.riksdagen.se/webbnav/index.aspx?nid =101&bet=1994/95:102 [accessed 21 April 2008].

Koch, L. and Svendsen, M.N. 2005. Providing solutions – defining problems: the imperative of disease prevention in genetic counselling. *Social Science & Medicine*, 60(4), 823–32.

Komiteanmietintö 1969:A3. Kansanterveystoimikunnan mietintö [Public Health Committee Report].

Kääriäinen, H. 1994. DNA–laboratoriosta kliiniseen työhön [From DNA–laboratory to clinical work]. *Duodecim*, 7: 757–61.

Kääriäinen, H. 1998. Geenitekniikan lupaukset ja uhkakuvat [The promises and threats of genetechnology]. *Duodecim*, 23: 2461–4.

Kääriäinen, H. 2000. Geeniseulontojen riskit ja haitat [The risks and harms of genetic screening]. *Duodecim*, 8: 909–13.

Kääriäinen, H. 2002a. Perinnöllisyysneuvonta – tietoa ja tukea perheille [Genetic counseling – information and support for families]. *Kätilölehti* 3: 94–6.

Kääriäinen, H. 2002b. *Sinun geenit ja minun: perinnöllisyystietoa perhettä suunnitteleville* [Your Genes and Mine: Genetic Information for those Planning a Family]. Helsinki: WSOY.

Laurén, M. et al. 2001. Prenatal diagnosis in the lay press and professional journals in Finland, Greece and The Netherlands, in *Before Birth: Understanding Prenatal Screening*, edited by E. Ettorre. Aldershot: Ashgate.

Leisti, J. 1992. Perinnöllisyysneuvontaa kaikille vuoteen 2000? [Genetic counseling for everyone by 2000?], in *Haasteena harvinaiset harmit. Väestöliiton perinnöllisyysklinikka 20 vuotta*, edited by R. Norio, Helsinki: Väestöliitto.

Lippman, A. 1999. Choice as a risk to women's health. *Health, Risk & Society*, 1(3), 281–91.

Meskus, M. 2009. *Elämän tiede: Tutkimus lääketieteellisestä teknologiasta, vanhemmuudesta ja perimän hallinnasta.* [Science of Life: A Study on Medical Technology, Parenthood and the Government of Heredity.] Tampere: Vastapaino.

Norio, R. 1970. Vajaamielisyys käytännön ongelmana [Feeblemindedness as a practical problem]. *Kätilölehti*, 75: 467–75.

Norio, R. 1975. Perinnöllisyysneuvonta [Genetic counseling]. *Duodecim*, 8: 503–8.

Norio, R. 1983. Sikiödiagnostiikan eettiset näkökohdat [Ethical aspects of prenatal diagnosis]. *Lääketiede*, 83: 294–5.

Norio, R. 1989. Tietämisen tarve, turva ja tuska perinnöllisissä sairauksissa [The need, reassurance and pain of knowing in the case of hereditary disease]. *Duodecim*, 105: 1872–6.

Norio, R. 1991. Lääketieteellisen genetiikan eettiset ongelmat [The ethical problems of medical genetics], in *Tiede ja etiikka*, edited by P. Löppönen et al., Porvoo, Helsinki: WSOY.

Norio, R. 1994. Suomalaisen tautiperinnön tulevaisuus [The future of the Finnish disease heritage]. *Duodecim*, 7: 640–3.

O'Malley, P. 2000. Introduction: configurations of risk, *Economy and Society*, 29(4), 457–9.

Palotie, L. 1993. DNA-tekniikat tautien diagnostiikassa ja preventiossa [DNA–techniques in the diagnosis and prevention of diseases]. *Sosiaalinen aikakauskirja*, 5: 17–21.

Palotie, L. and Ranki-Pesonen, M. 1994. Geenidiagnostiikan uudet ulottuvuudet [The new dimensions of genediagnosis]. *Duodecim*, 7: 647–653.

Peltonen-Palotie, L. 2001. Miten perimähankkeen valmistuminen vaikuttaa mahdollisuuksiimme selvittää sairauksien patogeneesiä?' [How will the accomplishment of the human genome project affect our possibilities to investigate disease pathogenesis?] *Duodecim*, 9: 939–44.

Petersen, A. and Bunton, R. 1997. *Foucault, Health and Medicine*. London: Routledge.

Petersen, A. and Bunton, R. 2002. *The New Genetics and the Public's Health*. London: Routledge.

Petschesky, R.P. 1987. Fetal images: the power of visual culture in the politics of reproduction. *Feminist Studies*, 13(2), 263–92.

Prenatal diagnostik – etiska aspekter. 1993. Riktlinjer från Läkaresällskapets etikdelegation. *Läkartidningen*, 23: 2232–6. [Prenatal diagnosis – ethical aspects.]

Rapp, R. 1995a. Risky business: genetic counselling in a shifting world, in *Articulating Hidden Histories: Exploring the Influence of Eric R. Wolf*, edited by J. Schneider and R. Rapp. Berkeley: University of California Press, 175–89.

Rapp, R. 1995b. Heredity, or: revising the facts of life', in *Naturalizing Power: Essays in Feminist Cultural Analysis*, edited by S. Yanagisako and C. Delaney. London: Routledge, 69–86.

Rapp, R. 2000a. *Testing Women, Testing the Fetus: The Social Impact of Amniocentesis in America*. London: Routledge.

Rapp, R. 2000b. Extra chromosomes and blue tulips: medico-familial interpretations, in *Living and Working with the New Medical Technologies*, edited by M. Lock et al. Cambridge: Cambridge University Press, 184–208.

Rose, N. 1989. *Governing the Soul: The Shaping of the Private Self*. London: Routledge.

Rose, N. 1999. *Powers of Freedom: Reframing Political Thought*. Cambridge: Cambridge University Press.

Rose, N. and Novas, C. 2005. Biological citizenship, in *Global Assemblages: Technology, Politics, and Ethics as Anthropological Problems*, edited by A. Ong and S.J. Collier. Oxford: Blackwell Publishing, 439–63.

Rothman, B.K. 1994. *The Tentative Pregnancy: Amniocentesis and the Sexual Politics of Motherhood*. London: Pandora/HarperCollins.

Ruhl, L. 1999. Liberal governance and prenatal care: risk and regulation in pregnancy. *Economy and Society*, 28(1), 95–117.

Ryynänen, M. et al. 1990. Downin syndrooman seulonta sikiöiltä äidin verikokeen avulla [The screening of Down's syndrome with maternal serum test]. *Duodecim*, 21: 1431–6.

Salonen, R. .1989. Mitä informaatiota missäkin pisteessä [Which information at what point?]. *Lääketiede*, 89: 121–2.

Santalahti, P. 1995. Naisten tieto, päätöksenteko ja kokemukset sikiöseulonnoista [Women's knowledge, decision–making and experiences of prenatal screening], in *Näkökulmia sikiöseulontoihin*, edited by P. Santalahti. STAKES: Aiheita 21.

Santalahti, P. 1998. *Prenatal Screening in Finland: Availability and Women's Decision-making and Experiences*. STAKES, Research Report 94.

Santalahti, P. and Hemminki, E. 1995. Johdanto [Introduction], in *Näkökulmia sikiöseulontoihin*, edited by P. Santalahti. STAKES: Aiheita 21.

Santalahti, P. and Hemminki, E. 1998. Use of prenatal screening tests in Finland. *European Journal of Public Health*, 8(1), 8–14.

Seulontatutkimukset ja yhteistyö äitiyshuollossa (1995), STAKES, Oppaita 27. [Screening tests and co-operation in maternity care.]

Sikiön kehityshäiriöiden seulonta: opas äideille. No date. [Screening of foetal developmental disorder: a guide for mothers.]

Sipponen, M. et al. 1999. Askarruttavatko suvun perinnölliset taudit mieltä? [Preoccupied by the hereditary diseases of your family?] *Kätilölehti*, 2: 24–6.

Sipponen, V. 1995. Sikiötutkimus ei takaa tervettä vauvaa [Prenatal testing does not guarantee a healthy baby]. *Hyvä Terveys* 6: 50–3

Tiedote kehityshäiriöiden seulontatutkimuksesta Keski–Suomen läänin alueella. No date. [Developmental disorder screening leaflet of the County of Central Finland.]

Tupasela, A. 2008. *Consent Practices and Biomedical Knowledge Production in Tissue Economies.* University of Helsinki, Department of Sociology, Research Reports No. 256.

Wahlström, J. 1998. Enklare fosterdiagnostik ger nya etiska problem [Easier prenatal diagnosis causes new ethical problems]. *Läkartidningen*, 12: 1270–4.

Wrede, S. 2001. *Decentering Care for Mothers: the Politics of Midwifery and the Design of Finnish Maternity Services.* Åbo: Åbo Akademi University Press.

Chapter 4

Visualizing and Calculating Life: Matters of Fact in the Context of Prenatal Risk Assessment

Nete Schwennesen and Lene Koch

Introduction

In the last decades, we have witnessed a proliferation of the production and circulation of what has been called the 'facts of life' (Franklin 2000, Rose 2001) – made in the context of pregnancy. When a woman becomes pregnant she is followed closely by doctors and midwifes who, through different techniques of surveillance, produce knowledge about the condition of foetal life. New dilemmas and problem spaces arise, as expecting couples are increasingly confronted with such knowledge and inhabit the new spaces of action and decision-making which grows out of it. This paper focuses on prenatal risk assessment (PRA) for Down's syndrome as one such site of knowledge production. PRA is a non-invasive risk assessment carried out in the first trimester of pregnancy (11–13 weeks of gestation) and involves a blood test and an ultrasound scan. PRA is presented as being 'the most accurate way of estimating the risk of a foetus having Down's syndrome' (http://www.fetalmedicine.com/fmc/ultrasound/11–13-weeks-scan/) on the market and is seen as an improvement on second trimester serum screening for Down's syndrome, which has an established place in antenatal care in Western countries (Williams et al. 2002: 1984, Meskus, this volume). In the context of PRA, facts about foetal life, presented to the couple in the form of a visual image and a risk figure, are seen as means to provide the pregnant woman and her partner with objective data on the basis of which they can make rational decisions about future pregnancy/foetal life. In the following, we illustrate the process through which facts about foetal life are produced and made meaningful at an ultrasound clinic in Denmark. On the basis of ethnographic observations and interviews with couples undergoing PRA, we trace the production of knowledge of foetal life as it is configured and reconfigured in three different locations: as the foetus is *visualised* through an ultrasound scan, as knowledge about its health status is *quantified* through a risk figure, and as this knowledge is *interpreted* and made meaningful by the pregnant woman and her partner together with health professionals in the process of decision-making.

Our point of departure is the situation in Denmark. In September 2004, the Danish National Board of Health issued new guidelines for prenatal screening and diagnosis (Sundhedsstyrelsen 2003a, 2003b, 2004). These recommended that PRA should be offered to every pregnant woman, regardless of age, on the basis of the principle of informed choice. All 15 Danish counties decided to follow the recommendations and by June 2006, every county in Denmark was offering PRA (Ekelund et al. 2008). PRA has a high uptake in Denmark. One study covering two counties shows that only 2% of couples who were offered PRA in the period 1 July to 31 December 2005 actively refused and it is estimated that the overall current uptake is at least 90% (Tørring et al. 2008). In the Copenhagen area the uptake is estimated to be around 95% (Tabor 2006).

Denmark is a unique case, because it is one of the first countries in the world to have implemented the test at a national level through a publicly financed health system (Ekelund et al. 2008). Other welfare states have implemented the test, but not (yet) at a national level. In Norway, PRA is offered only to pregnant women above 38 and women who are known to be at increased risk of having a diseased child (Bioteknologinemnda 2005)[1]. In Iceland, every pregnant woman is informed about the possibility of undergoing PRA, but she has to pay for the examination herself (Kristjánsdóttir 2008). Both Sweden (SMER 2007) and Finland (Decree 1339/2006) have a system similar to Denmark's underway, but they have not yet been fully implemented. Worldwide, several countries are discussing the possibility of introducing PRA as a national screening strategy and the various problems in trying to achieve this, have been reported (Chang 2006, O'Leary 2006, Reddy 2006).

The arguments used by the Danish health authorities for offering PRA to all pregnant women – in contrast to the previous programme which offered invasive diagnostic testing to all women above 35 years of age – were strongly linked to the issue of self determination. In the guidelines which provided the ethical grounding of the implementation on prenatal risk assessment in the Danish health care system, the Danish Board of Health emphasized its commitment to the principle of patient autonomy by stating that the objective was not prevention of disease, which had been the self-evident reason for the previous screening programme:

> The purpose of prenatal testing is not to prevent the birth of children with serious disease, but rather to assist the pregnant woman in making her own choice. Objective and adequate information is a necessary condition to this end (Sundhedsstyrelsen 2003a).

In the guidelines, the ideal of informed choice served as a rhetorical tool to demarcate a past, prevention-oriented regime of prenatal testing from a future

---

1   Pregnant women who show an increased level of anxiety are also in some situations offered to undergo PRA. This possibility has been widely debated in Norway (Solberg 2008).

choice-oriented regime of prenatal testing (Schwennesen et al. 2009). The regime was now formulated as an option of individual choice, and not as a public programme of disease prevention.

Questions have been raised in the Danish debate about whether or not the policy of autonomous decision making in connection with prenatal risk assessment works as intended and studies have been conducted aimed at evaluating whether the users of risk assessment are well informed (Dahl 2006a, 2006b, Bangsgaard et al. 2007). In a European context autonomous decision-making has been seen as a key aspect of ethical health care in the context of prenatal testing (Marteau 2001a, 2001b, Harper 2004, Dahl 2006a, 2006b, Hunt 2006) and tools to measure the level of informed choice have been developed (Marteau 2001b, Van den Berg 2006). The idea of ethical health care in the context of genetic counselling has been framed in a language of choice and as a question of having the right information in order to perform a qualified choice. Peter S. Harper sums up the ambition of genetic counselling in a recent text book: '[I]t is not the duty of a doctor to dictate the lives of others, but to ensure that individuals have the facts to enable them to make their own decisions ...' (Harper 2004: 81). The rationale is that non-directive information, based on objective facts, will provide the ethical basis for autonomous decision-making.

In this chapter, however, we contest this representational view of knowledge production, upon which the idea of non-directiveness relies. Drawing on specific case studies, we argue that facts of foetal life are not simply pre-existing entities, existing out there, waiting to be represented – visualized and quantified by doctor to patient. Secondly, we challenge the idea that decisions are made by autonomous individuals, and suggest that decisions instead may be seen as processes and practices of boundary drawing and meaning-making taking place in the relational space of social and material knowledge production. Finally, we want to draw attention to possible implications for the ethical framework that currently regulates PRA.

Agential realism: A framework for knowledge production

In the following analysis we are inspired by the physicist and science studies scholar Karen Barad. Drawing on Danish physicist Niels Bohr's study of quantum physics, Barad develops her theory of agential realism and challenges the representationalist idea of knowledge production, which holds that facts, in the form of words or images are capable of objectively reflecting pre-existing things. The idea that representations and the objects they claim to represent are independent of one another, has been challenged by several science studies scholars (Hacking 1983, Collin and Yearly 1992, Latour 1993, Pickering 1995, Rouse 1996). Although these scholars differ in significant ways, attention has been drawn to how knowledge production must be analysed as a process through which both human and non-human forms of agency are involved, and that the coming together of the human and the non-human evolves through a process of co-production (Callon and Latour 1992, Pickering 1995). Likewise, Barad's theory of agential realism starts out from the premise that 'we need to understand in an integral way the roles of human and nonhuman, material and discursive, and natural and cultural factors in scientific and other practices' (Barad 2007: 25). Barad goes further, however, than the mere acknowledgement that material and human agency play a role in knowledge production. Her starting point is Niels Bohr's demonstration that classical correspondence theories of scientific knowledge fall short when trying to explain the classical wave-particle paradox; that light manifests particle-like properties under one set of experimental circumstances and wave-like properties under a different set of experimental circumstances (Bohr 1958, Barad 2007: 198). To a classical realist, who sees the relationship between scientific knowledge and the object under observation as a corresponding or mirroring relationship, this situation is paradoxical; 'the true ontological nature of light is in question; either light is a wave or it is a particle, it cannot be both' (Barad 2007: 198). Bohr resolves this problem, in Barad's interpretation, by installing 'phenomena' understood as the wholeness of the entity of observation and the apparatus of observation as the referent of knowledge instead of the duality of an independent observer and an observation-independent object. Although Bohr's theory is concerned with physical matter, Barad shows how his thinking can be made productive in a social science context. Taking into account Bohr's notion of phenomenon, Barad develops the concept of *intra-action* which underscores the sense in which entities emerge through their encounters with each other in a continual process of becoming (Barad 2007: 33). As opposed to the concept interaction, which suggest two entities given in advance that come together and engage in some kind of exchange, she suggests that distinct entities, be it human and non-human, the social and the material, do not precede practice. Rather, the components are only distinct in relation to their mutual entanglement: they do not exist as individual elements (Barad 2007: 33). This implies that configurations of apparatuses or agencies of observation – the tools we use in our observations of objects – should not be framed as passive or innocent tools to peer at the object of observation or offering constraints on what we can see. Rather, they should be conceived as productive and part of the phenomena which emerge through the process of knowledge production. That is, the measured object *and* agencies of observation form a non-dualistic physical whole: 'Phenomena are the ontological inseparability of agentially intra-acting components' (Barad 2007: 33) and it is this relational and multidimensional entity that comprises the phenomenon (Barad 2007: 205). On this basis, Barad develops what she calls a non-representationalist – but still realist – account of scientific practices that takes the *material* nature of knowledge practices seriously. Barad's work goes further than theories of co-production in its attempt to create a more robust understanding of materiality. In our view, she manages successfully to integrate a notion of nature/the material as fundamental for knowledge production without reinstalling it as something which is outside or pre-existing practice.

We have found Barad's approach challenging in our analysis of the way that human and non-human intra-actions constitute knowledge production but also in her way of explicitly drawing out the ontological, ethical and political implications. If we acknowledge that the basic units of reality are phenomena, understood as the ontological inseparability of emergent configurations of (human and non-human) agencies, then we are in part responsible for what there 'is' in the world: 'We are responsible for the world in which we live not because it is an arbitrary construction of our choosing, but because agential reality is sedimented out of particular practices that we have a role in shaping' (Barad 2000: 247). Following this, Barad suggests that ethical concerns must not simply be considered as supplemental to the practice of science, which has been the case in PRA, where ethical concerns are centred on questions of correspondence, such as how to produce objective facts and make possible non-directive communication. Rather, ethical concerns must be considered as an integral part of knowledge production and its consequences. In the final section of the chapter, we will return to this point.

In the following section we want to look at the practices through which a visual representation of the foetus is produced, and the interpretative procedures, which make the produced image meaningful to the actors involved. What emerges from these practices is a realization that what we term 'a foetus' is not a well-defined observation-independent object, but a phenomenon which cannot be known – virtually does not exist – independently of apparatuses of observation applied to bring about such knowledge. Whether we speak of ultrasound scans, risk figures or the sensations of the pregnant women, these are all apparatuses of observations whose measurements require interpretation before they may be acted upon. Here the implications for the ethics of PRA become obvious. If the meaning that people make of specific measurements, be they images, risk figures or just corporeal sensations is an element of the total phenomenon it becomes meaningless to speak of autonomous decision on the basis of objective facts. Rather, the whole arrangement which together makes up PRA, may be seen as part of the phenomenon which emerges, and thus as part of the decision which is made. In the following we want to explore the implications of a Baradian viewpoint when applied to empirical material. The analysis is based on observations and interviews with couples undergoing PRA in a Danish public hospital. Three case studies have been selected to illustrate how the facts of life are produced and contested in the context of PRA.

Visualizing the foetus in PRA-practice

Undergoing an ultrasound scan is the first obligatory point of passage for those women and their partners who have chosen to undergo PRA. In contemporary western societies, ultrasound has become routine practice for pregnant women (Getz et al. 2003) and it is common to find foetal ultrasound images immediately preceding pictures of newborns in family photo albums or on the internet. Moreover,

Lennart Nilsson's popular book with images of pre-birth foetuses, has brought pictures of 'life before birth' into public life (Nilsson 1977) and today images of foetuses can be seen in media such as advertising, magazines, films etc.

In interviews with pregnant women and their partners the practice was described as 'a routine act' and 'a normal and natural part of pregnancy' which was motivated by a wish to 'be assured that everything is ok' and 'to see that there actually is something in there'. As we have argued elsewhere, PRA appeared as a 'default pathway' (Webster 2007: 470) on the trajectory towards having a healthy baby (Schwennesen et al. 2008: 18). In the following, we apply Barad's notion of intra-action on our first case, where we follow a couple undergoing a nuchal translucency scan through ultrasound. In Barad's terminology apparatuses are not mere observing instruments but material-discursive boundary drawing practices through which differential boundaries are constituted between objects (non-humans) and subjects (humans) (Barad 2007: 140). Following this, we frame the practice of ultrasonography as a device for making and remaking boundaries and ask: What kind of phenomena is constituted during ultrasound and which boundaries are constituted around objects (non-humans) and subjects (humans) through this process?

The ultrasound scan

Ida is 25 years old. She has been with Mark for three years, and she is now pregnant for the first time. Today, Ida is 13 weeks pregnant, and she has an appointment at the local hospital to undergo an ultrasound scan. Ida and Mark feel that until now the pregnancy has been unreal to them, and especially Mark is having difficulties relating to the fact that he is going to be a father. They look forward to the scan and expect that by undergoing the scan they will be assured that a baby is actually developing within Ida's belly. Mark cannot see on Ida's body that she is pregnant, neither has she experienced the baby move. Ida has felt a bit sick during the last weeks, which she knows might be related to pregnancy, but the only outward sign has been the blue line on the strip of the pregnancy test-kit.

After informing the reception that they have arrived, a sonographer shows Ida and Mark into the room where the ultrasound scan is going to be performed. Ida lies down on the examination couch and the sonographer puts a fluid gel on her belly. The sonographer places the transducer on Ida's belly, and a black and white image emerges on the screen in front of them. The sonographer has her own screen, which she looks at, at the same time as she moves the transducer back and forth on Ida's belly. During the scan, the sonographer marks out specific points on the image on the screen; she measures the nuchal translucency fold and the crown-rump length. She also points out to Mark and Ida where vital organs are, such as the heart, the arms, the hands, the bladder and the umbilical cord and she states that this one is an active one. During the scan Ida and Mark agree gigglingly that the image on the screen looks like a little boy and Ida states excitedly, that he has Mark's chin. When the scan is over, Ida pulls up her trousers, and they walk into the hall and wait for the result. The sonographer walks into another room to calculate the risk figure (field note).

During the scan the foetus floats between a human and a non-human state. Before undergoing the scan, the foetus was hardly experienced as really existing. During the scan, however, the foetus is gradually constituted as an autonomous living being. The image on the screen is displaced from its location in Ida's body and emerges as a free-floating entity, autonomously located on the screen. It is presented out of scale with Ida's body (the uterus, placenta, amniotic fluid, her emotions etc.) and emerges on the screen, as if it existed out of place and out of space. Ida and Mark were not able to immediately understand or independently interpret what they saw on the screen. Having seen an ultrasound image before, they regarded the grey visualizations of reflected echoes as an image of a foetus. During the scan, the sonographer described the image to them in details, as she pointed out specific body parts and characterized the foetus as being active. Ida and Mark trusted her qualified interpretation of the image, commented on the characterizations and continued her interpretations in their conversation. Through this material-discursive process, the image emerged to them, as not only a foetus, but as a child with a specific sex, having specific physical characteristics. Thus,

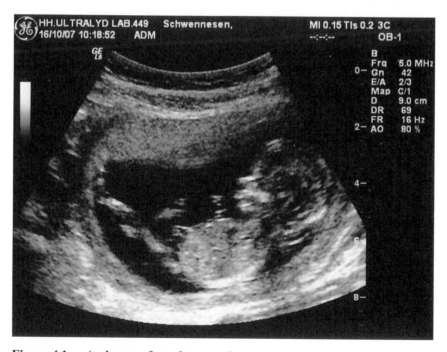

Figure 4.1   An image of an ultrasound scan

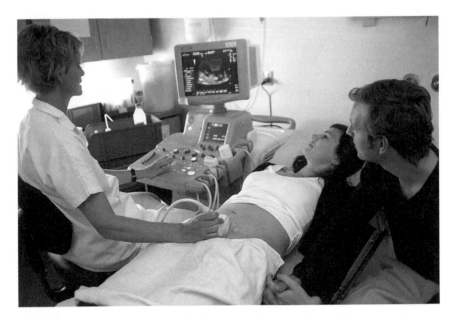

Figure 4.2. An ultrasound scan being performed

Source: Reproduced with the kind permission of Ann Tabor, Professor of Fetal Medicine, University of Copenhagen.

Ida and Mark became capable of reading the image on the screen as an image of a child through the sonographer's interpretation and their own interpretation of what she said. What Mark and Ida 'saw' on the computer screen, then, might well be interpreted as a relational entity of a phenomenon which emerged as a child through the temporal intra-action of 'agencies of observation': (the transducer), Ida's body, the sonographer's interpretation of the image and their own interpretation of what was said and shown to them. The transducer, the sonographer and Ida's body then seem to be intra-active agents and as such, part of the phenomena of the child in its emerging state. The collapsing of the image on the screen, with an ontologically stable level of an 'actually existing' baby (existing independently of material and social practices), had a strong emotional effect. After the scan Ida and Mark state that it was a very moving experience for them to undergo the scan:

> Ida: I was very moved during the scan. Moved that you could *actually* see that there was something in there with *hands and a heart* and everything, moved that it was *actually a human being* who was snuggling in there. I almost cried and now when I know that there is something, I experience a sort of a need to protect it.

Mark: When you see the ultrasound image, then it becomes *real and tangible*, right, then you begin to understand that a baby is on its way.

Ida elaborates: This is the first time that I have come to understand people who are against abortion. *Actually it is a three centimetre piece of life*, that there is in there, right? *Actually it is a person*, whom you may decide to kill, right?

Mark and Ida enact the scan as a window and representational space through which foetal life becomes visible, thus invoking ultrasound as a passive and neutral technology which mirrors the object under observation. They interpret the image as an accurate representation, and thus render the agency of the sonographer, Ida's body and the ultrasound scan invisible.

During the scan Mark and Ida's relationship to the pregnancy changed. Through this process the object under observation gradually emerged as an autonomous living being to them. Viewing and interpreting the image on the screen in intra-action, then, was also a process of humanization of the phenomenon under observation. Several feminist science scholars have drawn attention to how the temporal horizons of humanness are pushed further and further back, as new technologies of reproduction (especially imaging) have transformed current pregnancy (Petchesky 1987, Rothman 1994, Rapp 2000, Mitchell 2001). Moreover, as several authors have suggested (Braidotti 1994, Petchesky 1987), ultrasound has the capacity to alter the body boundaries of a woman by visualizing the inside of her body. The process of undergoing an ultrasound scan, however, blurs not only the corporal boundaries of the inside and outside of Ida's body, but also the temporal boundaries of being. By means of the ultrasound, the future was brought into the present and the social birth of a baby, came to precede the biological birth. This process also shaped Ida and Mark as prospective parents and they reacted with great affection on seeing the image on screen. This process, then, simultaneously marked a change in social status of both the foetus and Ida and Mark, whose developing identities as a responsible father and mother escalated by undergoing the scan.

Quantifying the foetus in PRA practice

After the scan, a risk figure is calculated in order to identify couples eligible for invasive tests such as chorionic villus sampling (CVS) or amniocentesis. These tests are said to be diagnostic, yet they do involve a risk of inducing a miscarriage (1%). The previous regime of prenatal testing in Denmark relied on an age limit, only women aged 35 or above were offered such tests. The new regime is organized around different access criteria in the shape of an established cut off point. The cut off point distributes foetuses into those at 'high' risk and thus eligible for further invasive tests, and those at 'low' risk and thus not eligible for further tests. The guidelines recommend that a cut off point at 1:250 should be implemented. When this study was carried out, the cut-off point was contested among Danish hospitals and ranged between 1:250 and 1:400 (Ekelund et al. 2008). The hospital where the fieldwork was undertaken, worked with a cut off point at 1:300, which is in accordance to the recommendations of the Fetal Medicine Foundation[2]. This allows for the use of a fetal medicine software program for calculating risk (Astraia, Germany) which is based on formulas derived from the Fetal Medicine Foundation. In January 2007, a common cut off of 1:300 was implemented in all Danish counties offering PRA (Ekelund et al. 2008). The first population based study on the impact of the implementation of PRA at a national level in Denmark, shows that the programme is very successful in terms of prevention. In the period 2000–2006 the number of infants born with Down's syndrome halved (from 55–65 pr. year during 2000–2004 to 32 in 2006) (Ekelund et al. 2008). Even though the Danish Board of Health does not characterize the new programme of prenatal testing in Denmark as a preventive screening programme, the study indicates that it is more effective in obtaining the goals of prevention than the previous programme.

The cut-off point is calculated on the basis of a large sample of epidemiological data (Nicolaides 2004) and expresses a relationship between detection rate, false positive rate and economic costs. If the cut-off point is high, only a few women will be given access to invasive tests, the detection rate will be low, the number of false positives will be low, and the socio-economic costs will be high (a greater number of children with Down's syndrome will be born, and require expensive care). Conversely, if the cut-off point is low, a high number of women will be given access to invasive tests, the detection rate will be high, the number of false positives will be high, and the socio-economic costs will be low (a lower number of children with Down's syndrome will be born, and require care). Thus, there is a trade-off between these factors, and where the exact limit is set is not objectively evident, but is based on normative and political decisions balancing the different interests. The cut off point may be seen as a moral assessment of threat or danger, as it points towards a certain action: undergoing an invasive test in order to know whether a foetus has Down's syndrome and to act on that basis. In this sense, it expresses normative and political intentions and values about the desired outcome of the programme on a population level. As Douglas argues, the moral dimension of risk arises in particular from the fact that 'risk is not only the probability of an event but also the probable magnitude of its outcome, and everything depends on the value that is set on the outcome. The evaluation is a political, aesthetic and moral matter' (Douglas 1990: 10). However, the implicit cost-benefit considerations were not mentioned in the guidelines as they were in the previous ones (Ministry of the Interior 1977) and no official discussions on the right balance between the different interests have been initiated.

---

2   The Fetal Medicine Foundation is based in London and lead by Professor Kypros Nicolaides. It is a registered charity that aims to improve the health of pregnant women and their babies through research and training in fetal medicine (<http://www.fetalmedicine.com/fmf/>).

Calculating a specific risk figure in the context of PRA is a complex matter. Three different parameters are taken into account: the pregnant woman's age related risk; a measurement of biochemical markers in the pregnant woman's blood (serum-free β human chorionic gonadotrophin and pregnancy-associated plasma protein A) called the double test; and the size of the nuchal translucency (obtained through the nuchal translucency scan). Blood samples for the double test are collected at the hospital in between weeks 8–13 of pregnancy. The sample is sent to a laboratory (Statens Serum Institut) for biochemical analysis. The sonographer receives the results the day the nuchal translucency scan is performed via the computer. After the scan has been carried out, the sonographer feeds the data into the software programme, and an overall risk figure is calculated and communicated to the couple. The calculation of the risk figure involves apparatuses such as blood, ultrasound, a trained sonographer[3], epidemiological data, computers, specific software and a pregnant woman's body. As such, the risk figure itself, may be seen as a phenomenon emerging in intra-action as a result of a complex configuration of apparatuses of observation.

Floating risk/floating foetuses

While a risk figure in an epidemiological setting is about relationships on a population level, its role in a clinical setting is to assist in the diagnosis and management of a *specific* patient (Gifford 1986: 221). Thus, in PRA practice a risk figure is transformed from characterizing the population to saying something about a specific foetus. When communicated to the pregnant woman and her partner, the task is now to translate this risk figure into a characterization of the specific foetus, and to make it useful as a basis for action. In the following, the practice of risk communication and decision-making is framed as a knowledge producing practice, which aims at saying something about the foetus. Even though the risk assessment does not involve biological material from the foetus (as invasive tests do) the underlying question of PRA is whether or not the foetus is at risk of having Down's syndrome and eventually how to act on this basis. Below we focus on the process through which the risk figure is made meaningful and boundaries around high risk and low risk are made. The point here is that for a while the foetus retains a certain ambiguity – and floats between not only a human and a non-human state but also a healthy and a non-healthy state. These potentialities are gradually resolved during the PRA process.

---

3   An international training programme for carrying out PRA for Down's syndrome has been established by the Fetal Medicine Foundation in London. In Denmark nuchal translucency ultrasonography is carried out by nurses, midwifes, and doctors certified by and in accordance with the guidelines of the Fetal Medicine Foundation (<http://www.fetalmedicine.com/fmf/training-certification/certificates-of-competence/>).

In the interviews underlying this paper, the risk figure was not seen as immediately meaningful by the couples undergoing PRA. It only became so, by being related to other entities. A number of the interviewees received a risk figure higher than expected. This was the case for Caroline, who is 40 years old, and has tried to conceive without any success the last three years. When she was interviewed, she was pregnant for the first time, after undergoing IVF. Caroline perceives herself as being rather old for a woman who is expecting her first child and she describes this pregnancy as '*her last chance*'. She did not think much about whether or not to undergo the risk assessment. To her it was '*a natural thing to do*'. Undergoing the scan was a very positive experience for her. She says '*during the scan, I experienced very positive feelings and happiness over actually seeing the baby for the first time. It was a great joy to see that there actually was a baby in there*'. Caroline received a risk figure of 1:164, and she was offered to undergo an amniocentesis. Caroline thought a lot about whether or not she should opt for an amniocentesis and the risk of abortion that it would involve:

> At first I was like, well I do not want to take that risk, now when I have seen the little miracle in there, I just did not want anything to happen with it. So it was these motherhood feelings, I think, which came to me. I thought a lot about that if this is my last chance and if it failed, then I would never be able to forgive myself for wasting this opportunity before even knowing whether something was wrong with this child.

During the scan, the object under observation emerged to Caroline as a baby and she experienced for the first time during pregnancy, what she calls 'maternal feelings'. Receiving a high risk figure according to the cut off point, however, reconfigured her interpretation of the object under observation. For Caroline the scan and the risk figure enacted two contradictory objects and with these, two possible futures. One, a foetal patient at-risk who might be eligible for 'treatment' (which in this context means abortion), the other a potentially healthy baby. This co-existence of different versions of the object under observation and what the future will bring created a sense of ambivalence for her and she experienced difficulties in acting on this basis. At first Caroline decided against having an amniocentesis, and thus preserved the phenomenon as a healthy baby, but after a week she reconsidered her decision.

After receiving the risk figure Caroline did not perceive it as immediately meaningful, and it did not guide her towards a clear decision. It only became so by relating it to other figures she was presented with, such as the cut off point, her age-related risk and the risk of inducing a miscarriage by undergoing an amniocentesis. Caroline negotiated her interpretation of the object under observation through this process of intra-action. The most powerful element in this process was the cut off point, which in the end worked as the categorical norm that eventually stabilized her interpretation of the object under observation as 'high risk'. Here one specific part of the apparatus of observation, the cut off point, seems to shape the emerging object with greater authority than other parts and thus directs Caroline towards a certain decision, e.g. to undergo an amniocentesis:

> I received a risk figure of 1:164, which is a tremendous improvement from my age risk. So, in that case it was a *positive risk figure*. However, there is still a long way to the cut-off point of 300. So, I still thought that it was a *big risk* seen in some kind of relationship. It is difficult to see through how much *age* counts alone, or if there also are other things in it. I did not know anything about that, because it is just a calculation. But still this risk was lurking in the back of my mind. In my head it was something like, when you are so far from the boundary [the cut-off point], well, maybe it is OK to be far from the boundary, but I had actually expected that I would receive a risk closer to 300, definitely around 200 or so.

Even though she found it difficult to relate to the cut off point, Caroline trusted this boundary and attributed authority to it. Thus it became the most important 'apparatus of observation' through which the meaning of the risk figure emerged as high-risk – and requiring amniocentesis. In Caroline's case social trust in the cut off point, and thereby in the Danish Health care sector, was used as a strategy through which complex risk knowledge was ordered and became meaningful. As we have shown elsewhere (Schwennesen et al. 2008) the couples undergoing PRA seek to reinstall authority and demonstrate a sturdy trust in the health professionals in the process of making risk knowledge meaning-full. This is similar to the Finnish experience, where a 'remarkable trust' in the public health system and maternity care has been identified (Meskus, this volume).

During the process of decision-making the enactment of the object under observation as a healthy baby receded into the background, and the enactment of it as being a high risk foetus possibly with Down's syndrome was fore-grounded. Through this process, a fearful version of the future was mobilized into the present. Caroline explains how it was difficult for her to face up to the decision and to take responsibility for it:

> The risk figure was explained to me in a very professional manner, and I was not able to make sense of it. They, of course, have to be very careful not to indirectly indicate anything. They emphasised over and over again, that it, well, it is your choice…. So I had to take responsibility for this all alone… Normally I like to take responsibility and make decisions; I like being responsible and being able to influence things. It fits very well with my personality. But in this situation it was not really a good experience, because I felt like, well, the health professionals are the experts and I know nothing and I was like, well, it is their field and they have the professional knowledge, so it should be possible to get more information or advice. I felt like that… at the same time I knew that I could not demand that. Eh… so I did not really like the responsibility I had. It was not

a decision I felt like facing up to… at the same time I knew that I was the only one who was capable of doing that.

In the situation of risk assessment, Caroline became a mother to a child at risk, but also a person responsible for making decisions. This case shows how apparatuses of observation do not only create objects but also subjects which are shaped in certain ways, in this case as a mother to a possibly diseased baby and simultaneously an actor who must choose and thereby take responsibility for the choice which is made.

Negotiating risk

In the interviews, the cut off point worked as a powerful disciplinary apparatus through which the phenomenon under observation emerged as either a high-risk foetus or a low-risk foetus. A recent survey covering pregnant women undergoing PRA in Denmark in 2006, however, shows that 10.27% decided not to accept the offer of an invasive test, even though they were offered one (Ekelund et al. 2008). In this sense it seems that PRA creates a certain space for action where it is possible to resist the disciplining effects of the cut off point, and interpret 'the facts' in alternative ways. This is illustrated in Lise's case, below. In her case we see very clearly how the apparatuses of observation not only create objects and subjects but also a certain space for action, where the disciplinary effects of the cut off point are challenged and even resisted. Lise is 43 years old and when we spoke to her, she was pregnant with her second child. After undergoing the scan, she received a risk figure of 1:262. She did not choose to proceed with further testing, even though she was offered a CVS. When explaining her reasons why, Lise talks about a past experience she had when she was pregnant with her first child. She was offered an amniocentesis (because of her age-related risk) and accepted the offer. Lise explains that on the way home from the hospital on the day she had undergone amniocentesis she met a boy with Down's syndrome:

> When I went home from the hospital that day in the bus, a grown up boy with Down's syndrome came into the bus and sat with his ticket. It was clear to me that he had a life which, eh, which he was able to live and it was not hopeless… With Down's syndrome you can live about 45–50 years, and there are a lot of, sort of help facilities, you will not be hidden away as you would 100 years ago.

Lise explains how she, on the basis of that experience, changed her image of a child with Down's syndrome. This made her reconsider what she would do if the amniocentesis were positive. Lise explains how she felt she had a very different relationship to children with Down's syndrome than the health professionals had during her last pregnancy:

They are very concerned about telling you that there is no guarantee for a perfect child. But they do not understand the opposite end of the scale. They don't understand how people might not have anything against having a child with Down's syndrome... maybe some are a bit cautious about getting rid of a child who is not perfect. This aspect they do not get.

Today, on the basis of these past experiences, Lise does not perceive her risk figure at 1:262 as high risk. She would not abort the child if she found out that it had Down's syndrome. A future with a child with Down's syndrome does not frighten her. Lise's past experiences, then, worked for her as an apparatus of observation through which the risk figure did not appear as high risk. She thereby challenged the cut-off point, and the image of a future with a child with Down's syndrome as risky and dangerous and in doing so she mobilized into the present the somehow marginalized image of a child with Down's syndrome as congruent with a good life.

Conclusion: Towards an ethics of mattering

In this chapter we have illustrated different ways in which 11–13-week old foetuses are made to matter in the context of PRA and PRA-related processes of decision-making. By giving analytical priority to emerging phenomena over pre-existing stable objects, we have shown how the object under observation in the practice of PRA emerge as different phenomena, be it human/nonhuman, high risk/low risk, as it is visualized through the ultrasound scan, as it is quantified through a risk figure, and as these technologies are interpreted and made sense of by the pregnant woman and her partner in the process of decision-making. We have illustrated that the foetus retains a certain ambiguity and emerges as different phenomena, while different configurations of apparatuses of observation are used to produce knowledge about it and that not only social but also material agency is involved in the process of bringing about phenomena.

On this basis we suggest that PRA may be seen as a process of *mattering,* where foetuses emerge as different forms of phenomena, as different configurations of apparatuses of observation are used. An understanding of PRA as a process of mattering has implications for how to think about accountability and responsibility in the context of PRA. In the following, we want to draw out two implications. As noted earlier, ethical health care in the context of PRA has mainly been concerned with how to produce and communicate objective facts in a non-directive way, so as to make possible a truly informed, rational and autonomous choice – as illustrated by attempts to create a measure for informed choice (Marteau et al. 2001). In this view, ethics is seen as a technicality which is supplemental to the practice of knowledge production and raises questions of correspondence such as how to produce objective facts and communicate them in a non-directive way. It relies on the view that knowledge concerns a pre-existing object which can be transmitted by doctor to patient as a bounded package which exists independently of social and material practices.

This study, however, suggests that we instead may think about ethics as an *integral part* of knowledge production. Whether the foetus emerges as a thing or a child, healthy or non-healthy in the process of PRA is not a matter of correspondence. The constitution of these boundaries is not given in the matter of the 'thing' in itself, but involves the whole configuration of apparatus (an ultrasound scan, a cut off point, epidemiological data, a computer, software, a sonographer, a foetus, a pregnant woman's body, prior experiences, discursive interpretations, expectations, etc.) which produces the phenomena in intra-action. Moreover, this process not only concerns the production of phenomena but has consequences for how subjects understand themselves as parents or not, responsible or irresponsible and simultaneously produces and forecloses possible spaces of action.

In sum, PRA intervenes in the way the world is made intelligible to us and gives shape to how we think about ourselves. This is not to say that the world is an effect of arbitrary choice, but to emphasize that we have a role in shaping the particular practices through which the world is made intelligible. This leads us to our second point where we contest the idea that decisions are individual undertakings made on the basis of objective facts. In this view, decision-making is seen as resting with the pregnant woman (and her partner), implying that responsibility for the choice being made and the futures made possible/impossible through this choice is located solely with her/them.

This study suggests that we may change the way we talk about prenatal decision making and look at decisions as *trajectories of boundary drawing practices* around phenomena which come to matter through processes of social and material intra-actions. Such a view on decision-making and knowledge production raises another kind of question than those concerned with how to produce and communicate correct facts. It focuses on how and which phenomena are enacted, what is excluded during this process and what the implications are for those involved. It shifts the focus from ethical principles to ethical practices which take place in particular places, and which are situated both temporally and physically. This paper then, is an argument for not only taking ethical account of how to pursue value-neutrality and non-directiveness in PRA, but also for being accountable and taking responsibility for the way PRA engages in a continual process of mattering, which has real consequences for those involved.

References

Bangsgaard, L. and Tabor, A. 2007. Are pregnant women and their partners making an informed choice about first trimester risk assessment for down's syndrome? *Ultrasound Obstet Gynecol*, 30: 376.

Barad, K. 1998. Getting real: technoscientific practices and the materialization of reality. *Differences: A Journal of Feminist Cultural Studies*, 10(2), 87–126.

Barad, K. 2003. Posthumanist performativity: how matter comes to matter. *Signs: Journal of Women in Culture and Society*, 28(3), 801–31.

Barad, K. 2007. *Meeting the Universe Halfway*. London: Duke University Press.

Bioteknologinemnda 2005. *Søknad om å tilby blodprøverundersøkelser ("dobbeltest" og trippeltest") til gravide kvinner som opfyller et teller flere av dagens vilkår for fosterdiagnostik*. Oslo: Biotechnologinemda.

Braidotti, R. 1994. *Nomadic Subjects: Embodiment and Sexual Difference in Contemporary Feminist Theory*. Columbia: Colombia University Press.

Bohr, N. 1958. *Atomic Physics and Human Knowledge*. New York: John Wiley and Sons inc.

Callon, M. and Latour, B. 1992. Don't throw the baby out with the bath school! A reply to Collins and Yearly, in *Science as Practice and Culture*, edited by A. Pickering. Chicago: University of Chicago Press, 343–68.

Casper, M. 1998. *The Making of the Unborn Patient: A Social Anatomy of Fetal Surgery*. New Brunswick, N.J.: Rutgers University Press.

Chang, T.C. 2006. Antenatal screening for Down's syndrome in New Zealand: time for a national screening policy? *Aust NZ J Obstet Gynaecol*, 42: 92–96.

Collins, H.M. and Yearly, S. 1992. Epistemological chicken, in *Science as Practice and Culture*, edited by A. Pickering. Chicago and London: University of Chicago Press, 301–26.

Dahl, K., Kesmodel U., Hvidman, L. and Olesen F. 2006a. Informed consent: attitudes, knowledge and information concerning prenatal examinations. *Acta Obstetricia et Gynecologica Scandinavia*, 85(12), 1414–19.

Dahl, K., Kesmodel U., Hvidman, L. and Olesen F. 2006b. Informed consent: providing information about prenatal examinations. *Acta Obstetricia et Gynecologica Scandinavia*, 85(12), 1420–25.

Decree 1339/2006. *Decree of the Council of State on Screening* [Online]. Available at: www.finlex.fi/fi/laki/alkup/2006/20061339 [accessed 20 January 2009].

Douglas, M. 1990. Risk as a forensic resource. *Daedalus* 119(14), 1–16.

Ekelund, C.H., Jørgensen, F.S., Petersen, O.B., Sundberg, K. and Tabor, A. 2008. Impact of a new national screening policy for Down's syndrome in Denmark: population based cohort study. *British Medical Journal*, 337: a2547.

Franklin, S. 2000. Life itself: global nature and the genetic imaginary, in *Global Nature, Global Culture*, edited by S. Franklin et al. London: Sage, 188–227.

Getz, L. and Kirkengen, A.L. 2003. Ultrasound screening in pregnancy: advancing technology, soft markers for fetal chromosomal aberrations, and unacknowledged ethical dilemmas. *Social Science & Medicine*, 56(10), 2045–57.

Hacking, I. 1983. *Representing and Intervening*. Cambridge: Cambridge University Press.

Harper, P.S. 2004. *Practical Genetic Counselling*. London: Arnold.

Hunt, L.M., Castaneda, H., de Voogd, K.B. 2006. Do notions of risk inform patient choice? Lessons from a study of prenatal genetic counselling. *Medical Anthropology*, 25(3), 193–219.

Kristjánsdóttir, H. 2008. President for the Nordic Foundation for Midwifes. Personal Communication.

Kerr, A. 2004. *Genetics and Society: a Sociology of Disease.* London: Routledge.

Latour, B. 1993. *We Have Never Been Modern.* Cambridge: Harvard University Press.

Marteau, T.M. and Dormandy, E. 2001. Facilitating informed choice in prenatal testing: how well are we doing? *American Journal of Medical Genetics,* 106(3), 185–190.

Marteau, T.M., Dormandy, E. and Michie, S. 2001. A measure of informed choice. *Health Expectations,* 4: 99–108.

Nicolaides, K.H. 2004. *The 11–13 Week Scan.* London: Foetal Medicine Foundation.

Nilsson, L. and Hamberger, K. 1977. *A Child is Born.* Delacorte Press/Seymour Lawrence.

Ministry of the Interior 1977. *Report about Prenatal Genetic Diagnosis.* Copenhagen: The Danish Publishing House.

Mitchell, L. 2001. *Baby's First Picture: Ultrasound and the Politics of Fetal Subjects.* Toronto: University of Toronto Press.

O'Leary, P., Breheny, N., Reid, G., Charles, T., Emery, J. 2006. Regional variations in prenatal screening across Australia: stepping towards a national policy framework. *Aust NZ J Obstet Gynaecol,* 46: 427–32.

Petchesky, R.P. 1987. Fetal images: the power of visual culture in the politics of reproduction. *Feminist Studies,* 13: 263–92.

Pickering, A. 1995. *The Mangle of Practice: Time, Agency, and Science.* Chicago: University of Chicago Press.

Rapp, R. 2000. *Testing Women, Testing the Fetus: The Social Impact of Amniocentesis in America.* London: Routledge.

Reddy, U.M., Mennuti, M.T. 2006. Incorporating first-trimester Down syndrome studies into prenatal screening: executive summary of the National Institute of Child Health and Human Development Workshop. *Obstet Gynecol,* 107: 167–73.

Rose, N. 2001. The politics of life itself. *Theory, Culture and Society,* 18(6), 1–30.

Rothman, B.K. 1994. *The Tentative Pregnancy: Amniocentesis and the Sexual Politics of Motherhood.* London: Pandora/HarperCollins.

Rouse, J. 1996. *Engaging Science: How to Understand Its Practises Philosophically.* Itacha, New York: Cornell University Press.

Schwennesen, N. Koch, L. and Svendsen, M.N. 2009. Practising informed choice: decision-making and prenatal risk assessment – the Danish experience, in *Disclosure Dilemmas: Ethics of Genetic Prognosis After the 'Right to Know/ Not to Know' Debate,* edited by C. Rehman-Sutter and H. Müller. Farnham: Ashgate.

Schwennesen, N., Svendsen, M.N. and Koch, L. 2008. Beyond informed choice: prenatal risk assessment, decision-making and trust. *Etikk i praksis,* 1: 11–31.

SMER (Statens medicinsk-etiske råd) 2007. *Yttrande om en ny metod för riskbedömning vid fosterdiagnostik*, 2007–09–24 Dnr 08/07 [Online]. Available at: www.smer.se/Bazment/106.aspx http://www.smer.se/Bazment/106. aspx[accesed: 20 January 2009].

Solberg, B. 2008. Associate Professor in bioethics, NTNU Norway, Personal communication.

Sundhedsstyrelsen [Danish Board of Health] 2003a. *Fosterdiagnostik og risikovurdering* [*Prenatal Diagnosis and Risk Assessment*]. Copenhagen: Schultz Information.

Sundhedsstyrelsen [Danish Board of Health] 2003b. *Notat vedrørende nye retningslinjer for fosterdiagnostik.* [*Note Regarding New Guidelines of Prenatal Diagnosis*]. Copenhagen: Danish Board of Health.

Sundhedsstyrelsen [Danish Board of Health] 2004. *Nye retningslinjer for fosterdiagnostik* [*New Guidelines for Prenatal Diagnosis*]. Copenhagen: Danish Board of Health.

Tabor, A. 2006. Professor in Foetal Medicine, Rigshospitalet. Personal communication.

Tørring, N., Petersen, B.B.O., Holmskov, A., Hertz, M.J. and Uldbjerg, N. 2008. Prænatal diagnostik i Århus og Viborg Amter efter implementering af første trimester-risikovurdering. *Ugeskrift for læger*, 170: 50–54.

Van den Berg, M., Timmermans, D.R.M., ten Kate, L.P., van Vugt, J.M.G. and van der Wal, G. 2006. Informed decision making in the context of prenatal screening. *Patient Education and Counseling*, 63(1–2), 110–117.

Webster, A. 2007. Crossing boundaries: social science in the policy room. *Science, Technology & Human Values*, 32(4), 458–78.

Williams, C., Sandall, J., Lewando-Hundt, G., Heyman, B., Spencer, K. and Grellier, R. 2002. Women as moral pioneers? Experiences of first trimester antenatal screening. *Social Science & Medicine*, 61(9), 1983–1992.

<http://www.fetalmedicine.com/fmc/ultrasound/11–13–weeks-scan/> [accessed: 20 January 2009].

<http://www.fetalmedicine.com/fmf/training-certification/certificates-of-competence/> [accessed: 20 January 2009].

<http://www.fetalmedicine.com/fmf/> [accessed: 20 January 2009].

Chapter 5
Serious Disease as Kinds of Living

Ayo Wahlberg

In December 2003, a Church of England curate from Chester in North West England challenged West Mercia police's failure to investigate the termination of a pregnancy in 2001 involving a 28-week-old foetus which had been diagnosed with a cleft lip and palate using ultrasound technology. In England, medical termination after 24 weeks is only allowed to save the pregnant woman's life, to prevent grave permanent injury to the health of the pregnant woman or if it is judged that the future child would be 'seriously handicapped' (United Kingdom 1991).[1] The curate's charge was that this termination had in fact been an unlawful killing because there was no risk to the life or health of the woman nor was there any risk that the child would be born seriously handicapped.

Just over a year later, in March 2005, the Crown Prosecution Service informed the curate that she had lost her challenge. The issue to be determined, according to the Crown prosecutor, had been 'whether the two doctors who had authorized the termination were of the opinion, formed in good faith, that there was a substantial risk that if the child were born it would suffer from such physical and mental abnormalities as to be seriously handicapped' (Crown Prosecution Service 2005). Following a review of the patient's medical records, guidance from the Royal College of Obstetricians and Gynaecologists (RCOG) on medical termination of pregnancy as well as evidence from a number of professionals involved in the patient's counselling and treatment and other medical experts, the Crown prosecutor concluded that 'the abortion was due to a bi-lateral cleft palate and was legally justified and procedurally correctly carried out' (EWHC 2003). He would later add, 'I consider that both doctors concluded that there was a substantial risk of abnormalities that would amount to the child being seriously handicapped' (cited in Gledhill 2005). The case, which has been debated widely in the UK (see Scott 2005a), is a helpful starting point for a chapter aiming to explore the terms and conditions that allow for normative estimations of 'good life' in reproductive medicine today.

Studies of the social, legal and ethical implications of selection practices in reproductive medicine today have in large part focused on four key areas: the

---

1   Up to 24 weeks, medical termination in the UK may take place if two doctors agree that continued pregnancy would involve 'risk of injury to the physical or mental health of the pregnant woman or any existing children of her family… greater than if the pregnancy were terminated' (United Kingdom 1991).

problem of (non-)directive counselling (Pilnick 2002, Rapp 1988, Williams et al. 2002b); debates about how to (and who should) define what a 'life worth living' and a 'serious disease' are and where to 'draw the line' when it comes to selective reproductive practices (Scott 2005b, Williams et al. 2002a, Williams et al. 2007); whether or not new reproductive technologies are a form of 'backdoor eugenics' and/or increasingly used to produce 'designer babies' (Duster 2003, Gosden 1999, Shakespeare 1998); and finally what the responsibilities and duties of prospective parents are in reproductive medicine as compared to the rights of an unborn child (Clarkeburn 2000, Vehmas 2002). In this chapter, I will focus on a different problem, namely how assessments of 'good life' are made technically feasible during the course of selective reproductive practices. Rather than attempting to resolve very much open ethical questions – e.g. What is a life worth living? Is termination of pregnancy acceptable under any circumstances? Who should make decisions about whether or not to terminate a pregnancy? – I will instead map out the practices that currently enable assessments of vitality, however contested these assessments may be.

To do so, I will examine ongoing attempts to stabilize and delimit the contested category of 'serious disease' in the context of selective reproductive practices in England today. In accordance with principles of informed choice and consent, it is emphasized that decisions about whether or not to begin or terminate a pregnancy must be made by prospective parents in consultation with their doctors. As Rosamund Scott (2005a, 2005b) has shown in her analysis of the cleft-palate case, the legal definition of 'seriousness' remains contested. When asked to clarify their position, the Royal College of Obstetricians and Gynaecologists has suggested that since 'there is no precise definition of "serious handicap"... the RCOG believes that the interpretation of 'serious abnormality' should be based upon individual discussion agreed between the parents and the mother's doctor' (RCOG 2008).

There have been a number of studies that have focussed on the interactions that take place in such consultations between health practitioners and patients in the context of carrier, preimplantation and prenatal testing. For example, in an analysis of health practitioners' views on 'non-directiveness', Williams et al. suggest that 'for practitioners, the boundary between choice and coercion... is not a clearcut one' (2002b: 345). Based on observations of genetic counselling sessions, Pilnick has argued that 'one of the reasons why genetic counsellors may appear to give advice or suggest courses of action in the face of the stated aim of non-directive counselling may be due to [an] ambiguity of role [since] the work of genetic counsellors may encompass anything from facilitating decision making in relation to genetic testing through to diagnostic news delivery' (Pilnick 2002: 85). Franklin and Roberts have analyzed preimplantation genetic diagnosis patients' deliberations in terms of 'reproductive accounting' – 'how couples weigh their odds or chances in order to reach a decision about continuing treatment, and how they account for, or explain their actions' (2006: 164). And Rayna Rapp has argued that when communicating the results of amniocentesis to pregnant women, 'counselors are caught between the need to sound authoritative and the desire to "glide on the patient's wavelength"' (1988: 151).

What I will focus on instead is the burgeoning literature – in the form of pamphlets, booklets, parent guides, handbooks and websites – aimed at parents who are contemplating undergoing or have undergone carrier testing, preimplantation genetic diagnosis or prenatal diagnosis. Such information is prepared by reproductive medicine clinics, patient support groups, the National Health Service as well as disease advocacy organizations. I will also cover documents and public consultations prepared by such organizations as the Human Fertilisation and Embryology Authority (HFEA), the Royal College of Obstetricians and Gynecologists (RCOG) and the Human Genetics Commission specifically on the topic of selective reproductive practices.

By analysing these materials with a specific focus on Spinal Muscular Atrophy (SMA), Cystic Fibrosis (CF) and Down's syndrome, I will show what concepts, norms and techniques are deployed in attempts to determine what good life is, and how these in turn are used to situate and justify selective reproductive practices. My key argument will be that while each of these three conditions have been researched and characterized in terms of their biological aetiology and pathology, what is of crucial importance in decisions about selection is how these conditions are seen to impact on a person's and/or family's 'quality of life'. Building on Ian Hacking's work around 'human kinds' (Hacking 1995, 2002), I will suggest that not only do Spinal Muscular Atrophy, Cystic Fibrosis and Down's syndrome entail certain biological 'modes of living' in Canguilhem's sense (Canguilhem 1989), they also entail certain 'kinds of living'. In this latter sense, life is not an anatomical, cellular or molecular affair, rather it is something that is lived, experienced, coped with, taken advantage of and improved in terms of 'quality', 'hope', 'capability' or 'happiness' (Wahlberg 2007).

Detecting abnormality

It is vitality that is at stake in practices of selective reproduction. If in the past, selective reproduction was about protecting and improving some kind of collective vitality (e.g. 'population stock' or 'population quality') by preventing persons of 'inferior quality' from reproducing, these days it is argued that selective reproductive practices are aimed at protecting/ensuring the individual vitality of pregnant women (as well as that of their family members) and/or her future child by allowing couples to make informed choices about whether or not to begin or terminate a pregnancy. Carrier screening, preimplantation genetic diagnosis (PGD) and prenatal screening are all elements in this process. Each involves some kind of 'non-directive counselling' where medical experts aim 'to explain the facts as clearly as possible, giving the person or family accurate information on their options in a way which they can understand' (Clinical Genetics Department 2008).

In each of these forms of selective reproductive practice – carrier testing, embryo biopsy and prenatal diagnosis – it is primarily[2] the possibility of a child being born with a disease or condition (whether hereditary or congenital) that is being addressed. Carrier testing aims at identifying 'a healthy "carrier" whose children could be affected with a particular genetic condition… [that] can cause problems', thereby affecting 'family planning decisions or other plans for the future' (Clinical Genetics Department 2008, Guy's and St Thomas's Hospital 2002). Carrier testing for conditions such as Tay Sachs Disease and Cystic Fibrosis, has been available in the UK for so-called 'at risk' (because of family history or ethnic background) populations since the 1980s. Individuals or couples identified by such testing as being substantially at risk of transmitting a disease through 'natural conception' can choose between accepting the risks, having no children, adopting, using gamete donors or using PGD and/or prenatal testing.

PGD, where a couples' gametes are fertilized in vitro and the resulting embryos are biopsied before a decision is made about which embryos to implant, is described by the Clinical Genetics Department at Guy's Hospital in London as 'a specialized treatment for couples who carry an inherited genetic defect that could cause serious health risks for their children' (Guy's and St Thomas's Hospital 2008). It is still a relatively new technique with 134 cycles of PGD carried out in the United Kingdom in 2005, resulting in 17 live births. At Guy's Hospital, one of the leading PGD centres in the UK, a total of 100 PGD babies had been born by the end of 2006. Neither carrier testing nor PGD involves medical abortion as they take place before pregnancy commences, either prior to conception or prior to implantation. Still, according to the logic of these practices, there are some inheritable conditions which some parents may wish to prevent being transmitted to future offspring.

Prenatal diagnosis using amniocentesis or chorionic villus sampling, on the other hand, can lead to the termination or continuation of a pregnancy depending on the decision of the couple. Following blood tests, ultrasound examinations, amniocentesis, chorionic villus sampling and/or, more recently, 'free foetal DNA' testing, prospective parents are given information concerning the chances that their child will be born with a certain chromosomal abnormality, hereditary disease or congenital malformation. Based on this information and following discussions with their doctor, couples will then make 'informed decisions' about whether they will continue their pregnancy or terminate it by assessing on the one hand, whether

---

2   PGD can also be used to select embryos which have a better chance of leading to pregnancy, for sex selection or to select an embryo which would result in a so-called 'saviour sibling', and PND techniques can also be used to determine the sex of a foetus which may lead some couples to terminate a pregnancy for 'social reasons' (even though abortion in the UK is not permitted on the grounds of sex alone). Indeed, it is the increasing use of selective reproductive techniques for 'non-medical' purposes that is seen by some as a dangerous slippery slope (see Duster 2003; Kerr and Shakespeare 2002). In this chapter, I will focus on carrier testing, PGD and PND to prevent transmission of disease.

there is a substantial risk that the child will be born 'seriously handicapped', and on the other, whether they would be able to cope with caring for a child with a particular condition. As described by the NHS, prenatal testing is 'a method of detecting serious, or potentially serious, disorders in the unborn child... If a serious abnormality is detected, amniocentesis gives parents the choice of whether they want to have a child with the abnormality, or whether they would prefer the pregnancy to be terminated at an early stage' (NHS 2009).

Of the almost 198,500 legal abortions carried out in England and Wales in 2007, about 1% of them (1,939) were because a substantial risk of serious handicap was deemed (see Table 5.1). And so, despite advances in forms of genetic testing and reproductive medicine, termination of pregnancy remains the most prevalent form of selective reproduction.

Most of the different forms of testing require biological samples obtained through biopsy. Originating from a prospective parent (blood, saliva), pregnant woman (blood, amniotic fluid), an embryo (blastomere) or a foetus (free foetal DNA, chorionic villus), such samples are biochemically and genetically analysed to detect abnormalities in alpha-fetoprotein levels using blood chemistry analysis techniques, numerical and morphological chromosome abnormalities using karyotyping techniques or the presence of specific gene defects using Polymerase Chain Reaction DNA-analysis techniques. Ultrasound visualizing technologies, on the other hand, allow for biometric assessment of foetuses to detect abnormalities in the amount of fluid at the back of a foetus' neck, femur length, biparietal diameter, abdominal circumference or head circumference. They also allow for morphological assessment as doctors look for 'lemon signs', 'banana signs',

Table 5.1   Number of legal terminations according to grounds given, 2007

	No.
Risk of injury to the physical or mental health of the pregnant woman or any children in her family, account may be taken of the pregnant woman's actual or reasonably foreseeable environment (so-called 'social abortions')	195,826
Substantial risk that child would be 'seriously handicapped'	1,939
To prevent grave permanent injury to physical or mental health of pregnant woman	622
Risk to woman's life, to save woman's life	112

Source: Department of Health (2008)

'strawberry-shaped heads', 'golf balls' or other abnormal shapes which have been associated with certain conditions such as spina bifida or Edwards syndrome.

The point being that each of these diagnostic tests has been designed to detect abnormalities using genetic, chromosomal, biochemical, morphological or biometric markers associated with specific diseases or conditions. Abnormalities are detected against 'normal' blood substance levels, gene sequences, karyotypes and foetal morphologies which have been stabilized through cumulative aggregation of clinical data. And so it is *elevated* blood substance levels, *irregular* numbers or arrangements of chromosomes, *deleted* or *mutated* gene sequences in a chromosome, *deviating* biometrics, and/or morphological *anomalies* that are singled out for further attention following diagnostic tests. Information is conveyed to prospective parents in the form of probabilities and chances as individual markers or combinations of markers are used to calculate risks. For example: if both prospective parents are identified as carriers of Cystic Fibrosis there is a 25% chance that a 'natural' pregnancy would result in a child with CF; levels of alpha-fetoprotein in a pregnant woman's blood together with her age are used to calculate chances of having a pregnancy with Down's syndrome (if the risk is calculated at more than 1 in 250, the pregnancy is classed as 'high risk'); and karyotype analysis following amniocentesis is considered to be 95–99% accurate in identifying chromosomal abnormalities in a foetus.

Now, what is important to underscore is that while these various diagnostic tests generate biological results which give parents an idea of the chances that their child will be born with a certain disease or condition, they do not tell them anything about whether or not the disease or condition in question is serious. This involves an entirely different form of assessing vitality, and it is this form of vital assessment that will be the focus of the remainder of this chapter. In the following, I will show how the question of 'seriousness' is contested and stabilized in screening for Cystic Fibrosis carriers, PGD embryo screening to avoid transmitting Spinal Muscular Atrophy disease and prenatal screening to identify Down's syndrome pregnancies. In each case, we will see how the problem of selection (i.e. whether to begin, terminate or continue a pregnancy) is linked to estimations of 'seriousness' which in turn rely on temporal notions of onset and life expectancy on the one hand, and experiential notions of severity, suffering and quality of life on the other. Indeed, I will suggest that in reproductive medicine today, it is serious disease as certain 'kinds of living' rather than as biological abnormality, error or inferiority that informs selective practices.

'Faulty' modes of living

In his analysis of how different concepts of pathology have historically instigated novel understandings of biological normativity, Georges Canguilhem concludes that 'there is no life whatsoever without norms of life, and the morbid state is always a certain mode of living' (Canguilhem 1989: 228). With disease come

Table 5.2　　Breakdown of prenatally-diagnosed conditions resulting in termination, 2007

	No.
Congenital malformations – nervous system	**473**
-　anencephaly	144
-　spina bifida	117
-　other malformations of the brain	78
-　encephalocele	33
-　hydrocephalus	31
-　other	70
Congenital malformations – other	**412**
-　musculoskeletal system	125
-　cardiovascular system	114
-　urinary system	74
-　respiratory system	11
-　other	88
Chromosomal abnormalities	**747**
-　Down's syndrome	437
-　Edward's syndrome	129
-　Patau's syndrome	63
-　other	118
Other conditions	**307**
-　family history of heritable disorders	145
-　fetus affected by maternal factors	101
-　hydrops fetalis	32
-　gestation and growth disorders	12
-　other	17

Source: Department of Health (2008)

new vital norms as bodies adapt to new conditions. 'Life does not recognise reversibility'[3] and 'every state of the organism, insofar as it is compatible with life [for however long], ends up being basically normal' (ibid.: 196, 200). His point being that until death silences the organs once and for all, all modes of living, even morbid ones, have their biological normality which in turn normalizes the 'sick living being' in defined, if not narrowed conditions of existence. And so, however serious they might be considered, Cystic Fibrosis, Spinal Muscular Atrophy and

---

3　As Sarah Franklin has pointed out, the development of Somatic Cell Nuclear Transfer or 'cloning' techniques in the 1990s has troubled this 'biological fact' as 'adult body cells are induced to deliver functions they were formerly presumed to have lost', i.e. recapacitated (Franklin 2007: 32–43). The same can be said of recent development of induced Pluripotent Stem cells through genetic reprogramming.

Down's syndrome nevertheless result in certain biological modes of living for those affected by them, albeit ones which, as we will see, are judged by some to be of lower quality because of the restrictions and limitations they entail. So, how is value attached to certain modes of living over others? To answer this, let us first look at what modes of living these diseases or conditions are seen to engender.

Before any kind of diagnostic tests are carried out, prospective parents are advised to prepare themselves well by knowing their options and deciding which of these options are appropriate for them – e.g. continuing or terminating a pregnancy following prenatal diagnostic tests. It is also recommended that this preparation includes getting to 'know more about the disorder or disorders which can be detected' (RCOG 2006: 7), 'it may be important to you in the future to know that when you made your decisions, you had all the information you needed' (Antenatal Results and Choices 2007: 2). As a consequence, there is an abundance of detailed information made available to prospective parents in the form of hospital leaflets, booklets and pamphlets prepared by the National Health Service, patient groups, disease advocacy organisations not to mention a wealth of internet sites. Such information papers, parents' guides and websites have been designed to give people a concise idea of what a particular condition consists of so that they can envisage the prognosis for a child born with the condition. This includes information about the biological causes of the diseases or conditions as well as related diagnostic options.

In literature aimed at prospective parents, CF, SMA and Down's syndrome are each described as resulting from errors – mutations (3 deleted base pairs) in the cystic fibrosis transmembrane conductance regulator (CFTR) gene on chromosome 7, a missing or altered survival motor neuron (SMN1) gene on chromosome 5, and an extra chromosome 21 respectively. It is these genetic errors and resulting modes of living that are identified as the causes of the pain, discomfort and/or limitations experienced by those who are born with these conditions. With Cystic Fibrosis, parents are informed, 'the faulty gene allows too much salt and not enough water into your cells, which results in a build up of thick, sticky mucus in your body's tubes and passageways' (NHS 2008a). For a person with SMA, the missing SMN1 gene:

> makes them unable to produce Survival Motor Neuron protein. Without this protein, motor neuron cells in part of the spinal cord deteriorate and die. As a result, nerve impulses are unable to get through to the muscles that these motor neurons control, which become weaker and shrink due to lack of use. (NHS 2008b)

Down's syndrome, on the other hand, is not a single-gene disorder but rather a chromosomal disorder and it is not known exactly how an extra chromosome 21 leads to the learning difficulties, reduced muscle tone (hypotonia), flat facial profile, upward slanting eyes as well as health problems that prospective parents are told can characterize a person with Down's syndrome (see DSA 2006b).

Usually, the nucleus of each cell contains 23 pairs of chromosomes – 23 we inherit from our mother and 23 we inherit from our father. In people with Down's syndrome the cells contain 47 chromosomes, with an extra copy of chromosome 21. This additional genetic material results in Down's syndrome. As yet we do not know what causes the presence of an extra chromosome 21. It can come from either the mother or the father. There is no way of predicting whether a person is more or less likely to make an egg or sperm with 24 chromosomes. (DSA 2006b: 1)

In contrast, in the cases of Cystic Fibrosis and Spinal Muscular Atrophy, parents are told that they may be 'carriers' of the culpable genetic errors and therefore may be at risk of transmitting these errors to an offspring. As such, parents are advised that while carrier testing is relevant for CF and SMA, it is not applicable for Down's syndrome which at this time can only be detected after conception. Moreover, since it is almost impossible to predict which couples will conceive a child with Down's syndrome, PGD is rarely a realistic option, whereas couples where both partners are known to be carriers of CF or SMA may well opt for PGD as they are informed they have a 25% chance of giving birth to a child with that condition. Prenatal testing for Down's syndrome is offered to those prospective parents who are judged to be 'at risk' following routine antenatal ultrasound scans.

Normal lifespan and spans of normal life

As I have already suggested, conditions like CF, SMA or Down's syndrome do not only denote certain 'faulty' modes of living, they also denote particular 'kinds of living'. This becomes clear in the descriptions given to prospective parents of the symptoms and limitations *experienced* by those individuals who have been born with CF, SMA or Down's syndrome, i.e. the impact they have on individuals' lives. With Cystic Fibrosis, the National Health Service informs parents that 'many parts of the body are affected including the pancreas and its secretions, which leads to malabsorption, malnutrition and vitamin E deficiency, and the lungs, which results in frequent chest infections and lung damage... Median life expectancy for patients with CF is around 31 years' (NHS 2008a). And, in their information materials, the Cystic Fibrosis Trust describes it as 'the UK's most common life-threatening inherited disease... affect[ing] over 8,000 people', again highlighting that 'average life expectancy is around 31 years, although improvements in treatments mean a baby born today could expect to live for longer' (Cystic Fibrosis Trust 2000).

Spinal Muscular Atrophy is described by the Jennifer Trust for SMA as affecting 1 in 6,500 babies born (about 260 per year) and as the 'biggest genetic killer of infants in the UK' (Jennifer Trust 2008b). As a condition it is divided into 4 types which have been graded by the Trust in terms of severity, with life expectancy being one of the key indicators of this severity (see Table 5.3).

Table 5.3   Types of SMA

Type 1 (Severe)	Also known as Werdnig-Hoffman Syndrome. Onset before or shortly after birth. Unable to sit. Do not usually survive past 2 years old.
Type II (Intermediate)	Onset between 3 months and 2 years. Able to sit, but not stand without aid. Survival into adulthood possible.
Type III (Mild)	Also known as Kugelberg-Welander Disease. Onset usually around 2 years. Able to walk. Normal lifespan.
Adult Onset SMA	Number of forms differing in age of onset. Degree of weakness is variable.

Source: Jennifer Trust (2008a)

While stressing that Down's syndrome is 'not a disease', the Down's Syndrome Association (the UK's largest support group for people living with Down's syndrome) describes it as one of the most common genetic conditions affecting around 60,000 people in the UK. In 2006, 1,877 diagnoses of Down's syndrome were made in England and Wales of which 1,132 (60%) were prenatally diagnosed. There were an estimated 749 live births, although following confirmed prenatal diagnosis an estimated 1,000+ pregnancies were terminated with 436 of these terminations primarily justified on the grounds of a substantial risk that if born the child would be 'seriously handicapped' (Department of Health and National Statistics 2007, NDSCR 2006).[4] Nevertheless, although there are clearly many prospective parents who do view Down's syndrome as serious enough to warrant a termination of pregnancy, information available to prospective parents considering their options inform them of dramatic improvements in a Down's syndrome child's prognosis over the last half century or so:

> In the 1950s, many people with Down's syndrome did not live past the age of
> 15. However, due to a better understanding of the condition, and advancements

---

4   While there are no available statistics on this, presumably the other 500+ terminations were carried out on the legal grounds that a medical termination of pregnancy was necessary to protect the pregnant woman's physical and mental health (Scott 2005b: 310). Also, a recent survey by the Down's Syndrome Associations showed that in 2006 for the first time there were more live births (749) than in 1989 (717) when screening became available, a 15% rise after taking into account the UK's overall rise in birth rates (BBC News 2008).

in treatment and care, the average life expectancy of someone with Down's syndrome is now 60–65 years of age. (NHS Choices 2008)

Survival then, is one factor used to gauge seriousness. Yet, while a 'normal lifespan' is one of the norms against which seriousness is measured, there is no clear cut off point but rather continuums. The genetic errors behind CF, SMA and Down's certainly can impact catastrophically on bodily vitality and thereby shorten a person's lifespan (compared to average life expectancy) even to under two years in the case of severe SMA, yet others can live to 30 or even over 60 years.

Another temporal component in determinations of seriousness is that of onset, and again we can see that there is considerable variability with some conditions manifest at birth, some manifesting themselves 'around 2 years' and others much later in adulthood. Indeed, in 2006, the HFEA for the first time approved embryo testing for susceptibility genes associated with inherited cancer pointing out that 'these conditions differ from those already licensed before because people at risk do not always develop cancer, it may occur later in life and some treatments may be available' (HFEA 2006). So, in some cases, the mere possibility that a condition will set in at a later point (perhaps never) is deemed 'to be sufficiently serious to merit the use of PGD embryo testing' (ibid.) so as to avoid implanting susceptibility-gene-affected embryos, or put in another way, to prevent potentially faulty modes of living from coming to term.

With onset, it is not so much a 'normal lifespan' as a span of 'normal life' (prior to onset) that is the norm against which seriousness is measured, and again, onset appears as a continuum with no clear cut off point.[5] In terms of selective reproductive practices, some of the targeted serious diseases are congenital (present from birth) while others may appear in an affected individual much later in life (if ever). It is noteworthy that in their report on new reproductive technologies the Human Genetic Commission suggested that 'a distinction may be drawn between the moral status of an unimplanted embryo and a fetus in an established pregnancy, and that this distinction may be used to justify the use of PGD for certain conditions where prenatal diagnosis cannot be regarded as appropriate or acceptable' (Human Genetics Commission 2006: 49). One such case was testing for serious late onset conditions.

Normal lifespan and span of normal life are social rather than biological norms which, in a sense, organize disease variability in terms of vital continuums that are used to prognose a patient's vitality over time. The former allows for

---

5   Barbara Katz Rothman (1998: 186) captured this gradated fluidity in her reflections on 'spoiled pregnancies': 'Anencephalic babies live for a few days. Tay-Sachs babies live for a few years. Children with cystic fibrosis lived a decade or two, longer now with better treatment; some of the familial cancers come in people's 30s; Huntington's disease comes at midlife. There is no point, we say, in continuing the pregnancy if the baby is going to die right away. How about soon? How soon?'

assessment of a disease in terms of its impact on the length of an affected person's life – by how much is a disease expected to shorten a person's life when compared against some kind of (usually national) average life expectancy? The latter, on the other hand, provides an indication of how much 'normal life' an individual can expect to live before he or she is affected by a disease that lies dormant in his/her genes. Upholding both norms is some kind of notion of a 'normal life' as opposed to an affected life. That is to say, CF, SMA and Down's syndrome are diseases or conditions which can be accounted for not only in terms of faulty gene expression or regulation, but also as certain 'kinds of living'. With this term I borrow from Hacking's notion of a 'human kind' which he argues differs from a 'natural kind' because 'the classification of people and their acts can influence people and what they do directly' (Hacking 1992: 190). Diagnosis is a prevalent act of classification and although the genetic errors that are seen to cause CF, SMA and Down's syndrome as modes of living are a necessary diagnostic criteria, it is social rather than biological norms that are invoked when ascertaining the 'severity' or 'seriousness' of a particular disease or condition. As kinds of living, diseases or conditions can be deemed inferior both in terms of shortened lifespan and/or in terms of a shortened span of 'normal life' for the affected individual. Value is attached to living long (as related to average life expectancy), unaffected (compared against 'faulty' modes of living) lives.

Living with…

But it is not only temporal norms of vitality that are relevant in deliberations about the seriousness of a disease or condition. Perhaps more important is the concept of 'quality of life' and the vital norms it entails, as further to the clinical descriptions of symptoms, onset and life expectancy discussed above, prospective parents are also provided with considerable amounts of qualitative information based on interviews with people who have been diagnosed with a certain disease as well as their parents and siblings. These booklets and websites have titles like 'Living with Cystic Fibrosis', 'Down's syndrome – a new parents guide', 'Personal stories – Type 1 SMA' or 'Cystic Fibrosis and You'. In these accounts, it is not so much genetic errors, medical symptoms and life expectancies that inform prognoses, rather it is patient experiences, coping strategies and condition management advice. Whatever the limitations imposed on a child by these conditions (learning difficulties, immobility, tiredness, pain, poor immunity, etc.), it is argued that they can nevertheless be fulfilling according to their own terms.

For example, the UK's Down's Syndrome Association argues that if individuals with Down's syndrome have had a low quality of life this has more to do with prejudice than with their condition:

> In the past it was believed that there were many things that people with Down's syndrome could not do when in fact they had never been given the opportunity

to try. Today these opportunities have never been greater with many people with Down's syndrome leading rich and varied lives. People with Down's syndrome are now leaving home, forming relationships, gaining employment and leading independent and active lives with differing levels of support. The quality of life, life expectancy and role in the community for adults with Down's syndrome has been transformed as education, support and opportunities have improved. (DSA 2007: 12)

With CF, it is stressed that '50% of people with CF now live into their late 30s but the condition can severely affect their quality of life' (CGE 2007: 3–4) making it 'vitally important that those with Cystic Fibrosis receive appropriate healthcare to ensure a better quality and length of life' (Cystic Fibrosis Trust 2008a). At the same time, it is also highlighted that most children with CF will just want to go on leading 'a normal life' at school, with friends, etc. – 'I just want to live a normal life really, just get on with it. Brave is a horrible word, never use it' (Youth Health Talk 2008).

'Even' in cases of SMA Type 1 where life expectancy is rarely above 2 years of age and the child suffers from poor cough, poor feeding and chest infections, information for parents includes 'Tips to Improve Quality of Life' such as providing the child with 'Light and Sound toys of all types to stimulate your child's imagination' (Jennifer Trust 2008d). A study from 2003 which compared healthcare professionals' assessment of quality of life of children with SMA Type 1 with that of their primary carers concluded that 'although there is a widespread perception that spinal muscular atrophy type 1 children have a poor quality of life, this perception is not shared by their care providers' (Bach et al. 2003: 137).

What is more, in patient literature about each of the three conditions it is consistently pointed out that 'individuals [with SMA] vary enormously' (Jennifer Trust 2008a), 'there is no such thing as a typical person with Down's syndrome... some have more serious difficulties than others' (NHS 2006: 3) or that 'CF affects people in a lot of different ways – some have it severely, but many have it mildly or moderately' (Cystic Fibrosis Trust 2000: 7). The way in which each condition affects individuals can be graded according to severity understood as a kind of intensity of symptoms, limitations or suffering.

Notwithstanding these abundantly available 'living with' accounts of certain diseases or conditions which maintain that all modes of living (however 'faulty'[6])

---

6   The question of whether or not there are any kinds of living that are so poor as to be not worth living has been discussed by many (see Brody 2002; Reuter 2007). Some argue that 'only the most devastating diseases, such as Tay-Sachs disease or Lesch-Nyhan disease... involve so much pain and suffering before death with so little in compensating benefits that those suffering from them are properly described as having lives not worth living' (Brody 2002: 347), while others maintain that '*every life* is worthy of our protection, our care, and our welcome. No one should ever discount the difficulties of dealing with children who are born with severe genetic abnormalities or serious diseases... Nevertheless,

have some kind of quality, normative estimations about the quality of life of persons affected by CF, SMA or Down's are a key component in deliberations about whether to begin, terminate or continue a pregnancy. The Cystic Fibrosis Trust, for example, which helps families and individuals who suffer from CF underscores that 'while there have been great improvements in the length and quality of life for people with CF, it still remains a serious condition and carrier couples should think very seriously before undertaking a pregnancy' (Cystic Fibrosis Trust 2002: 7). And a father of a child who died from SMA writes on the Jennifer Trust's website:

> Why use PGD? Because it works! Individual families known to be carriers of genetic disorders are always faced with difficult decisions when contemplating the start or the continuation of family life... Saying that it would be better for a child to be free of the disease does not necessarily reflect on attitudes towards those with the disease... For anyone who knows what it is like to care for a severely disabled child, the difference between having a child with and without a condition is not one of love and care of the child but about the impact that the extreme disability has on the family and affected child. (Jennifer Trust 2008e)

When the HFEA approved PGD for certain late onset diseases they made a point of stressing that:

> The role of medicine has always been to try to relieve pain and suffering and to try to improve the quality of life for people... [Our] decision today deals only with serious genetic conditions that we have a single gene test for. We would not consider mild conditions – like asthma and eczema – which can be well-managed in medical practice... The Authority agreed that we should consider the use of PGD embryo testing for conditions such as inherited breast, ovarian and bowel cancers given the aggressive nature of the cancers, the impact of treatment and the extreme anxiety that carriers of the gene can experience. (HFEA 2006)

With so many variables in play (severity, suffering, pain, dependency, immobility, disability), it is little wonder that there is no consensus when it comes to determining which diseases are serious using quality of life criteria. The UK's Human Genetics Commission has summed up such variability as follows:

---

these are the very same issues we will all face in terms of issues at the end of life, and at many points between birth and death' (Mohler 2006, emphasis original). In a parent's guide, one couple describes the moment they decided not to have their son who had Tay Sachs disease resuscitated: 'one day when he was about 2½ and had to be admitted to the hospital. He was very weak. He was having trouble eating and drinking. We knew at this point it was not possible for him to have any quality of life, and it was at this point we made that decision. It was very difficult to make, and prior to his getting this sick I would not have been able to make that decision.' (Borfitz and Margolis 2006: 11).

it has proved difficult to define what is meant by 'serious'. One way of doing this would be to draw up a list of conditions that are considered to lead to a very poor quality of life... However, this approach fails to recognise that quality of life judgements are subjective, and that genetic disorders are variable in terms of severity and health outcomes. There is evidence to suggest that people with genetic disorders, their families and professionals all have different views about which conditions give rise to a poor quality of life. In general, those who have direct experience of *living with a genetic disorder* are likely to rate the quality of their lives more highly than would medically qualified professionals. (Human Genetics Commission 2006: 36, emphasis added)

Similarly, in connection with recent parliamentary debates to amend the Human Fertilisation and Embryology Bill in early 2008, the Royal College of Obstetricians and Gynaecologists argued that:

a strict definition [of what constitutes a serious abnormality] is impractical because we do not have sufficiently advanced diagnostic techniques to detect malformations accurately all of the time and it is not always possible to predict the 'seriousness' of the outcome (in terms of the long-term physical, intellectual or social disability on the child and the effects on the family). The RCOG believes that the interpretation of 'serious abnormality' should be based upon individual discussion agreed between the parents and the mother's doctor. (RCOG 2008)

And so it is in practice; agreement on termination of pregnancy on the grounds of substantial risk that the child, if born, would be seriously handicapped, comes about through consultation between prospective parents and their doctors, with two doctors having to authorise the termination by signing a so-called Certificate A form. The point being that determination of 'seriousness' has less to do with biochemical or genetic test results from the laboratory and much more to do with discussion and information exchange between prospective parents and doctors about what living with a certain disease or disorder entails. To reach agreement on whether a disease or condition is serious, prospective parents are not given blood substance level values or karyotype maps, rather they are provided with qualitative information which presents other patients' and families' experiences of 'living with a genetic condition'.

Once again, vital norms emerge in attempts to organize variability of 'interpretation' along continuums of quality of life, where value is attached to living independently, having social relationships, gaining employment and of course not suffering from the symptoms caused by genetic conditions. As kinds of living, CF, SMA and Down's syndrome have their own particular vital norms which make space for, albeit narrowed, continuums of not just lifespan and onset, but also quality of life particular and relevant to these conditions. Borrowing from Canguilhem, we might say there is no living without norms of living, and living with a genetic disease or condition is always a certain kind of living. Yet, at the same time, these kinds of living are also assessed against the norms of living associated with those who lead a 'normal life'. This is the case when some prospective parents decide that there are some kinds of living which should be prevented from coming into being for the sake of the child; that some 'faulty' modes of living are not worth living. And so, where some might consider Down's syndrome serious enough to warrant termination of pregnancy because of the condition's potential impact on the future child's quality of life, others would vigorously dispute this by arguing that people with Down's syndrome can 'live full and rewarding lives' (DSA 2008). Such contradictions are not resolvable by recourse to biology.

Coping

When it comes to living with a genetic condition it is of course not only the affected individual who is living with the condition. In a very concrete and intimate sense, so too are the parents and siblings of the affected individual as it is they who will, in by far most cases, be caring for the affected child from birth and often throughout his or her life. We have already seen how, in cases where parents are considering termination of a pregnancy, negotiation of what constitutes seriousness currently takes place in consultation between prospective parents and their doctors. To carry out PGD in the UK, on the other hand, clinics must be licensed to do so and may only offer PGD for diseases and conditions that have been approved by the Human Fertilisation and Embryology Authority. In both cases, it is not only the impact of the condition on the child (if born) that is taken into consideration, it is also 'the effects on the family' (RCOG 2008) or 'the way it affects the family' (HFEA 1999). Moreover, as we saw earlier, the decision to license some late onset disorders for PGD was partly based on 'the extreme anxiety that carriers of the gene can experience' (HFEA 2006). As put by the Human Genetics Commission, '[reproductive] decisions are often linked to whether the family feels it could cope with the demands of a child with such problems, the impact it would have on other children, or on the carers' (2006: 3).

As such, literature provided to prospective parents also includes information on the difficulties that other parents have had in coping with caring for a child with a genetic disorder. Prospective parents are also encouraged to get in touch with other parents who have given birth to and cared for a child with a similar genetic condition. Through such interaction, parents are reassured that they are 'not alone' as they learn how 'most parents find out that their baby has Down's syndrome soon after the birth and the news is a great shock', how parents can be left 'feeling confused, angry, alone or afraid' after a diagnosis of SMA or how 'coping with CF at the time of diagnosis... can be challenging' (Cystic Fibrosis Trust 2008b, DSA 2007, Jennifer Trust 2008b).

Carers' descriptions of living with a genetic condition in terms of coping are of course not limited to the moment of diagnosis, for once a diagnosis is confirmed parents will often want to do everything to ensure that their affected child is given the best possible life under the circumstances. This can be a challenging task to say the least:

> Parents' ways of coping with their children with CF differ as widely as the condition of the children themselves. The whole family – the parents, the child or children with CF, other siblings – will all be affected by the psychological pressures arising from the chronic nature of CF, the uncertainty about the future, the genetic aspects, worry, depression and the tiring routines of physio and supervising medication. (Cystic Fibrosis Trust 2008b: 9)

> The demands of living with a young child can be overwhelming particularly when the fact that your child has Down's syndrome may lead to extra appointments with doctors and therapists and anxiety in the early years. (DSA 2007: 11–12)

> At the back of our minds we did keep alive the possibility that she might not have Down's syndrome but we knew that we would be able to cope if she did – there's so much out there for her. Schools are integrated and there are even actors with Down's syndrome. There's a worker at our local supermarket who has Down's syndrome and we think that it doesn't need to hold you back. (BBC News 2008)

> We were determined that Amar [diagnosed with SMA Type 1] would have the best time we could imagine... We never complained about the sleepless nights, possibly three hours of sleep a night on average. My wife stayed at home with Amar all day, every day, until I came home from work in the evening. He stayed with me, so I could give my wife a break. We were committed and got used to it, and enjoyed it, even though it was hard. We never complained. We coughed every cough for him; we wanted him to stay as well as possible. (Jennifer Trust 2008c)

The argument that the impact of a genetic condition on a family's life is relevant when determining what constitutes seriousness is perhaps one of the most controversial. As Scott has shown, in a 'wrongful birth' case from 2000 in East Dorset which was brought by parents who argued that they had lost the opportunity to abort a child with Down's syndrome because of a breach of duty, the presiding judge concluded that 'the birth of a disabled child will dramatically affect the quality of life of both parents and it is to be inferred that a reason why they would have terminated the pregnancy was to avoid such a loss of amenity in their lives' (cited in Scott 2005a: 402). A distinction is made between caring for a 'normal child' and one affected by a condition such as Down's syndrome ('She will need care and supervision for the rest of her life' (ibid.: 401)). What is more, it is a normative distinction since looking after an affected child is seen to negatively impact the quality of life of the couple.

Such arguments have been controversial especially because they are considered to discount the interests of the future child in favour of the 'selfish' interests of the parents. It is also suggested that once the future child's interests are set aside, the problem of 'serious disease' can very quickly become framed in terms of burden, whether this burden is considered psychological, social, emotional, financial or genetic. For example, Tom Shakespeare has argued that if sufficient care is not taken 'decisions about reproductive choices are likely to be influenced by the fact that an unjust society means that having a disabled child places a severe financial and practical burden on a family' (Shakespeare 1998: 679). And if reproductive selection becomes a matter of alleviating burdens for collectives (e.g. 'family', 'society', 'population', 'human gene pool') then reproductive medicine is once again well on its way down the slippery slope to eugenics (see also Wahlberg 2008).

Notwithstanding these controversies, it is clear that the circumscription of genetic conditions as 'kinds of living' takes place not just as regards the affected individual but also his or her carers. The perceived impact a genetic disease or condition has on a family's quality of life is a central element in deliberations about what constitutes a serious disease. Indeed, in the case of the termination of a pregnancy in week 28 following prenatal diagnosis of a cleft palate with which I started this chapter, the curate argued that it was an 'error of law' that the medical practitioners who authorised the termination 'took into account the views of the parents involved' (cited in Scott 2005b: 309). In contrast, as we saw earlier, the RCOG suggests that interpretation of what is meant by 'seriously handicapped' should be resolved between parents and doctors.[7]

The birth of a child affected by a genetic condition also introduces a new 'kind of living' for carers and siblings as their lives are transformed. Since there is no living without norms of living, it follows that this new kind of living for families will have its own norms, however 'narrowed'. And, just as there is no consensus concerning how good a quality of life persons affected by genetic conditions can have, there is no consensus on whether a family's quality of life will necessarily deteriorate as a result of caring for a person with a genetic condition. Indeed, in many of the parental accounts of living with a genetic condition, it is often pointed out how such an experience can in fact enrich and strengthen family life – 'I can only describe how much joy my son [who has Down's syndrome] has given me' (DSA 2006a: 7).

---

7   Williams et al. (2002a: 65) have also shown how some practitioners find it hard to 'draw the line' with one of their respondents arguing: 'I mean, I've seen a woman who had a cleft lip and palate herself, her first child had a cleft lip and palate, she had another baby with a cleft lip and palate and she said, "I want a termination". Now who am I to say to her that I know more about cleft lip and palate than she does?'

Conclusion – modes and kinds of living

In this chapter, I have investigated how the estimations of vitality that inform attempts to circumscribe and stabilize 'serious disease' as a legal and medical category are made feasible and practicable. While the diagnosis of a certain disease or condition in reproductive medicine relies on biochemical and genetic analyses of biological samples and/or biometric and morphological analyses of ultrasound scans, there is nothing in the laboratory techniques of Polymerase Chain Reaction analysis, blood substance level analysis, karyotyping or sonography that can qualify a disease or condition as 'serious', 'intermediate' or 'mild'.

Instead, I have shown how value is formed in the transmogrification or looping of certain diagnosed 'faulty' modes of living into kinds of living. As modes of living, hereditary and congenital conditions are characterized in terms of genetic errors which are ultimately seen as narrowing, to varying degrees, an individual's biological conditions of existence. As kinds of living, these same conditions are characterized in terms of their constraining/negative impact on 'normal life' or 'quality of life' – immobility, dependence, learning difficulties, premature death, poor immunity, pain, suffering, etc. It is in this circumscription of genetic conditions as kinds of living that phenomenological nosologies emerge, making it possible, for example, to classify SMA Type 1 as 'severe', SMA Type 2 as 'intermediate' and SMA Type 3 as 'mild', to suggest that 'some have CF severely, but many have it mildly or moderately', or to classify breast and bowel cancer as 'serious' and asthma and eczema as 'mild'. As, we have seen, such attempts to grade the seriousness or severity of certain diseases or conditions are often described as subjective and therefore inconsistent. Such variability and inconsistency has nevertheless not prevented ongoing efforts to do exactly this, especially when decisions about whether or not to begin or terminate a pregnancy must comply with law.

What I have argued is that when attempts are made to classify conditions or diseases according to gradations of seriousness or severity, this has been made possible by norms of living which have emerged out of qualitative interviews with individuals affected by these conditions, their parents and families as well as medical doctors. Such qualitative or human technologies – 'technologies that take modes of being human as their object' (Rose 1996: 26) – are not somehow abstract or 'merely' subjective when compared to the laboratory technologies used to diagnose certain conditions, rather they are concrete and palpable, resulting in parent guides, ranking of different Types of SMA according to severity, coping strategy manuals, guidelines for termination of pregnancy, etc. It is the social norms of living ('normal lifespan', 'normal (quality of) life', 'normal family life') that these human technologies have generated which in turn allow for assessments of a certain condition's likely impact on the life of a child and her/his family. At the same time, they have also generated new norms of living that are particular to the limitations and restrictions attributed to a disease or condition on an individual and his/her family. These condition-specific norms of living are what allow parents to nevertheless do everything they can to give the best possible lives to their affected children. There are no clear cut off points, rather there are continuums of lifespan and quality of life which are used as navigation aids in deliberations over whether or not to begin, terminate or continue pregnancies that may result in a child being born with a serious disease or condition.

References

Antenatal Results and Choices 2007. *A Handbook to be Given to Parents When an Abnormality is Diagnosed in Their Unborn Baby*. London: ARC.

Bach, J., Vega, J., Majors, J. and Friedman, A. 2003. Spinal muscular atrophy type 1 quality of life. *American Journal of Physical Medicine & Rehabilitation*, 82(2), 137–42.

BBC News 2008. Society 'more positive on Down's', [Online, 24 November] Available at: news.bbc.co.uk/1/hi/health/7746747.stm [accessed: 24 November 2008].

Borfitz, J. and Margolis, M. 2006. *The Home Care Book – A Parent's Guide to Caring for Children With Progressive Neurological Diseases*, Brookline: National Tay-Sachs & Allied Diseases Association, Inc.

Brody, B. 2002. Freedom and responsibility in genetic testing. *Social Philosophy & Policy*, 19(2), 343–59.

Canguilhem, G. 1989. *The Normal and the Pathological*. New York: Zone Books.

CGE 2007. Fact Sheet 35: Tay-Sachs Disease and other conditions more common in the Ashkenazi Jewish community. The Australasian Genetics Resource Book. Centre for Genetic Education.

Clarkeburn, H. 2000. Parental duties and untreatable genetic conditions. *Journal of Medical Ethics*, 26: 400–3.

Clinical Genetics Department 2008. *Genetics* [Online] Available at: www.guysandstthomas.nhs.uk/services/managednetworks/genetics/genetics.aspx [accessed: 14 October 2008].

Crown Prosecution Service 2005. CPS decides not to prosecute doctors following complaint by Rev Joanna Jepson. Press Release. 16 March 2005.

Cystic Fibrosis Trust 2000. *Cystic Fibrosis and You*, Kent: Cystic Fibrosis Trust.

Cystic Fibrosis Trust 2002. *Genetics, Carrier Testing, Tests During Pregnancy and For Newborn Babies*, London: Cystic Fibrosis Trust.

Cystic Fibrosis Trust 2008a. *Cystic Fibrosis Care* [Online]. Available at: www.cftrust.org.uk/aboutcf/cfcare/ [accessed: 1 October 2008].

Cystic Fibrosis Trust 2008b. *School and Cystic Fibrosis: A Guide for Teachers and Parents*. Kent: Cystic Fibrosis Trust.

Department of Health and National Statistics 2007. Abortion Statistics, England and Wales: 2006. *Statistical Bulletin*, 2007(1).

Department of Health and National Statistics 2008. Abortion Statistics, England and Wales: 2007. *Statistical Bulletin*, 2008(1).

DSA 2006a. *Continuing Pregnancy with a Diagnosis of Down's syndrome: A Guide for Parents*. Middlesex: Down's Syndrome Association.

DSA 2006b. *People with Down's Syndrome: Your Questions Answered*. Middlesex: Down's Syndrome Association.

DSA 2007. *Down's Syndrome: A New Parents Guide*. London: Down's Syndrome Association.

DSA 2008. Our position on pre-natal testing for Down's syndrome [Online]. Available at: www.downs-syndrome.org.uk/news-and-media/policy/statements /231–pre-natal-testing.html [accessed: 15 November 2008].

Duster, T. 2003. *Backdoor to Eugenics*. New York: Routledge.

EWHC 2003. *Jepson v. The Chief Constable of West Mercia Police Constabulary*. 3318, England and Wales High Court: 2003 WL 23145287, 58.

Franklin, S. 2007. *Dolly Mixtures: The Remaking of Genealogy*. Durham N.C.: Duke University Press.

Franklin, S. and Roberts, C. 2006. *Born and Made: An Ethnography of Preimplantation Genetic Diagnosis*. Princeton: Princeton University Press.

Gledhill, R. 2005. Curate loses legal challenge over cleft-palate abortion. *The Times*, London, 17 March 2005.

Gosden, R.G. 1999. *Designer Babies: The Brave New World of Reproductive Technology*. London: Gollancz.

Guy's and St Thomas's Hospital 2002. *The Genetic Testing of Children*. London: NHS Trust.

Guy's and St Thomas's Hospital 2008. Pre-implantation genetic diagnosis (PGD) [Online], Clinical Genetics Department, available at: www.guysandstthomas. nhs.uk/services/managednetworks/womensservices/acu/pgd.aspx: [accessed: 10 October 2008].

Hacking, I. 1992. World-making by kind-making: child abuse for example, in *How Classification Works: Nelson Goodman Among the Social Sciences*, edited by M. Douglas and D. Hull. Edinburgh: Edinburgh University Press, 180–238.

Hacking, I. 1995. The looping effects of human kinds, in *Causal Cognition: A Multidisciplinary Debate*, edited by D. Sperber et al. Oxford: Clarendon Press, 351–83.

Hacking, I. 2002. *Historical Ontology*. Cambridge, Mass.: Harvard University Press.

HFEA 1999. Letter to all IVF clinics regarding Preimplantation Genetic Diagnosis: CE13/08/1999. 13 August 1999.

HFEA 2006. Authority decision on PGD policy, 10 May 2006 [Online]. Available at: www.hfea.gov.uk/en/1124.html [accessed: 15 October 2008].

Human Genetics Commission 2006. *Making Babies: Reproductive Decisions and Genetic Technologies*. London: Human Genetics Commission.

Jennifer Trust 2008a *Background to Spinal Muscular Atrophy* [Online]. Available at: www.jtsma.org.uk/sma0.html [accessed: 2 November 2008].

Jennifer Trust 2008b. *Key Facts about SMA* [Online]. Available at: www.jtsma. org.uk/press_office.html [accessed: 2 November 2008].

Jennifer Trust 2008c. Personal stories – Type 1: Raj, Priti and Rishi [Online]. Available at: www.jtsma.org.uk/ps8.html [accessed: 24 October 2008].

Jennifer Trust 2008d. Personal stories – Type 1: Sue, David and Abigail [Online]. Available at: www.jtsma.org.uk/ps3.html [accessed: 5 October 2008].

Jennifer Trust 2008e. Preimplanation Genetic Diagnosis (PGD) [Online]. Available at: www.jtsma.org.uk/info_pgd.html [accessed: 12 November 2008].

Kerr, A. and Shakespeare, T. 2002. *Genetic Politics: from Eugenics to Genome*. Cheltenham: New Clarion Press.

Mohler, A. 2006. Are all lives worth living? A dangerous idea moves front and center. *The Albert Mohler Programme*. March 13, 2006.

NDSCR 2006. *The National Down Syndrome Cytogenetic Register – 2006 Annual Report*. London: Queen Mary's School of Medicine and Dentistry.

NHS 2006. *Testing for Down's Syndrome in Pregnancy: Choosing Whether to Have the Tests is an Important Decision, for You and for Your Baby*. Antenatal and Newborn Screening Programmes: UK National Screening Committee.

NHS 2008a. *Causes of Cystic Fibrosis* [Online]. Available at: www.nhs.uk/ Conditions/Cystic-fibrosis/Pages/Causes.aspx?url=Pages/what-is-it.aspx [accessed: 1 October 2008].

NHS 2008b. *Causes of Spinal Muscular Atrophy* [Online]. Available at: www. nhs.uk/Conditions/Spinal-muscular-atrophy/Pages/Causes.aspx?url=Pages/ Overview.aspx [accessed: 23 October 2008].

NHS 2009. *Amniocentesis* [Online]. Available at: www.nhs.uk/Conditions/ Amniocentesis/Pages/Why-should-it-be-done.aspx?url=Pages/ what-is-it.aspx [accessed: 12 January 2009].

NHS Choices 2008. *Down's Syndrome* [Online]. Available at: www.nhs.uk/ conditions/downs-syndrome/Pages/Introduction.aspx?url=Pages/what-is-it.aspx [accessed: 10 October 2008].

Pilnick, A. 2002. 'There are no rights and wrongs in these situations': identifying interactional difficulties in genetic counseling. *Sociology of Health & Illness*, 24(1), 66–88.

Rapp, R. 1988. Chromosomes and communication: the discourse of genetic counseling. *Medical Anthropology Quarterly*, 2(2), 143–57.

RCOG 2006. *Amniocentesis: What you Need to Know*. Royal College of Obstetricians and Gynaecologists: London.

RCOG 2008. Q&A: Abortions for fetal abnormality and sydromatic conditions indicated by cleft lip and/or palate – the O&G perspective [Online]. Available at: www.rcog.org.uk/index.asp?PageID=2550 [accessed: 2 November 2008].

Reuter, S. 2007. The politics of 'wrongful life' itself: discursive (mal)practices and Tay-Sachs disease. *Economy and Society*, 36(2), 236–62.

Rose, N. 1996. *Inventing Our Selves: Psychology, Power, and Personhood*. Cambridge: Cambridge University Press.

Rothman, B.K. 1998. *Genetic Maps and Human Imaginations: The Limits of Science in Understanding Who We Are*. New York: W.W. Norton & Company.

Scott, R. 2005a. Interpreting the disability ground of the abortion act. *Cambridge Law Journal*, 64(2), 388–412.

Scott, R. 2005b. The uncertain scope of reproductive autonomy in preimplantation genetic diagnosis and selective abortion. *Medical Law Review*, 13(Autumn), 291–327.

Shakespeare, T. 1998. Choices and rights: eugenics, genetics and disability equality. *Disability & Society*, 13(5), 665–81.

United Kingdom 1991. Abortion Act 1967 (c. 87). UK: Ministry of Justice.

Vehmas, S. 2002. Parental responsibility and the morality of selective abortion. *Ethical Theory and Moral Practice*, 5: 463–84.

Wahlberg, A. 2007. Measuring progress: calculating the life of nations. *Distinktion – Scandinavian Journal of Social Theory*, 14: 65–82.

Wahlberg, A. 2008. Reproductive medicine and the concept of 'quality'. *Clinical Ethics*, 3(4), 189–93.

Williams, C., Alderson, P. and Farsides, B. 2002a. 'Drawing the line' in prenatal screening and testing: health practitioners' discussions. *Health, Risk & Society*, 4(1), 61–75.

Williams, C., Alderson, P. and Farsides, B. 2002b. Is nondirectiveness possible within the context of antenatal screening and testing? *Social Science and Medicine*, 54: 339–47.

Williams, C., Ehrich, K., Farsides, B. and Scott, R. 2007. Facilitating choice, framing choice: staff views on widening the scope of preimplantation genetic diagnosis in the UK. *Social Science and Medicine*, 65: 1094–105.

Youth Health Talk 2008. *Jodie's Story* [Online]. Available at: www.youthhealthtalk. org/InterviewTranscript.aspx?Interview=1554&Clip=0 [accessed: 28 October 2008].

Chapter 6

From Society to Molecule and Back: The Contested Scale of Public Health Science

Susanne Bauer

'X may increase your risk of Y by a factor of Z'. It is in this format that the results of epidemiological studies are often communicated. Associations between factors expressed as quasi-causal relations or as risk figures seem ubiquitous in health research and beyond. They circulate in consultation rooms, in preventive medicine and public health recommendations, but also in lifestyle magazines and popular culture. Statements on risk are expressed in terms of quantitative relations, with reference to specific subgroups, or with estimates on trends or interactions between several factors. 'Risk assessments' and 'risk factors' are pervasive in policy discourses and practices of public health and health care systems. But how do the categories X, Y, and Z come about; how are they selected, connected and stabilized? By what means are subpopulations categorized, aligned and tied together (or separated) in statements about health risks?

Many of the statements of health risks originate in epidemiological research. The science of epidemiology has often been defined as the study of distributions and determinants of health and disease in terms of population patterns (Last 1993). Epidemiological studies bring together variables from otherwise separate contexts, which can range from molecular analyses of a blood sample to the small details of everyday life, like cups of tea consumed per day, and more macro categories such as education, income or social networks.

This chapter will take a closer look at the 'production side' of scientific risk assessments and examine the relevant infrastructures to such knowledge generation in science and society. Risk estimation is a burgeoning industry and the epidemiological gaze has extended to almost all corners of society: the range of potential risk factors that have come under epidemiological scrutiny appears nearly unlimited. Among the many categories and dichotomies at work in the field, I will trace some shared features of epidemiological inquiry at the 'population level' and address current movements within emergent epidemiological data assemblages[1] – i.e. that of molecularization and a subsequent turn to interaction and complexity. Within a context of contested frameworks of disease causation –

---

1 Originally a Deleuzian term, Paul Rabinow (1996) and Aihwa Ong and Stephen Collier (2005) have taken up this term to describe the heterogeneous and temporal constellations e.g. of recent biomedicine.

from sociopolitical to biomedical – it was precisely the conceptual openness of risk factor epidemiology that made its methodological approach immensely successful (Aronowitz 1998)[2]. While parts of epidemiology have strived to integrate social and biological variables, the divides between the social and the biological have persisted in the organization of its sub-disciplines – for instance in the different research agendas of social epidemiology and genetic epidemiology.

Although a part of biomedicine, the scale of epidemiological investigations extends far beyond the laboratory to society at large. Different from the confined spaces of biomedical laboratories and their material objects, in observational epidemiology the population of an entire country or region can be subject to investigation. The research questions in applied health science emerge not only from biomedicine but also from clinical practice, patient organizations or public health agendas. For example issues of health promotion are then rendered compatible with the formats, protocols and logics of epidemiological study designs. Evaluations of population health guided by an epidemiological toolbox – that comprises a set of study designs and statistical methodologies – have become the common denominator for much of contemporary health research. It even seems that in the second half of the 20th century, risk factor epidemiology became a knowledge regime or an 'obligatory passage point' (Callon 1986) for any statements about public health. Whether it was biomedical, environmental, social or economic parameters affecting health, proof needed to be established with analytical study designs[3] in order to count as evidence for decision-making or policy.

Social studies of the health sciences have taken issue with the effects of 'biologization' and 'genetization' of the social as well as with emerging risk discourses and their modes of governmentality (Lupton and Petersen 1997, Petersen and Bunton 2002, Brown and Webster 2004). Some more recent studies have closely examined settings of epidemiologic knowledge production, bringing to attention, for example, data collecting as a process of social exchange, the epistemological significance of data infrastructures and population health modelling and simulations (Trostle 2005, Mattila 2006, Bauer 2008). Building on these approaches, this chapter discusses some of the key categories – such as individual and population, genes and environment – which have structured much of contemporary epidemiology.

Interestingly, in epidemiology and public health sciences themselves, the social has not been an ignored category; on the contrary, efforts have been made to operationalize the social within the framework of risk factor epidemiology – for instance, through different categories such as social class, socioeconomic status, education, occupation or income. As a category to explain 'population health',

---

2   See Aronowitz (1998) for an account of the development of risk factor epidemiology, in particular in the US context.

3   Different from so called 'ecological studies', the analytical designs of risk factor epidemiology required data on exposure and disease at the individual level.

social categories have been reintroduced into the biomedical sciences in particular by social epidemiologists; in this context 'ecosocial frameworks' that take into account the social without ignoring biology have been proposed (Krieger 2001). While the development of epidemiological methods has been closely linked to biomedical concepts, epidemiologic methods also share common features with quantitative social sciences.

Taking its points of departure in the epidemiologic negotiation of health and disease, this chapter examines how categories can be both rigid and flexible in the process of knowledge production. Empirically, I draw on published and archival materials, observations and expert interviews, in particular related to local long-term studies conducted in Copenhagen. The case of the Nordic countries in general, is of particular interest here, due to the important role of epidemiological research in local health policy as well as internationally-oriented research agendas.

The first part of this chapter describes the relationship of the 'individual' and the 'population' in an epidemiological study and develops how, from a large study collective, quantitative risk estimates are produced at the population level and translated to the individual level in preventive medicine. Here, I am particularly interested in the movement from observational to interventional approaches and in how a collective population past and individualized futures are joined in risk prediction. The second part describes how, with the new genetics, sequence data have entered risk factor epidemiology: data collected locally are enrolled into multinational genomics consortia and the matrix of disease causation is reorganized with the concept of 'genetic susceptibility'. On a more general level, for 'population health science', this chapter addresses how, in the research process, categories such as nature and nurture, inside and outside of the human body, past and future, local and global are no longer separable but deeply entangled. Thus, this part of the chapter will be about categorizations in public health science and epidemiology, a field which forms a particularly 'thick' site at the intersections of the two-way traffic between biomedicine and society at large.

Risk factor epidemiology: Investigating states of population health

Infrastructures for research

Perhaps the most important category along which public health science works is 'population health' as its overarching epistemic object. It is 'population health' and a toolbox of specific study designs that tie together an otherwise heterogeneous field. Performing epidemiological studies requires extended data infrastructures; here the conditions in the Nordic countries have often been depicted as particularly favourable, since a host of individual data for the entire population are traceable (Olsen et al. 2004). This is due to a network of central registries that collect population statistics making it possible to follow individuals through their contacts with the public services including healthcare (for instance diagnoses and prescriptions), education and employment. In the Nordic countries, there is a strong research tradition of comparing disease statistics among different population subgroups (e.g. groups with different socioeconomic status or occupational exposures) through registry-based research.

Similar to the large-scale cardiovascular risk study of Framingham in the US (Dawber 1951), a new type of follow-up investigation was introduced in the mid-1960s, as epidemiology had broadened much beyond its original context of infectious disease. In particular in the study of cardiovascular disease, epidemiologists actively gathered data from large population samples in order to discern the contribution of lifestyle risks to disease. This was to establish a research infrastructure that would allow long-term data collection (through medical examinations and questionnaires) from study participants who were identified ((by age and residence) using population registries.

The cardiovascular risk studies initiated in the Nordic countries in the 1960s and 1970s were aimed at the investigation of prevention possibilities. Like elsewhere, prevention concepts at the time were mainly conceived of in terms of changing 'individual lifestyles'. As a first step, local scientific inventories of cardiovascular risk factors were established as 'reference values' (Hagerup 1981, Appleyard 1989). In that way, a data infrastructure would help identify prevention opportunities and secure rational ways to improve population health. However, there were many clinicians at the time who considered a study that examined healthy people a 'waste of resources' (Jørgensen 2004). To most clinicians, medicine was made up by the two pillars of diagnosis and therapy, and therefore these early studies in the general population started as rather marginal undertakings. Following in part the Framingham approach, local epidemiological questionnaires focused first and foremost on behavioural factors – lifestyle was understood as controllable if not 'chosen' by the individual. However, social factors could in principle be incorporated into the risk factor concept and in some instances items on occupation, education, and income were included in the questionnaires. With each resident in Denmark having a unique registration number (CPR-number) since the system was introduced in 1968, yet more linkage opportunities to retrieve data at an individual level became available. Whereas, in similar epidemiological studies in the US context, social conditions were often addressed in terms of 'psychosocial' variables only, several analyses for the Danish dataset also included 'the social' in terms of 'social class', 'social conditions' or 'socioeconomy' (Møller et al. 1991, Osler 1993).

In epidemiological fieldwork, data collection starts at the individual level; the steps of data organization and analysis perform aggregations at population levels. In the statistical processing and modelling of data, measures of disease frequency are brought in relation to factors of exposure or lifestyle. These frequencies are internally compared in order to quantify risk in relation to disease, for instance as increases or decreases in relative risks with the amount of alcohol consumed or with the degree of physical activity. Different from environmental or occupational studies that often follow two groups with different exposure characteristics, lifestyle risk factor studies work with multiple comparisons between flexible subgroups defined by selected lifestyle variables. It is the individual level at which data have been collected that epidemiologists draw from when they perform hypothesis testing,[4] which brings disease frequencies in relation to aetiological factors. Risk estimates are calculated for multiple risk factors and under adjustments (controlling) for a range of further correlated factors. Multivariate analyses produce adjusted risk estimates for the entire study population as well as by subgroup – this includes tabulations of subgroup-specific risks. Aggregating and processing data in population databases reshuffles data and their different categories – from individual datasets into population subgroups by age, gender, socioeconomic status or polymorphism. For each of these subgroups, risk estimates can be calculated – the formal model of analysis is flexible and not limited to a context or specific source: the statistical procedures deal with determinants, variables and parameter estimates independent of the categories investigated, i.e. whether those relate to contexts of individual biology such as biomarker status or to social networks. Once part of the study, the information collected for study participants – i.e. the data that was generated using a questionnaire, an examination or a lab test – becomes part of the population database and is processed in multivariate regression analyses. As inscriptions from the individual obtained via questionnaire or medical examination, the data is stored in a population database and used to calculate risk estimates; the latter then leave the modelling procedure and the context of the study – and begin travelling as 'immutable mobiles' (Latour 1987) that are stabilized to the extent that they circulate as facts.

From observation to intervention

Most early studies in cardiovascular prevention of the 1960s and 1970s made use of observational designs to investigate population health: they performed comparisons based on study groups that differed by 'exposure', comprising mainly environmental or lifestyle factors. In epidemiology these types of observational studies are sometimes referred to as 'natural experiments' (Roberts 1978, 187). Identifying and evaluating 'natural experiments' – analytically making use of or 'taking advantage' of differences in exposure within the population – has been a key concept in the tradition of observational studies. Groups that differed by exposure were compared with respect to disease statistics and, from there, risk estimates were derived which would then inform public health planning.

At the same time, clinical research in particular began relying on 'experimental' designs such as the randomized comparison of different treatments. And, when prevention studies began going beyond the investigation of disease determinants

---

4   Analytical studies involve statistical modelling of health and disease in relation to individual determinants as opposed to descriptive comparisons between regions such as in 'ecological studies'; in the latter, exposure information is based on areas, while in the former individual exposure estimates are needed.

or causes (aetiologies), they also started to make use of experimental designs similar to clinical trials for prevention research. In contrast to hitherto purely observational approaches, 'experimental' interventions to facilitate lifestyle change were organized. For instance, a large-scale prevention trial was set up in greater Copenhagen in the 1990s. In this 'non-clinical' trial, participants were randomly assigned to three groups: one group was offered a 'lifestyle change intervention' that included a consultation with a general practitioner (GP) and support groups; the second group was offered a conversation with a GP only and the third group remained without intervention (Jørgensen et al. 2003). The effect of these interventions was measured by three subsequent examinations and comprehensive questionnaires on lifestyle changes (e.g. dietary habits, smoking, alcohol intake and physical activity) after one, three and five years. All three 'arms' of the trial – two groups with interventions at different intensities (high and low) and one group without – were followed up with questionnaires.

With the randomized allocation of participants to different interventions, this experimental set up was designed to follow the principle of clinical trials. With the emergence of evidence-based medicine, the randomized controlled trial (treatment versus placebo in its classical version) had developed into a methodological gold standard of research. While 'experimental studies' in this format were most influential in the context of clinical medicine,[5] research on prevention, has gradually adopted the new concepts, e.g. in 'evidence-based prevention' that privileged 'non-clinical intervention trials' since, in this understanding, the technique of randomization controls for unknown confounding factors.[6]

When epidemiology extended from the study of risk factors towards the study of interventions in preventive medicine, the mode of evidence that was demanded to justify action through public health interventions and policies was contested: what kind of proof was deemed necessary to show that an intervention works? With the emerging paradigm of evidence-based medicine, study designs were designed to mimic 'true experiments'. Just like in clinical medicine 'experimental studies' that statistically adjust for the influence of unknown factors by means of randomization were increasingly used in public health in order to meet the new evidence level requirements (The Cochrane Collaboration 1993, Sackett et al. 1996, Weisz 2005). Allocation into the different arms of the trial was randomized – and thereby the problem of confounding by unknown or unaccounted factors statistically controlled. This meant that such a study would have a superior status compared to observational study designs: according to the classifications of the Oxford Center for Evidence Based Medicine (2001), results of randomized studies rank higher in the evidence hierarchy. In that sense, the intervention trials are not only about going beyond the mere identification of aetiological factors in order to facilitate improvements of population health; they are also about improving the

---

5   For a history of clinical trials, see Marks (1997).

6   For a review of the development of non-clinical randomized trials in psychology and social policy, see Dehue (2001).

quality of evidence in accordance with more recent standards. This improvement is achieved by 'experimental comparison' of different 'intervention options'.

Epidemiological field research through empirical observation maps out large scale social settings of differences in exposures or interventions, which renders 'population health' not only into an object of investigation but also of management and optimization. With the application of the model of clinical trials to population studies, preventive medicine has also taken on a specific social epistemology. By conducting 'experimental' trials with different methods and intensities of a public health measure, research extends to a much larger space of social experimentation that has been highly influential also in psychology and social policy (Dehue 2001). This is part of a much more fundamental epistemological condition that conceives of society and social change in terms of scientific – and economic – governance. This emerging mode of scientific governance also plays out in what is often termed 'evidence-based policy'. In many policy fields, outcome studies and quantitative evaluations have acquired a key role in balancing size, costs and efficiency in the implementation of interventions.

Predicting individual futures from the population's past

Long-term epidemiological studies of population health have recently also been used to 'translate' risks calculated for populations back to the individual patient or citizen. Since the late 1990s formal tools for 'individualized' cardiovascular risk assessment have entered the consultation rooms of general practitioners. In Denmark, for example, GPs were offered a software tool for individual risk assessment to be used in preventive consultations with patients. This tool was based on local epidemiological studies and became fairly widespread – around 30% of GPs reported having the tool installed and using it in 2000 (Bonnevie et al. 2005).[7] The software applies a risk score to the individual patient based on his or her profile (that is composed of variables such as gender, age, blood pressure, weight, cholesterol, smoking, etc.). The goal of the tool was to help general practitioners and patients negotiate individual plans on how to reduce risk factors; measures to reduce risk could also include preventive medication.[8]

The individual profile is composed of a list of parameters divided into so-called 'non-modifiable risk factors' (sex, diabetes, previous heart disease, family history, height) and 'modifiable risk factors' that will become subject to intervention (blood pressure, cholesterol, smoking, weight and HDL[9]). A risk score based on the underlying epidemiological data is used to compute the 'individual risk' – here of stroke – as a probability (in %) for the next 10 years (or next 20 years, 5 years,

---

7   Further marketing was planned although now the software has mostly been replaced by the successor software (HeartScore).

8   For the role of pharmaceuticals in the history of chronic disease in the US in the second half of the 20th century see Greene (2006).

9   HDL: high density lipoprotein, a blood lipid parameter.

1 year). By performing this risk calculation, the individual is localized through extrapolation from the population experience; through population subgroups according to the parameters included in the modelling, an 'individualized' risk value is assigned.[10] The calculations are offered for four different disease categories, i.e. 'stroke', 'coronary heart disease', 'acute myocardial infarction', or general 'fatal event' based on the average population experience for the profile in the underlying dataset. The output is given as a visual graph, with pie charts that display the calculated risk contribution of specific 'intervention options' – smoking, weight, cholesterol, blood pressure. Temporal graphs give an evaluation on whether the lifestyle intervention has been successful and reached its target. The patient is given a results sheet with prewritten texts, explaining the probabilistic character of the assessments:

> If I had 100 patients with the same risk profile as you, I would expect that 24 persons would experience a heart attack over the coming 10 years, while 76 of them would not. Naturally I do not know if you belong to the group with 24 persons or the group with the 76 persons. However, if the same 100 persons reach the recommended treatment goal I would only expect that 6 persons would experience a heart attack in the same period of time while 94 would not – but still I do not know if you belong to the 6 or 94 (PRECARD Software 2004).

Here the individual patient obtains a prediction based on a calculation performed at the population level; this calculation addresses her/him as a member of a statistically defined risk group. Particularly in secondary prevention the use of this tool was reported as accommodating, as the consultation enables patients to be active in improving their health. When applied in primary prevention – confronting the 'healthy patient' with risk estimates according to his/her profiles in the consultation room – the 'translation tool' can however also have come to function in a different mode: effects include the enrolment of individuals into preventive 'treatment' and management of risk factors that may or may not lead to disease in the future. As a tool for prevention, risk figures call upon the individual to act in terms of normalizing his or her risk factor profile – this process can be understood as an interpellation of the subject (Althusser 1979). In this context, it is less an ideological apparatus than an 'apparatus of observation' (Barad 2007; Schwennesen and Koch, this volume) entrenched in the health care system together with a performative process of a preventive consultation that creates the patient/ citizen both as object and subject at the same time. The process of encountering

---

10   Methodologically, this works only for large numbers: as stated in the limitations section of the risk assessment software, the predictions are only valid for risks between 5% and 40% and in a certain age group, becoming highly problematic for strata with small numbers. Although it may seem straightforward, 'individualizing' a probabilistic risk estimate by subgroup categories is complex and not uncontested in statistical theory.

and negotiating the calculations result in the actual enactment of the risk score that enrols the citizen into self observation and preventive risk optimization.

There is a further entanglement occurring in the application of risk calculations to individuals – that of two different temporal regimes. Sometimes notions of temporality are addressed explicitly by epidemiologists, in the sense that mortality is understood as referring to the past, morbidity to the present, while thinking in terms of risk factors bears implications for the future. Yet, when looking at the practices of epidemiological risk assessment, the temporal economies prove more complicated: Risk scores are calculated from the observational data of the 'past experience' in the study population, which is then projected into the future. For this example, the population experience of the past, i.e. of two decades – mainly late 1970s to early 1990s – are used for the extrapolation of individual futures. Performing the risk assessment is joining two different time regimes, i.e. that of the past and the future but also that of the population and the individual. In the calculations carried out, the individual future refers to 1–20 years in the 21st century, while the population experience which the data represents comes mostly from the 1980s – the score then carries the earlier empirical situation with it into the predicted future – a deferral in time regimes that aligns a statistical version of the past with individual futures.

Based on a select number of significant categories, risk estimates are derived and spelled out for subgroups and differentiated according to profiles and reapplied to individuals. The software computes risk figures which are mobilized in the consultation room to activate individuals and to engage them in risk optimization. In evidence-based prevention, risk prediction has increasingly constituted its own grammar of population health considerations which now also is called upon to remodel individual lives. Epidemiologic risk estimates are turned into a prognostic tool for individuals – in a mode of reasoning in terms of governmentality and optimization that is characteristic of risk assessment regimes.

Interestingly, neither social factors nor genetic markers were included into risk assessment tools for cardiovascular prevention in the late 1990s. This was because, after accounting for the 'major' lifestyle risk factors, not much precision was added to the prediction; when accounting for more than 10 factors, the overall predictive capacity of the risk score would not improve significantly. While genetics in terms of family history plays some role in the risk assessment tool and genotyping and other biomarkers are applied to some degree in treatment decision-making, they have rarely reached preventive medicine so far. Still, future inclusion of genetic factors into such tools is envisioned by genetic epidemiologists.

Genomic variables as a source of contestation?

From risk factor epidemiology to genomics (and back)

When the editors of *Genetic Epidemiology* advocated an epidemiological approach to genetics, they envisioned fundamentally new understandings of disease causation which would possibly revolutionize treatment and prevention. It was epidemiological methods that should 'sort out the complex mix' (Neel 1984) of aetiological factors, including genetic predisposition. This was what research at the population level – the study of outcomes (disease) dependent on multiple determinants – could contribute to genetics. The fundamental micro-unit of epidemiological statistics, the '2x2 contingency table',[11] is based on the distribution of exposure and disease in the population sample under study. The mode in which exposure and disease are linked here is statistical; classical epidemiological studies do not draw on knowledge of biological pathways in disease causation. When expanding the focus towards molecular mechanisms and intermediate biomarkers, epidemiologists envisioned being able to open this 'black box between exposure and disease'. This was the contribution genetics and in particular genomics should make to epidemiology and many epidemiologists see the future precisely in that form of public health genomics (Khoury and Little 2000, Khoury et al. 2004, Knoppers and Brand 2009).[12]

In the local studies in Denmark, genetic epidemiology was only one among many research lines pursued in cardiovascular epidemiology. Some genetic markers for cardiovascular disease and diabetes have been looked at since the 1980s, but in general genetics played only a minor role before the 1990s. The main lines of investigations were lifestyle risk, blood lipids as risk factors and potential early predictors, socioeconomic factors and, occasionally, environmental or occupational exposures. By the late 1990s, with sequencing technologies broadly available, research into the influence of genetic variation has developed into a major research direction, in particular the study of candidate genes and single nucleotide polymorphisms (Nordestgaard et al. 1994). Established epidemiological databases and sample repositories were drawn upon to produce data on genetic variation;

---

11   Based on a categorization of the data set in a 2x2 contingency table (into 'diseased and exposed', 'diseased and non-exposed', and 'non-diseased and exposed', 'non-diseased and non-exposed'), estimations of relative risks between these groups are calculated.

12   In the last decade, research centres dedicated to 'public health genomics' or 'public health genetics' have been established at many universities and governmental research institutions as well as intense networking to promote the field. See, e.g. the office of Public Health Genomics at CDC, Atlanta, USA (http://www.cdc.gov/genomics/), Public Health Genomics European network (http://www.phgen.nrw.de/typo3/index.php), The Post-Genomic Public Health Cluster (GENPUB), University of Copenhagen (2008) (http://www.pubhealth.ku.dk/postgeno_en/).

new epidemiological studies integrated biobanks and genetic epidemiology components from their very start.

Some epidemiologists discussed genetic epidemiology as a way to reorient and improve observational and environmental studies. For instance, it has been argued that studies of genetic variation were 'inherently randomized': following the concept of 'Mendelian randomization', i.e. 'the random assortment of genes from parents to offspring that occurs during gamete formation and conception' (Davey Smith and Ebrahim 2003), epidemiologists proposed to take advantage of this 'inherent randomization'. Then, the evidence for genetic factors would be equally valued as the gold standard of medical science—the randomized clinical trial (Davey Smith and Ebrahim 2003). Therefore, some advocate the study of genetic determinants as being methodologically superior, when compared to observational designs.

Nevertheless, wherever possible, epidemiologists adjust for known confounders; the decision on how many variables to adjust for in a particular context, however, is a complex issue. In a conversation about which variables should be adjusted for when studying single nucleotide polymorphisms (SNPs), a genetic epidemiologist states that his group adjusts for whatever the reviewers want them to adjust for, since they can access most variables reviewers would come up with – either from their own database or with record linkage to the central registries. It is this linkage capacity that makes the population registries in the Nordic countries into highly productive resources for biomedical research, which are being deployed using epidemiological techniques. Moreover, these infrastructures represent a resource and continual methodological advantage, which is used to falsify hypotheses suggested by smaller studies conducted elsewhere.

Despite early visions of opening black boxes, gaining fundamental insight and producing applied predictive knowledge by including genetic variation, many of the early expectations – hopes and fears – have not been actualized in the results that these studies yielded. It has rather remained the case that, as it was put much earlier, 'the genetic epidemiologist is slave to the concept of multiple causation' (Neel 1984). The initial enthusiasm for the new genetics has declined after only few polymorphisms have been found to play a significant role; in particular 'low penetrance genes' are hardly significant with respect to genetic testing. Nevertheless, as a consequence of the broad availability of data on genetic variation, the mode of epidemiological research has changed considerably: For example, biobanking is integrated in most epidemiological studies by design – this is also where funding has been available in the age of genomics. Together with other techniques such as linkage analysis, studies on candidate genes and SNPs have played an important role in the early phase of genetic epidemiology. In genomics, epidemiological methods were instrumental in making sense of sequence data at the population level. Most recently, fields such as environmental, nutritional, cardiovascular or cancer epidemiology have been concerned with the study of gene-environment and gene-lifestyle interactions. Thus, epidemiology has developed into a tool to study genetic variation – yet as part of an increasingly complex 'web of causation'.

Gene-lifestyle assemblages

Among the many analyses conducted for the intervention trial described above, this section will focus on an association study of the relationship between genetic variation, lifestyle variables and a biological marker known as a risk factor for cardiovascular disease. As a result of that study, an interaction between genotype and smoking with respect to the concentration of this biomarker was established (Husemoen et al. 2004). This association study can serve as an example for an aetiological re-assemblage of genotype, lifestyle and disease risk. In what ways are differences in disease risk examined within these assemblages and how are variables selected for these models of multiple-causation? As a rule, a first selection step is done in the study design and a further one in the selection of variables for that particular study – a step that depends on both conceptual considerations and data availability. Subsequently, the selection of variables for the final model equation is done following a statistical technique that uses significance levels as cut off marks for the inclusion or exclusion of variables. In this case, for instance, the variables 'tea consumption, intake of dessert wine and spirit, physical activity, body mass index, triglyceride, and presence of chronic disease' were not found significant and therefore excluded. The final model included:

> sex, age MTHFR(C677T) genotype, social class, systolic blood pressure, total cholesterol, smoking status, dietary habits, coffee and wine and beer consumption, including interaction terms between age and MTHFR(C677T) genotype, smoking status and MTHFR(C677T) genotype, smoking status and sex, and beer consumption and age. (Husemoen 2004, 1147)

This set of factors may at first look arbitrary and somewhat surprising, yet from the epidemiologic point of view it performs the selection of significant variables for a particular outcome based on the empirical dataset. The variables chosen to be the potential parameters then make up the epistemic grid with which the aetiology of disease causation or, in this case, associations between genotype and risk factor are statistically 'modelled'. Based on multivariate regression modelling, quantitative risk estimates are derived. Decisions concerning the variables to be included (sex, age MTHFR(C677T) genotype, social class, systolic blood pressure, total cholesterol, smoking status, dietary habits, coffee and wine and beer consumption) and those excluded from the final model (tea consumption, intake of dessert wine and spirit, physical activity, body mass index, triglyceride, and presence of chronic disease), are taken based on statistical significance testing: What is below a certain quantitative level of significance is dropped (as non-significant) in the process of statistical analyses. Using the level of statistical significance (95% as a rule, sometimes 90%) as a 'cut-off point' is an established practice, based on technical standards and consensus in the field.

Just like other 'risk factors', markers of genomic variation have entered the epidemiological matrix, as potential risk factors for disease or related to susceptibilities to the disease. While relating to routines of falsification and explicit or implicit concepts of causality, the choice of the initial categories (before selection via modelling) depends on data opportunities and judgement from experiences with other studies; only then is it narrowed down with the help of statistical techniques. The resulting model ties together micro and macro contexts in one model equation, drawing on their availability in the database (going back to questionnaires, data from population registries, or using proxies that denote further influences that are not directly recordable).

It should be noted here, that the association investigated in this case is not between 'exposure' and 'disease' in the sense of classical epidemiology; but the same epidemiological methods are used to study early mechanisms of later potential. Here, the association between a genetic polymorphism and a biomarker that was previously established as a risk factor for cardiovascular disease is investigated. This illustrates how epidemiological analyses can be used in a flexible way with analytical practices transferred across levels and stages: a SNP takes the role of what used to be 'exposure' in traditional epidemiology and what was 'disease' is now a biomarker understood as an independent risk factor for disease. Both the shifts to the molecular level and to prevention possibly work towards a kind of biomedical governmentality of preventive risk optimization, which operates at the levels of both the population and the individual.

Epidemiology in large networks

With the ever larger amounts of variables generated by 'omics' technologies, the infrastructures and logistics required for epidemiologic analyses have also become more complex. These requirements cannot be met by single studies due to their lack of statistical power when it comes to simultaneously studying large numbers of variables. As a result, epidemiological studies are increasingly conducted as multicentre studies or single studies pooled by larger consortia. Coordination and pooling of epidemiological studies is, however, not new. Although initially first and foremost local projects, some population studies have been part of larger international networks well before the rise of genetic epidemiology, e.g. the Seven Countries Study conducted between 1958 and 1970 (Keys 1970, Mariotti et al. 1981). A large multinational study *Monitoring of Trends and Determinants in Cardiovascular Disease* (*MONICA*) was launched in the early 1980s by the WHO (WHO 1988, Tunstall-Pedoe et al. 2003) and included 39 centres in 26 countries (besides European countries the study included for instance partners in Canada, US, Soviet Union, China, Australia and New Zealand); for Denmark, the Glostrup studies were invited to be part of that effort. The rationale for this concerted effort of research into cardiovascular prevention was to secure sufficient statistical power to identify risk factors across populations. This 'largest cardiovascular risk factor study conducted ever' (Tunstall Pedoe et al. 2003), included standardized data collecting and validation procedures performed centrally at the *MONICA* data centre at the National Public Health Institute of Finland in Helsinki as well as storage of biological material and genetic analyses. While centrally analysed, each participating centre was granted access to genotype information on their own samples. As much as the international project relied on cooperation and continuous efforts on the part of the local studies, the latter substantially benefited from the joint protocols, validation and quality control.

By the end of the 1990s, project coordinators of this large study initiated a follow-up project *MOnica Risk, Genetics, Archiving and Monograph* (*MORGAM*) to maintain and develop the already established datasets. During this transition, the multicentre network was redefined, with a shift in research focus towards two main goals; i.e. improving derived risk scores and, most importantly, deploying the stored DNA in studies of the genetic variation on multi-factorial disease. A key part of *MORGAM* consists of genotyping the polymorphisms that were assumed to influence other cardiovascular risk factors (Tunstall-Pedoe et al. 2003). Such large population databases that store biological materials with lifestyle and health information are attributed 'unique research potential'. Beyond *MORGAM*, the collaboration is being continued within the framework of a European funded consortium 'EU Genome Twin'[13] that aims at the investigation of genetic markers of chronic disease. Here, together with the twin registries of Europe, the network provides opportunities to pool data and samples from more than 1 million participants in a large consortium. The aim of these global networks is to study multiple gene-environment interactions, taking into account novel parameters and biomarkers, which is only statistically meaningful with very large samples.

The networking does however not stop there: 'GenomeEUtwin' has, in turn, joined a recently initiated global network, the 'Public Population Project' (P3G)[14], which lists a large number of publicly funded epidemiological studies that store biological materials. This network connects cohorts and their resources for potential pooled investigations. The rationale in sharing study profiles, developing standards for lab practices and catalogues of questionnaires, is to eventually negotiate mutual access and shared use of biomaterials from millions of participants, which is only feasible through collaboration.

In terms of any analytical categories of the global and the local, epidemiological data and samples are both at the same time: the very same population dataset is both investigated with highly local concerns and simultaneously part of a globally networked 'big science' that requires standardization. Networking and data exchange has only become possible with new information technologies that allow data transfer of large data sets and rapid statistical processing. Often the development of epidemiological methods was made possible and spurred by information technologies on the one hand, while there was a need for new methods due to the large amounts of data generated by new genomics technologies on the

---

13   http://www.biocompetence.eu/index.php/kb_1/io_3205/io.html [accessed January 31, 2009].

14   The Public Population Project. http://www.p3gconsortium.org/ [accessed January 31, 2009].

other hand. It was also this dynamics that has changed epidemiology from rather local studies into a big science conducted in large multinational consortia.

Both public health genomics networks and international data infrastructures are being established as a response to quests for larger samples and pooled studies mostly coming from agendas in genomics and molecular epidemiology (e.g. Emerging Risk Factors Collaboration 2007). While genomic technologies are ubiquitous in much of the life sciences, the study of genetic variation has become far more complex and moved away from 'genetic reductionism'. Rather than conceptualized as deterministic, the genome is seen as imprinted and influenced by multiple environments – from epigenetics to the social environment.

Susceptibility research and epigenetic environments

Conceptually, genomic variables have been integrated into risk models and population health concepts by drawing on the concept of susceptibility. The latter and the notion of individual predisposition can be traced back to the 'epidemiologic triangle of host, agent and environment'. The 'host characteristics' and the 'healthy carrier' in bacteriological concepts of the late 19th century, as well as in early 20th century constitutional medicine became more complex with broad epidemiological research (MacMahon et al. 1960, Mendelsohn 1998). In recent debates, the endeavour to include genetic variation as markers for susceptibility is often presented as tackling the molecular mechanisms between exposure and disease, formerly not accessible – and therefore black-boxed – to epidemiologic investigation. It is the usage of molecular markers for increasingly specific profiling that gives rise to expectations of a more 'personalized' medicine. Moreover, these visions of individualized medicine have been linked to a potential reduction of expenses in the health care sector with more efficient treatment of individual patients; in public health, more targeted interventions directed at the most 'susceptible' subpopulations are envisioned (Villadóniga 2008, Knoppers and Brand 2009).

The concept of susceptibility draws together both epidemiology and genetics: susceptibility is conceptualised as genetic polymorphisms as haplotype patterns are dealt with in bioinformatics and statistical modelling. The notion of susceptibility here moves centre stage as a key 'boundary concept'[15] that is meaningful in both worlds of epidemiology and genetics. A combination of genetics and epidemiology is by no means new; it has a long pre-genomics tradition in population genetics, biometry and physical anthropology. Early textbooks introduced the beginning of genetic epidemiology – as the 'middle ground' (MacMahon 1978) between genetics and epidemiology; they also stress the commonality to both disciplines of path analysis as an approach to causation. For MacMahon (1978), both epidemiology and genetics deal with gene-environment interactions – just that for

---

15   My use of the term 'boundary concept' is inspired by the notion of 'boundary object' (Star and Griesemer 1989).

genetics, the determinants are now 'intrinsic to the species' as their environmental origins are located way back in time. For epidemiology, however, the environment is a factor that co-constitutes actual lifetime events. Yet the integration sought in today's public health sciences 'from molecule to society'[16] seems to aim at a more comprehensive project; it extends from genetic biomarkers to macro economy and ecology.

With susceptibility research as part of epidemiological studies of gene-environment interactions, the focus remains on variables that can be individualized; the preferred combination of lifestyle and genetics is in line with the biomedical paradigm as much as with the risk factor epidemiology approach. However, social epidemiologists continue to criticize the lack of attention to the broader social and environmental factors; all too often, in their views these are reduced to a set of covariates or confounders that need to be statistically controlled for rather than becoming an object of investigation in themselves. In that context, 'public health' and, sometimes, 'population health' are used to put emphasis on the social determinants of health and disease in terms of a public health agenda (Kindig and Stoddart 2003, Labonte et al. 2005), as opposed to 'reductionist' biomedical models. Yet, the key concepts of differences in susceptibility to disease can be found in much of the public health literature. The issue of inter-individual variation in health – of 'why some are healthier than others' – seems to have moved centre-stage in the study of population health (Evans et al. 1994). The population gaze upon the individual can be viewed as performative with respect to producing differences and population subgrouping. In conceptualizing this difference, it seems that there is an oscillation between heredity and genes versus environment and social contexts throughout the history of 'modern epidemiology' – from bacteriology to the age of genomics (MacMahon et al. 1970; Mendelsohn 1998). The 'epidemiological triangle' of host susceptibility, exposure and disease agent of the 19th century appears recurrent in western biomedical health discourses. The notion of host susceptibility has assumed different degrees of importance across history – it has been actualized not only in genetic epidemiology, but also in constitutional medicine, behaviourist approaches to public health and some concepts of lifestyle risk. As close studies of scientific practices demonstrate, the nature/nurture opposition is – and perhaps always has been – much more entangled and blurred.

A closer look at the category of the environment, in the age of genomics and postgenomics shows that the term 'environment' is often used to encompass all non-genetic risk factors: physical activity, for example, became an 'environmental' factor as opposed to genetic risk factors. Moreover, the environment is no longer limited to the physical environment outside the body – in terms of environmental compartments of air or water and their composition – but it is also within the

---

16   'From molecule to society' is the subtitle that appears on the website of the Faculty for Health Sciences: 'fra molekyle til samfund' http://sund.ku.dk/ (last accessed 8 January 2009).

body and part of an individualized notion of this body's 'lifestyle'. Sometimes, the environment refers to the molecular environment of DNA, as in the notion of 'epigenetic environment'. It is this 'environment' that has been conceptualized as the 'trigger' that sets off the effect of susceptibility genes (Olden and Wilson 2000, 149). More recently, variables much beyond genomics, have emerged from 'omics' technologies, i.e. proteomics, transcriptomics and metabolomics. Thus, with genomic epidemiology, the notion of the environment has changed: it is a different environment – molecular and beyond – that has changed from encompassing the sphere that surrounds the human body (in terms of social and physical environment) to one that reaches into the human body as well. Moreover, a blurring also occurs when one focuses on the other side of the dichotomy, i.e. on the gene itself: the genetic no longer stands alone, it is 'switched on or off', 'modulated' and 'imprinted' by this epigenetic environment. With the awareness of increasing complexity of epigenetic influence and of various 'embodiments' of social environments, there is not only a genetization or molecularization of life, there is also a movement back from molecule to the complex environments co-shaped by society.

Conclusions

This chapter has described how epidemiology performs categorical dichotomies but also how this discipline works across them, using techniques of information networking. It has attempted to sketch out how these dynamics co-shape both aetiologic research and contribute to preventive medicine. In particular genomics has recently brought about shifts in the conceptual matrix of disease causation. While genomics has not led to sustained straightforward determinisms, there are other effects brought about by the molecularization of public health matters, for instance a production of difference and 'individualization' based on more complex profiling techniques. Rather than genomics being directly 'translated' into public health, the reconfiguration of public health with genomics is taking place in different, more subtle ways that also include novel ways of incorporating social categories into epidemiological research.

The categories examined in this paper are entangled to an extent that some approaches of the social sciences – such as biologization of the social – are no longer sufficient: with postgenomics, the gene sequence is no longer a candidate for deterministic concepts; rather it represents one parameter among others that is in continuous interaction with its environment. This notion of the environment begins with the epigenetic space adjacent to the DNA and reaches into lifestyle, economic conditions and social networks. In view of the hybridity and blended categories of molecular epidemiology, it is helpful to complement the analytic tools of social studies of the biosciences with attention to the inherent epistemologies of these categories and the 'categorical politics' they perform. Health research, as a rule, pursues a pragmatic approach – often without making explicit the underlying concepts. While at the same time highly regulated procedures, epidemiological designs are pragmatically open to including variables from different contexts. In that sense, health and disease and the matrix of its determinants are under continual re-territorialization, as epidemiological studies range from the molecular level to the social sphere.

In a keynote on whether 'the epidemiologist [should] be a molecular biologist or a social scientist'[17] held in Copenhagen in 1999, Mervyn Susser argued for keeping the integrity of risk factor epidemiology and of the framework of multiple causation. In his understanding, risk factor epidemiology was precisely about combining factors from the microbiological and molecular world as well as from the social world; epidemiology should encompass and work at multiple levels. However, Susser also stressed the fact that it is hardly possible for a single researcher to extend 'beyond the current individual level of risk factor epidemiology to both the micro and macro level' (Susser 1999: S1019). Rather than turning either into a molecular biologist or social scientist, the epidemiologist 'must comprehend and deploy the basic premises and the nature of the information these other disciplines yield' (Susser 1999: S1019). In this conceptualization, the epidemiologist integrates new variables emerging from a broad range of disciplines – from molecular biology to macro-economy. This implies a key epistemological position for epidemiology that becomes the discipline to sort out and synthesize information from different levels and contexts.

This integration across scale of analysis – from molecular genetics to social networks – is different from a mere mutual overlap or stabilization of two sets of biological and social difference categories. In practice, it is a statistical process negotiated in view of emerging empirical data and conceptual issues – it is in this context where for instance concepts such as susceptibility reappear and are actualized.

With epidemiological registries, sample repositories and practices of record linkage and statistical modelling, categories such as the population, the individual, the gene and the environment are reconfigured and intertwine. The epistemologies and categorizations inherent in the modes and practices of knowledge generation have important consequences for how public health is understood – and eventually acted upon. Both in single studies and in multinational research consortia, risk scores are derived from the local data infrastructures for future domains of application in the clinic, in policy and everyday life. As this chapter has described, the implications of epidemiological projections are sometimes far-reaching in their applications: accounts of the collective past are mobilized as a predictor of individual futures in probabilistic risk assessment. The numerical 'population body' brought into being by epidemiology for

---

17 In the symposium 'The future of epidemiology' held at the Panum Institute of the University of Copenhagen in January 1999, leading epidemiologists were brought together to discuss fundamental concepts and future research priorities; these lectures were subsequently published in the *International Journal of Epidemiology* (Susser 1999).

preventive medicine is made up by data collected from individual bodies; in turn, this population knowledge then imprints on the ways individuals act with and relate to health issues. Accounting for the 'omics' level in epidemiology has led to a change in practice: recently, epidemiological research has become about facilitating and negotiating collaboration in large networks. Often, this includes access to data based on examinations, questionnaires, samples, lab results, clinical and socioeconomic data generated elsewhere – here, gene and environment, the local and global are entangled and, for instance in intervention studies, observation and experiment converge.

Genomic epidemiology performs specific categorical politics, in which the 'environment' is conceptualized as a 'trigger' that influences the genome. While parts of public health science have embraced the molecular level, much of the discipline is gradually on its way back to reposition the biological as co-shaped by much larger social influences. Engaging with those reformulations of 'the social' will be an emerging issue for public health science. Following these blended and hybrid categories and their transformations will remain an important analytical task for the social studies of epidemiology.

References

Althusser, L. 1971. Ideology and Ideological State Apparatuses (Notes towards an Investigation), in *Lenin and Philosophy and Other Essays*, edited by L. Althusser. New York/London: Monthly Review Press, 127–86.

Appleyard, M. 1989. The Copenhagen City Heart Study. Østerbroundersøgelsen. A book of tables with data from the first examination (1976–78) and a five year follow-up (1981–83), *Scandinavian Journal of Social Medicine*, Suppl. 41, 1–160.

Aronowitz, R.A. 1998. *Making Sense of Illness. Science, Society, and Disease*. Cambridge: Cambridge University Press.

Barad, K. 2007. *Meeting the Universe Halfway*. London: Duke University Press.

Bauer, S. 2008. Mining data, gathering variables and recombining information. The flexible architecture of epidemiologic studies. *Studies in History and Philosophy of Biological and Biomedical Sciences*, 39, 415–428.

Bonnevie, L. Thomsen, T. and Jørgensen, T. 2005. The use of computerized decision support systems in preventive cardiology – principle results from the national PRECARD® survey in Denmark. *European Journal of Cardiovascular Prevention and Rehabilitation*, 12(1), 52–55.

Brown, N. and Webster, A. 2004. *New Medical Technologies and Society: Reordering Life*. Cambridge: Polity Press.

Callon, M. 1986. Elements of a sociology of translation: Domestication of the Scallops and the Fishermen of St Brieuc Bay, in *Power, Action and Belief: A New Sociology of Knowledge?*, edited by J. Law. London: Routledge, 196–233.

Davey Smith, G. and Ebrahim, S. 2003. Mendelian randomization: can genetic epidemiology contribute to understanding environmental determinants of disease? *International Journal of Epidemiology*, 32, 1–22.

Dawber, T.R., Meadors, G.F. and Moore, F., E. Jr. 1951. Epidemiological approaches to heart disease: the Framingham Study. *American Journal of Public Health*, 41(3), 279–81.

Dehue, T. 2001. Establishing the experimenting society. The historical origination of social experimentation according to the randomized controlled design. *American Journal of Psychology*, 114(2), 283–302.

Emerging Risk Factors Collaboration (writing committee Danesh, J., Erqou, S., Walker, M., Thompson. S.G.) 2007. Analysis of individual data on lipid, inflammatory and other markers in over 1.1 million participants in 104 prospective studies of cardiovascular disease. *European Journal of Epidemiology*, 22(12), 839–869.

Evans, R.G., Barer, M.L., Marmor, T.R. 1994. *Why are Some People Healthier than Others. The Determinants of Health of Populations*. Berlin De Gruyter.

Greene, J.A. 2006. *Prescribing by Numbers: Drugs and the Definition of Disease*. Baltimore: Johns Hopkins University Press.

Hagerup, L., Eriksen, M., Schroll, M., Hollnagel, H., Agner E., and Larsen, S. 1981. The Glostrup population studies collection of epidemiologic tables. Reference values for use in cardiovascular population studies. *Scandinavian Journal of Social Medicine*, 20(Suppl), 1–112.

Husemoen, L. L., Thomsen, T.F. Jørgensen, T. 2004. Effect of lifestyle factors on plasma total homocysteine concentrations in relation to MTHFR(C677T) genotype. Inter99, *European Journal of Clinical Nutrition*, 58, 1142–1150.

Jørgensen, T., Borch-Johnsen, K., Thomsen, T.F., Ibsen, H., Glümer. C., et al. 2003. A randomized non-pharmacological intervention study for prevention of ischaemic heart disease: baseline results Inter99. *European Journal of Cardiovascular Prevention and Rehabilitation*, 10, 377–386.

Jørgensen, T. 2004. Epidemiologisk forskning gennem 40 år. Befolknings-undersøgelserne i Glostrup – Center for Sygdomsforebyggelse – Forskningscenter for Forebyggelse og Sundhed. *Ugeskrift Læger*, 166(15–16), 1425–1428.

Keys, A. 1970. Coronary heart disease in seven countries. *Circulation*, 41(Suppl), 1–211.

Khoury, M. J.; Little, J. 2000. Human genome epidemiologic reviews: the beginning of something HuGE. *American Journal of Epidemiology*, 151, 2–3.

Khoury, M. J., Little, J. and Burke, W. 2004. *Human Genome Epidemiology*. New York: Oxford University Press.

Kindig, D., Stoddart, G. 2003. What is population health? *American Journal for Public Health*, 93, 380–383.

Knoppers, B.M., Brand, A.M. 2009. From Community Genetics to Public Health Genomics – What's in a name? Editorial. *Public Health Genomics*, 12, 1–3.

Krieger, N. 2001. Theories for social epidemiology in the 21st century: an ecosocial perspective. *International Journal of Epidemiology*, 30(4), 668–677.

Labonte, R., Polanyi, M., Muhajarine, N., McIntosh, T., Williams, A. 2005. Beyond the divides: Towards critical population health research. *Critical Public Health*, 15(1), 5–17.

Last, J. 2001. *A Dictionary of Epidemiology*. New York: Oxford University Press.

Latour, B. 1987. *Science in Action: How to Follow Scientists and Engineers Through Society*. Milton Keynes: Open University Press.

MacMahon, B., Pugh, T. and Ipsen, J. 1960. *Epidemiologic Methods*. Boston: Little, Brown & Company.

MacMahon, B. 1978. Epidemiologic approaches to family resemblance, in *Genetic Epidemiology*, edited by N.E. Morton, C.S. Chung. New York: Academic Press.

Mariotti, S., Capocaccia, R., Farchi, G., Menotti, A., Verdecchia, A., and Keys, A. 1981. Differences in the incidence rate of coronary heart disease between North and South European cohorts of the Seven Countries Study as partially explained by risk factors. *European Heart Journal*, 3, 481–487.

Marks, H. 1997. *The Progress of Experiment. Science and Therapeutic Reform in the United States, 1900–1990*. Cambridge/New York: Cambridge University Press.

Mattila, E. 2006. Struggle between specificity and generality: how infectious disease models become a simulation platform, in *Simulation: Pragmatic Constructions of Reality*, edited by J. Lenhard, G. Küppers and T. Shinn. Sociology of the Sciences, Vol. 25. Heidelberg: Springer, 125–138.

Mendelsohn, A. 1998. From eradication to equilibrium: How epidemics became complex after World War I, in *Greater than the Parts: Holism in Biomedicine, 1920–1950*, edited by C. Lawrence and G. Weisz. Oxford: Oxford University Press, 303–331.

Møller L., Kristensen T.S., Hollnagel H. 1991. Social status og kardiovaskulære risikofaktorer *Ugeskrift Læger*, 154, 8–13.

Neel, J.V. 1984. A revised estimate of the amount of genetic variation in human proteins: implications for the distribution of DNA polymorphisms. *American Journal of Human Genetics*, 36(5), 1135–48.

Nordestgaard, B., Agerholm-Larsen, B., Wittrup, H.H. and Tybjærg-Hansen A. 1996. A prospective cardiovascular population study used in genetic epidemiology. The Copenhagen City Heart Study. *Scandinavian Journal of Clinical Laboratory Investigation* 56(Suppl 226), 65–71.

Olden, K., Wilson S. 2000. Environmental health and genomics: visions and implications. *Nature Reviews Genetics*, 1, 149–153.

Olsen, J. H., Mellemkjær, L. and Friis, S. 2004. Fra kræfttælling til cancerregister. *Ugeskrift Læger*, 166(15/16), 1458–1459.

Ong, A., Collier, S. 2005. *Global Assemblages: Technology, Politics and Ethics as Anthropological Problems*. Malden: Blackwell Publishing.

Osler M. 1993. Social class and health behaviour in Danish adults: A longitudinal study. *Public Health*, 107, 251–260.

Oxford Center for Evidence Based Medicine (2001), Levels of Evidence. http://www.cebm.net/index.aspx?o=1025 [accessed 31 Jan 2009].

Petersen, A., Lupton D. 1997. *The New Public Health. Health and Self in the Age of Risk*. London: Sage.

Petersen, A. and Bunton, R. 2002. *The New Genetics and the Public's Health*. London: Routledge.

PRECARD® 2001. Evidence-based prevention of cardiovascular disease. Software, registered at the Medical Museion (Object Registration Number: MM139:2007G), University of Copenhagen.

Rabinow P. 1996. *Essays on the Anthropology of Reason*. Princeton: Princeton University Press.

Roberts, C.J. 1978. *Epidemiology for Clinicians*. London: Pitman Medical Publishing.

Sackett, D. L., Rosenberg, W. M.C., Gray, J.A. M, Haynes, R.B. and Richardson, W.S. 1996. Evidence Based Medicine. *British Medical Journal*, 312, 71–72.

Star, S., L. and Griesemer, J.R. 1989. Institutional ecology, 'translations' and boundary objects: Amateurs and professionals in Berkeley's Museum of Vertebrate Zoology, 1907–39. *Social Studies of Science*, 19, 387–420.

Susser, M. 1999. Should the epidemiologist be a social scientist or a molecular biologist? *International Journal of Epidemiology*, 28, S1019–S1021.

The Cochrane Collaboration 2009 [1993], http://www.cochrane.org/ [accessed: 15 February 2009].

Trostle, J.A. 2005. *Epidemiology and Culture*. New York: Cambridge University Press.

Tunstall-Pedoe, H. 2003. *MONICA Monograph and Multimedia Sourcebook*. Geneva: World Health Organization.

Villadóniga J.I. (2008), A more accurate approach to molecular genetics analysis in vascular disease, *Cardiovasc Hematol Disord Drug Targets*, 8(3), 212–27.

Weisz, G. (2005), From clinical counting to evidence-based medicine, in *Body Counts. Medical Quantification in Historical & Sociological Perspectives*, edited by G. Jorland, A. Opinel and G. Weisz. (Montreal: McGill-Queen's University Press), 377–393.

WHO (The World Health Organization) 1988. MONICA Project (monitoring trends and determinants in cardiovascular disease): A major international collaboration. *Journal of Clinical Epidemiology*, 41, 105–114.

Chapter 7

Life Beyond Information: Contesting Life and the Body in History and Molecular Biology

Adam Bencard

Introduction

This chapter is a study of parallel obsessions; of intangible wires crossed, creating sparks of metaphors and bursts of imaginative energy. These obsessions run complicated courses through two seemingly distant scientific landscapes, those of molecular biology and history, but, as I will attempt to map out, there is a sense in which the preoccupations of post-genomic scientists and complexity-sensitive historians share a similar sense of a reconfiguration of their subject matter. Within molecular biology, this reconfiguration is tied to the intense interest in the protein, which increasingly is occupying centre-stage in post-genomic research; in this new development in the life sciences, life scientists 'can be seen turning from matters of code to matters of substance – that is, from spelling out linear gene sequences to inquiring after the three-dimensional materiality, structure, and function of the protein molecules' (Myers 2008, 163). This turn from matters of code to matters of substance is, as I will argue, echoed and reverberated in the preoccupations of a new orientation with the historical study of the body in history. Within history, and even in the humanities more generally, there seems to be a renewed desire to examine ourselves and the subjects we investigate as part of a material world, rather than one made from codes, language, symbols and discourses; as one German philosopher writes, it is as if 'we found ourselves in the middle of time and in the middle of objects, with a desire to become part of this material world' (Gumbrecht 2008: 522).

This chapter, then, traces the parallel track of the geneticist vision of the 'book of life' and what might be called the new cultural historical vision of 'the body as text'. These are two understandings of what constitutes life and the human form that are dissimilar in aims, methods and purpose, but that nonetheless share, as I will argue, certain metaphorical similarities. These similarities revolve around the notion of life as information, the body as text, and the notion of something semantic, almost non-physical which determines and inscribes the human form. The essay follows the parallel life of this informational metaphor, through its inception, its subsequent problematization and a possible move beyond it.

Within molecular biology the idea of the gene as the information that makes up the text of life developed from the 1960s onwards and came to a head in the 1990s with the publication of the human genome (Doyle 1997, Kay 2000, Keller 2002, Rose 2007). Parallel to this, within historical studies of the body a discursive model of the body developed in the 1960s out of the linguistic turn, and came to a head in the early 1990s (Frank 1990, Bynum 1995, Porter 1999, Jenner and Taithe 2000). But, as I will argue, it seems as if this informational gestalt/mindset is undergoing a change both within molecular biology and within the historical study of the human body and its relationship to the material world. After approximately 2000 it has increasingly been recognized that the informational metaphor is no longer adequate, and perhaps does not cover how 'life' functions. The move within biomedicine has instead been towards proteomics, which, as I will argue in the chapter, is a move that privileges spatial relations and materiality over informational metaphors (Kay 2000, Tanford and Reynolds 2001, Tyers and Mann 2003, Pappas 2006, Myers 2008). Similarly, within the humanities an increasing emphasis has been put on the concrete matter of the body and materiality, on spatiality, and the more-than-representational (Massumi 2002, DeLanda 2002, Olsen 2003, Gumbrecht 2004, Runia 2006, Ingold 2007, Thrift 2007).

What I will do in this chapter is to trace first the outlines of the informational mindset in the historical study of the human body in molecular biology, and then suggest that a change is under way in both mindsets, visible within molecular biology in a new set of metaphors surrounding proteonomics, and within the humanities in a new set of metaphors surrounding the study of the body and materiality. We are possibly witnessing a formation of new interests where people feel a greater need to understand not the history of something but rather the here and now – not the historical 'how' (how something came to be the way it appears to us) but the 'what' of the moment (what happens in the moments when things appear to us) (see Pred 2005 and Stewart 2007). History recedes in importance compared to figuring out what happens in the now, not only as a formation of earlier events, but also as something particular, something unfinished. This is paralleled within biomedicine, where there seems to be a sense in which 'the protein' is taking over for 'the cell' as a primary generator of metaphors/ways of thinking – this, of course, does not mean that cells are being abandoned as objects of scientific study, but rather that the cell is being studied from a different perspective, namely that of the proteome, and this changed perspective leads to the generation of new metaphors.[1] Comparatively, we might say that the somewhat vague term 'the non-representational' is taking over from various forms of representational preoccupations (Lorimer 2005, Thrift 2007). These are admittedly vague notions, but I will attempt to show, through examples from biomedical and historical discourse respectively, how the metaphors used seem to be shifting in such parallel ways. It is also important to note already at the outset that this is not a

---

1 Thank you to Thomas Söderqvist for bringing these developments to my attention. See http://www.corporeality.net/museion/2008/09/23/metaphors-for-proteins-and-proteomics/.

matter of clean breaks, radical shifts or paradigmatic revolution, but rather a series of minor steps that are slowly eroding the previous strong foundation of a specific set of metaphors, and the new metaphorical pathways that open as a result of this erosion. Genes are not being abandoned as objects of studies in the biomedical sciences, just as meaning is not being sidelined in historical sciences, but their status as the dominant generators of metaphors seems to be changing.

I will in no way suggest any causal relationship between the developments in genetics and the history of the body, since that would be almost impossible to verify in any form. It is hard to judge what informs what; the cultural chains of influence, inspiration and osmosis are too intangible and convoluted to unravel. But metaphors and models have a tendency to transcend different areas and move from one part of social, cultural and scientific life to another. Their specific articulation might vary tremendously, but certain metaphors have a relative strength at certain points in history – they grip us with the force of the new, the hitherto unseen after which everything will be slightly different.

The metaphors that are under investigation in this essay are ones that lay claim to ways of formulating the categories of life and the body. They are essential contestations of previous models, and thus partake in the ongoing and continual process of refiguring and contesting the categories most intimate and central to us. They are by no means the only available metaphors to describe those categories even in the period where they have had their prominence – categories such as life or the body are much too expansive and slippery to control through a single set of metaphors. I hope that this simple paralleling of two developments can suggest something about the complex ways in which our relationship to and thinking about categories such as the body interweaves and intermingles. What I would like to do in this essay is to suggest that the ways in which we think of categories such as life or the human body carries with it a set of internal momentums which make certain conclusions obvious and immediate while pushing certain agendas to the forefront. Intellectual development, be it within the humanities or molecular biology, depends on refiguring, re-conceptualizing that which is given and taken for granted.

Metaphors in science

This chapter, then, is a study of a set of metaphors of how to envision the functioning of the body, whether in history or as a biological organism. How the categories we operate with are framed and represented, and how this framing and representation affect our understanding and interaction with those categories, is a complex matter.[2] This is no less true for scientists; as Keller points out, 'like the rest of us, scientists

---

2   The study of metaphors has had something of a Renaissance recently, (see Franke 2000, 137–153) Also of note on the topic of metaphors and their complex interweaving with human practices is Hans Blumenberg's notion of a metaphorology (see Blumenberg 1997

are language-speaking actors. The words they use play a crucial (and more often than not, indispensable) role in motivating them to act, in directing their attention, in framing their questions, and in guiding their experimental efforts. By their words, their very landscapes of possibility are shaped' (Keller 2000: 139). This landscape of possibilities offered by language is particularly important when it comes to a complex and entangled issue such as the human body. These metaphors give the body a form and a shape, an internal logic, a sense of its functioning and of its place in the complex web between biology and culture. The metaphors might originate in specific scientific circumstances, where they have specific meanings, but their meanings are often stretched far beyond these circumstances and often take on a social, cultural, political and scientific life of their own – the history of science and technology are rife with examples of narrow scientific discoveries becoming powerful metaphors in a wider public domain. These metaphors are not tied down through strings of causality or logic, but function in a realm between on the one hand the known, the studied and the scientific and on the other the possible, the virtual and the potential.

In the preface to the now classic study on biological metaphors, *Refiguring Life – Metaphors of Twentieth Century Biology*, Evelyn Fox Keller notes that:

> Not all metaphors are equally useful or, for that matter, equally captivating. The effectiveness of a metaphor, like that of a speech act, depends on shared social conventions and, perhaps especially, on the authority conventionally granted to those who use it. It also depends on other family resemblances already in place. (Keller 1995: xii)

In order for a metaphor to be regarded as useful it needs a network of ideas, resemblances and practices that supports it and lends it an air of explanatory potential and applicability. The metaphors we use change as these networks change, and the seeming usefulness of the metaphor fades.

The two forces mentioned in the quote above that can support a metaphor – authority and resemblance – are both at play in the issues that I would like to explore in this essay. Notions of authority in metaphors are often silent and unrecognized, and the users draw unconsciously on the socially endowed strength of the metaphor in question. Whether in the realms of science, politics or culture, such metaphors allow its users to tap into discourses outside of itself and gain some sort of rhetorical and argumentative force by the implication. At times, such borrowing of metaphorical authority is creative and fruitful in that it spurs new debates and new ideas, and at times it is more like wielding a rhetorical hammer to bludgeon ideological opponents with or create guilt by association. These metaphors play an essential part in contesting the categories with which we apprehend the world around us. Metaphors often sweep people up in a flurry

---

and Adams 1991, 152–166). See also http://mason.gmu.edu/~montecin/metabiblio.htm for a comprehensive bibliography of studies of metaphors.

of enthusiasm, and carry with them seeming endless possibilities and promises of new paths to walk. New ideas need metaphors that fuel it by drawing on both authority from other often quite unrelated, fields and by resemblance. As philosopher Brian Massumi noted in an interview when describing Deleuze's idea of 'images of thought':

> Our words don't just describe, they intervene. They don't just reflect, they affect. They intervene in a web of relations that what is being talked about is already a part of, and that already includes ourselves and others. That web of relation is what made them noticeable to begin with. It is what recommended them to us, or committed them to our attention in the first place. (Massumi 2004: 60)[3]

Of course, such words and metaphors in no way make up the entirety of scientific practice or idea-making. They merely form a part of the ideological framework that supports an idea – both figuratively by strengthening arguments and promoting creative thought, and literally by providing financial and scholarly support. Biological, medical, social and philosophical thought interweaves in complex ways, and being attentive to the metaphorical content of this interweaving will potentially sensitize us to the complex politics of the moment. As one scientist writes on the power of metaphors:

> Of all intellectuals, scientists are the most distrustful of metaphors and images. This, of course, is our tacit acknowledgment of the power of these mental constructs, which shape the questions we ask and the methods we use to answer these questions. (Wolynes 2001: 555)

The rise of the informational model

Genetics and the rise of the informational model

The twentieth century inherited a model of the body from the nineteenth century that, as Foucault described famously in *The Birth of the Clinic*, rested on a clinical gaze as it was performed in the hospitals (Foucault 1994). It was a gaze that was

---

3   Massumi continues, noting the importance of understanding the degree to which our vocabularies should not be read in terms of right or wrong but rather through sets of social relations: 'So the question is not, right or wrong? But: important or unimportant, in what way and to whom, and moving in what direction? How can we modulate that emphasis, and with what consequences, by the way we address each other, taking into consideration the web that already involves us and our thinking and knits us to others and our things in a thoroughly social world?' Similarly, in this essay, I'm not concerned with whether or not the informational metaphor is right or wrong, but rather in tracing its coming into being and possible fading away.

drawn in detail on the anatomical atlas and studied carefully on the dissection table. This body was envisioned as a complete, unified whole, a system of systems. As Nikolas Rose writes, the skin was seen as enclosing 'a "natural" volume of functionally interconnected organs, tissues, functions, controls, feedbacks, reflexes, rhythms, circulations and so forth' (Rose 2007: 43–44). But during the 1930s, biology began studying life and thereby the body on a molecular level. This change was not merely a matter of finding new explanations on a molecular level, but comprised a complete reorganization of the gaze of the life scientists. This new gaze led to the formation of a new epistemological configuration, one based on information which became foundational for the next half century and into the new millennium.

This new gaze focused on the gene as the key to life itself. The groundbreaking discovery of the DNA double helix by Francis Crick and James Watson in 1953 lead to the belief, that this molecular structure was the primary agent of inheritance in all living things. This belief became known to molecular biologists as the central dogma of molecular biology, and is essentially the belief that an organism's genome, i.e. the sum total of its genes, accounts fully for its characteristic assemblage of inherited traits. This central dogma was a foundational part of the revolutions in molecular biology that took place in the latter half of the twentieth century (Kay 2000). It sought to focus inheritance entirely on the molecular level and was at once both simple, elegant, and easily summarised. The molecular agent of inheritance is DNA (deoxyribonucleic acid) which is essentially a very long molecule that lies coiled within the nucleus of each cell. Individual segments of DNA make up the genes that, through a series of molecular processes, give rise to each of our inherited traits (Keller 2000).

The genetic gaze was further strengthened and extended by a host of important discoveries which followed Watson and Cricks' groundbreaking insight. These were particularly the advent of the so-called recombinant DNA technology in the mid 1970s, the launch of the Human Genome Project in 1990, and the publication of the complete draft of the human genome in 2003. These scientific discoveries led to the formation, from the 1960s onwards, of what has been called an informational model of life generally including the human body. This model was specifically formulated through the metaphor of the 'book of life'. This image was particularly prevalent in the rhetoric surrounding the Human Genome Project (Nerlich, Dingwall and Clark 2002: 445–469). The genes were conceived of as a sort of digital manual for making a human being; thus while DNA itself is a spatial, physical structure, the way in which DNA was seen as functioning was shrouded in metaphors of code, information and text. Though problematic, this view of the genome as an information system, a linguistic text written in DNA code, has been guiding theories and practices of molecular biologists since the 1950s.[4] This view is summed up in the metaphor of molecular biology as being

---

4   For a case study of the early application of informational metaphors in molecular biology, see Brandt 2005.

involved in the decoding of the Book of Life, a metaphor that has taken on a life of its own:

> No longer taken as a metaphor, the chimera of the Book of Life, with all its incongruities and aporias, has become the dominant icon in the quest of biopower, genomic mastery predicated on 'DNA literacy', and control of the word; it professes both creation and revelation. (Kay 2000: 325)

This point is emphasised in the following quote from the former President Bill Clinton, taken from his speech on 26th of June 2000 at the press conference announcing the publication of the working draft of the human genome: 'Today, we are learning the language in which God created life. We are gaining ever more awe for the complexity, the beauty, the wonder of God's most divine and sacred gift. With this profound new knowledge, humankind is on the verge of gaining immense, new power to heal' (Dingwall and Clarke 2002: 445). The informational model promises us a chance to read the Book of Life, a work previously only accessible to its creator. In a similar vein, Hans Jörg Rheinberger has pointed out the fundamental change that recombinant DNA-techniques produced:

> With the advent of recombinant DNA technologies, a radical change of perspective ensued. The momentum of gene technology is based on the prospects of an intracellular representation of extracellular projects – the potential of 'rewriting' life. (Rheinberger 2000: 19)

Life, then, is something that is 'written' – it is fundamentally a code or a text, and it is a text that scientists have gained the ability not only to read, but to edit and rewrite.

Even if I go on to sketch how this model was complicated and that the focus in genetics seems to be shifting to proteomics, the importance of the informational model for the efforts in identifying the genomic foundation for vital biological processes such as aging and disease cannot be underestimated. It still commands metaphorical as well as economic, political and cultural clout, and it has a firm grasp on the public understanding of life and the body, even to the point of inducing a kind of 'genetic fetishism' (Haraway 1997, see also Kay 2000, Rose 2007).

Writing a completely historicized body

Within the humanities the informational model of the human body primarily took the form of what I have elsewhere called the historicized body (Bencard 2008). This model has, on the most general level, been a part of what has been called the linguistic turn. From the 1960s onwards, scholars in the humanities and social sciences, particularly within history and social sciences, have increasingly turned their attention to questions of language, identity, symbols and social constructions. Although this turn can be traced back to the mid-1960s with particularly the works of Michel Foucault as an early example, it had its main impact from the late 1970s and onwards. The linguistic turn was seen as an oppositional, progressive method that was used to break new ground in the struggle against more conservative or traditional understandings of the social, the cultural, nature, biology, knowledge, truth, and a host of similar foundational categories. At the most general level, the linguistic turn specifies a preoccupation with language as one, or even *the*, constitutive element of the social and the cultural – Jacques Derrida's proclamation in *Of Grammatology* that there exists no outside-the-text is a seminal moment in this turning towards language, which has dominated debates in history throughout the 1980s and 1990s. This linguistic approach, which is within history often summated as a post-modern historiography (with all the cumbersome imprecision of such labels), implies a challenge to early conventional certainties such as 'facts', 'objectivity', and 'truth' (see Berkhofer 1995, Jenkins 1997, Wilson 1999).

Historian Nancy Partner has summarized the linguistic challenge thus, suggesting the scope of the issues involved:

> The iconoclastic weapons of the 'linguistic turn' were the exposure of 'transparent' language as a rhetorical voice like any other; a destabilized theory of reference connected to semiotics: and the deconstructive analysis of historical 'facts' as constructed artefacts no different in cognitive origin than any other made thing of 'fiction'. (Partner 1992: 23)

This development has had several effects, including a destabilization of both the object and subject of historical knowledge and an emphasis on the performativity of texts. As Hayden White writes in the influential collection of essays *Probing the Limits of Representation*: 'There is an inexpungeable relativity in every representation of historical phenomenon. The relativity of the representation is a function of the language used to describe and thereby constitute past events as possible objects of explanation and understanding [...] stories, like factual statements, are linguistic entities and belong to the order of discourse' (White 1992: 42). White expressed one of the core arguments of the linguistic turn: that language is inherently unstable, and since it is involved in every act of representation, representations themselves are equally unstable.

The study of the body in history has been one of the pre-eminent ways in which this emphasis on narrativity and discourse manifested itself. Bodies have been a centrepiece of these new historiographical forms – as historian Roger Cooter notes, 'body studies were in many ways the epitome of the linguistic turn in cultural studies' (Cooter 2004: 319). The central themes of post-modernism – discourse, sexuality, textuality and power – all point to the body as a central object of study, a locus on which these themes register. The movements of poststructuralism in general were an important part in the rise of the body as a topic in the humanities and social sciences. This new history of the body was thus one which emphasised the historicity and constructed nature of the human body at its core. It focused on the body as a gateway to reading the complicated webs of the knowledge constructions in which it was perceived as suspended. In other words, it was an understanding of the body fuelled by a social constructionist anti-essentialism. This historicized body was seen as being in every pertinent way made up from the outside, it was constructed out of the information absorbed from cultural and societal forces around it – it was seen as totally imprinted by history. This is expressed here by Michel Feher in his introduction to the important three-volume study *Fragments for a History of the Human Body* in a quote which encapsulates much of what the notion of the historicized body aspires to:

> The history of the human body is not so much the history of its representations as of its modes of construction. For the history of its representations always refer to a real body considered to be 'without history' – whether this is the organism observed by the natural sciences, the body proper as perceived by phenomenology, or the instinctual, repressed body on which psychoanalysis is based – whereas the history of its modes of construction can, since it avoids the overly massive oppositions of science and ideology or of authenticity and alienation, turn the body into a thoroughly historizised and completely problematic issue. (Feher 1989: 11)

This sense of the body as a completely problematic issue is described by Londa Schiebinger, who herself participated actively in the historicizing of bodies, who wrote about her seminal work of body history, *Nature's Body – Gender in the Making of Modern Science*, that *Nature's Body* was published in the era when it was imperative to expose the privileged firstborn twins of modern science: the myth of the natural body and the myth of value-neutral knowledge' (Schiebinger 2004: ix). The will to expose the problematic nature of this axis – the naturalistic understanding of the body and the value-neutrality of scientific knowledge about it – is fundamental for the new cultural histories of the body. The new cultural histories of the body proceed from the insight that bodies have histories, that this presumed biological core is in fact a historical construction.

Complicating the informational model

Blurring the genetic code

The epitome of the information epistemology was the so-called 'gene for' thinking, i.e. the search for a single gene that coded for the varieties of life as seen in the search for the fat gene, the alcoholic gene, the homosexual gene and so on. While some scientists from the start cautioned against believing this rhetoric, it still took firm hold of the public imagination. But as molecular biology developed, an increasingly vocal group of scientists were pointing to the limitations of the model. It was increasingly realised that genes do not just code for one single thing. As Keller argues:

New kinds of data gathered over the last few decades have dramatically fleshed out our understanding of the parts played by genes in cellular and organismic processes, and in doing so they have made it increasingly apparent how far the weight of such a load exceeds what any one single entity can reasonably be expected to bear, and hence, how appropriate that it be distributed among many different players in the game of life. Indeed, even taking these burdens separately, evolution has apparently seen fit to distribute each of them amongst a variety of players. (Keller 2000: 145)

Genetic sequence data is still growing exponentially – Google's massive investment in the personalised gene date service 23andme.com is a perfect example of just how much emotion and economic attachment such data holds for us. But as several scientists have argued, these genomic visions are founded on a simplistic and reductionist understanding of the gene. Such sequence data seem to hold more data than they actually do, promising much more existential meaningfulness than they deliver. Transliterated DNA sequences are extremely polysemic and context-dependent, which goes against the underlying the faith in the explanatory powers of genomic sequences, since that is a belief founded on a relative straightforward correspondence between genes, structures and functioning. And it is increasingly being suggested that such a straightforward relation between genes and their expressions is not tenable. As one science blogger writes, the belief that life is programmed by DNA is falling apart:

This is essentially when the smoke from our pipedream of a molecular Grail was blown away by the harsh winds of reality. If DNA is the book of life, no one has the slightest idea of how to read it. One major reason for this is that making sense of the huge amount of data is too complex—when one focuses on the small details the complete picture becomes blurred.[5]

Life is being reconfigured from a straightforward instantiation of a molecular code to the mysterious transformation of the one-dimensional and comparatively simple genome to the three-dimensional and very complex system of the cell.

Thus what is changing is the faith in the genome as the key with which to understand, decipher and decode life itself, due to the realization that the translation process from gene to cell is a world unto itself. As Kay writes,

With transposons, exons, and introns, and with splicing and posttranslation modification, the relation is plastic, context-dependent, and contingent. In several laboratories around the world, genomics is now moving beyond monogenetic and polygenetic determinism, even beyond functional genomics, towards a phase concerned with nonlinear, adaptive properties of complex dynamic systems, where visions of linear causality would be replaced by analysis of networks

---

5   http://www.medbioworld.com/postgenomics_blog/?p=17 (accessed 27 June 2008).

interacting with the environment and operation across levels of regulations: genetic, epigenetic, morphogenetic, and organismal. (Kay 2000: 326)

The list of parts that the Human Genome Project revealed turned out not to be a complete wiring diagram that it was hoped to be. The history contained in the gene turned out to be only a part of what happens in the continuing series of events that make up life and the body – the historical 'how' did not fully encompass the continuing 'what' happens right now.

Critiquing the new discursive body

This split between the 'how' and the 'what' had a strong parallel in the history of the discursive body. A sense of dissatisfaction developed alongside the success of the historicized body. A critique of the lingualism of the new histories of the body was voiced, focusing particularly on a lack of the felt, experienced, lived body. In 1995, medievalist Caroline Walker Bynum wrote perhaps the most cited reflection of the current prevalence of body studies from a historian's perspective (Bynum 1995). The essay opens with an anecdote, relating how a colleague of Bynum's on her way to an Eastern European University in order to head up a woman's studies program bemoaned the then current state of affairs in body studies; 'There is so much written about the body,' she groans, 'but it all focuses on such a recent period. And in so much of it, the body dissolves into language. The body that eats, that works, that dies, that is afraid – that body just isn't there' (Bynum 1995: 1). Bynum identifies what she perceives to be a cardinal problem for the constructivist approach to the body: the body becomes a trap or a prison because it is seemingly powerless to resist or transform the social force which constructs it from the bottom up. The social system is watertight, so to speak, a level and unbroken discursive field. There is a sense of something being missed, of something important being phased out of the historical study of the body; a blind spot in discursive analysis. They all suggest that there is something being left out in the new history of the body, namely an experience of embodiment/lived experience.

Bynum's critique participated in a wider sense of disparagement with the discursive body that took form during the 1990s. The common point of this criticism was that the stress on the discursive in some sense left the material contexts of the body unexplored. One historian lamented the fact that the body in historical work is often 'an irritatingly non-physical abstraction' and has argued that instead we need an 'understanding of sexual difference which will incorporate, not fight against, the corporeal' (Roper 1994: 17–18). Similarly, Dorinda Outram accused the new cultural histories of the body of shying away from integrating subjectivity into their history of the body. She argued that without taking into account how people have felt about their own bodies, of how they come to terms with or remake them, something essential is edged out of the story about the body. If the historian of the body does not take subjective body experience into account, it becomes, she argues, all too easy, as well, to write the history of the body as the history of its representations. The body starts to resemble a creature of infinite plasticity, constantly culturally redefined and re-represented until it becomes difficult to understand why the body should ever have been portrayed as either prison, fortress, or temple, as in any way absolutely and ineluctable present. (Outram 1993: 348)

Subjective experience of the body is then, in Outram's view, what gives a sense of the inescapable presence of the body in our lives. From her perspective, much of the new history of the body seemingly rendered the historical actors silent about the experience of their bodies.

The idea that the body could be understood through discourse and language was contested by referencing a sense of lack originating in a perceived inability to capture experience in the body. The history of the body could not fully capture what having a body felt like, and thus the informational or discursive model of the body in the humanities was lopsided in relation to human experience. The discursive figure of the historicized body relied on an understanding of the expansiveness of language and text that hid some blind spots in the study of the body in history. The most prominent of these blind spots was that of a sense of life lived, of experiences in the body.

Beyond the informational model?

Proteomics and the new genetic reality

Proteins have a long and varied history in the life sciences (Kay 1993, Rheinberger 1997, Tanford and Reynolds 2001). Through the 1930s and 1940, up to the discovery of the structure of DNA, they were thought to be the material basis of heredity, and the investigation of their structures and activities dominated the new field of molecular biology (Law 1973). But the focus in the field was quickly changing, as Gunther Stent forecast in his much quoted lecture 'That Was the Molecular Biology That Was' from 1967, in which he foresaw the downfall of the structural school of molecular biology. Stent defended the idea that the physical function of the cell could be understood 'only in terms of the three-dimensional configurations of its elements', but acceded that the revolution in molecular biology was likely to come from a 'one-dimensional' or 'information school' (Stent 1968: 391). That school, described on the previous pages, led the way for the sequencing craze of the genomics revolution.

But there are signs that this structural school is returning to the forefront of molecular biology. The gene has, as Evelyn Fox Keller wrote some years ago, 'had a glorious run in the twentieth century' (Keller 2000: 147). But at the same time there is a sense in which the life sciences is at a juncture that requires new concepts, terms and metaphors to grasp life and the body in productive ways; there is a need to loosen 'the grip that genes have had on the imagination of life scientists these many decades' (Keller 2000: 147). These new concepts, terms and metaphors seem to be stemming from the study of proteins, the so-called proteomics. Proteomics is the large-scale study of proteins, particularly their structures and functions. On a biological level, proteins are a central part of living organisms, and are the main components of the physiological pathways of cells. The term 'proteomics' itself was coined to make an analogy with genomics, and there is talk of a Human Proteome Project, paralleling the Genome Project (see Pearson 2008).

The Proteomic project holds different metaphors and a different spirit than the Human Genome Project did. The reason is in part to be found in the biological reality – that the proteome is a much vaster and more complicated system to decipher. One of the central problems with carrying over the informational metaphors into the study of proteins is that protein structures defy reduction to metaphors of code or scriptures. The functioning of proteins is dependent on their shape, size, location and temporality – 'a protein may have more twists and bends than a bagful of pretzels' as one laboratory news release states, noting that 'while most objects – shirts, sheets, newspapers, camping equipment – are inoperative until unfolded, scientists agree that only when a protein folds is it able to act' (Sandia National Laboratory 1995). This dependency on folding means that information metaphors come up short. As Natasha Myers writes, this is 'in part because the three-dimensional conformation of a protein, and the paths through which a peptide folds into its active form within the cell, have yet to be successfully predicted entirely from the DNA sequence: no one has discovered a "code" that can predict protein form' (Myers 2008: 168). This is because while an organism's genome is rather constant, a proteome differs from cell to cell and constantly changes through its biochemical interactions with the genome and the environment. The expression of proteins can be completely and radically different in different parts of the same organism and it similarly might be radically different in different stages of its life cycle and under different environmental conditions. As an editorial in *Nature* stated:

> There was a certain intellectual allure about 'cracking' the human genome that, on the face of it, is lacking from cataloguing all the proteins. And although the human genome is finite, the proteome is almost boundless, because each of the body's proteins may be present in different forms and different amounts in each tissue – and even in precisely the same cell from one moment to the next. (Tyers and Mann 2003, 193)

The study of proteins is a field in explosive growth (the Protein Data Bank (www.pdb.org) contained as of the 24th June 2008, 47,526 proteins, with 5,000 new structures being released each year), and the study of proteins has made new ways of conceptualizing life and the body required. Working with proteins requires a different approach to the world, a form of thinking not based around information, because of the very nature of proteins – they are physical forms and need to be envisioned as such in order to understand their functioning. Working with proteins does not lend itself to the kind of informational thinking, and thus informational thinking no longer seems to provide answers to the questions that have arisen. Thus, rather than seeing life and the body as being determined by a code, proteomics is searching for the building blocks of life – which is a metaphor with different implications than that of a text. Building blocks denote structural form, three-dimensionality, relationality and morphology, whereas text leans towards information, meaning, code and intangibility.

Scientists involved in protein research use complex visualization techniques to render the folds, forms and movements of biological molecules in elaborate detail. Understanding the world of proteins means making sense of them as physical and spatially located structures, and the visualization they employ allows them to make interactive digital models to be used in analysis. Just how spatial proteins are was illustrated recently when scientists at the University of Washington released a computer game called Foldit, in which gamers can learn to fold proteins.[6] The game targets the mentioned problem for protein research, namely the vast number of possible protein combinations. Even with all the collected computer power on the planet at the moment, it would take several centuries to work through all the protein combinations and shapes of the 100.000 proteins in the body, so the idea behind the game is that the players can develop an intuition for how proteins connect and use it to target specific medical problems. Involving the general public in a project like this instead of leaving it to trained researchers is because a lot of what goes into protein folding has little to do with scientific knowledge, but is rather based on an intuition for shapes. As Natasha Myers writes in her study of the body-work done by those who work in protein crystallography:

> It is through the dimensionality of her body that she is able to appreciate the full three-dimensionality and movements of the protein model, so that she feels the spatiality and temporality of the molecule by virtue of the spatiality and temporality of her own body. (Myers 2008: 187)

Foldit illustrates both how scientific practices are changing, and specifically how protein research, and particularly protein modelling, requires a unique set of skills that have to do with intuition, spatial awareness and a sense of physical shapes. This emphasis, which is quite different from the informational, linguistic metaphors involved in genetic practices, means that protein research is developing a new set of practices and a new set of metaphors. The metaphors involved in protein research is turning from matters of code to matters of substance – that is, from interpreting linear gene sequences to inquiring after the spatial materiality of the protein, which make up the building blocks of life. These metaphors are still being fleshed out; the only major historical overview so far suggests that of

---

6   See http://www.sciencedaily.com/releases/2008/05/080508122520.htm. For more information on the game and the full version, see http://fold.it.

molecular machines or even 'nature's robots' (Tanford and Reynolds 2001), while others have likened the proteome to the cast of a play (Pappas 2006). Time will tell what metaphors end up being dominant in the rhetoric and practices of the new proteomic sciences, but it seems as if the informational metaphors of genomic science are loosening their grip on the categories of life and the body.

The body beyond language

The historicized notion of the body is predicated on a specific understanding of the role of language, and specifically the role of language in determining our engagement with the world around us. It is founded on a primacy of mind and consciousness. With the emphasis on language the new cultural history of the body has become a history of various meanings attached to the body, to the extent that any experience of this 'stuff' often becomes epiphenomenal and derivative of the cultural meanings surrounding it. For historical reasons (very valid ones at that) the predominant form of historical scholarship that engages with the body has been largely devoted to the meaning of the historical text, in part due to its reliance on Geertz' notion of cultural reality as text that can be read for symbolic meaning. As it has been argued, the core of cultural history is 'its attention to the making of meaning' (Fissel 2004: 365). Meaning, in this context, is specifically meaning as a linguistic phenomenon, meaning made coherent and accessible in language.

But the history of the body raises, in a particularly acute way, the problem of how to encompass those elements of embodiment that does not rest easily within a historical discourse primarily dedicated to representations. The metaphor of the historicized body had problems in capturing a sense of lived experience and relies on a blurring of the ontological separation between text and reality. As philosopher Michael Bentley has written, this emphasis on matters of language, epistemology and meaning has the consequence that matters of ontology were abandoned which in turn led to an evacuation of historical reality (Bentley 2006). He notes that in the twenty-five years after 1970 the intense preoccupation with the epistemological basis of historical work led theoreticians to lose sight of the object of study, namely historical reality. The past-in-itself, as he writes, 'became an absence, a nothingness, a page on which to write, a place for dreams and images. A constructed factuality announced itself as the past's sole presence, representation it's only strangulated voice, colligation its distant tyrant' (Bentley 2006: 349–350).

The study of the body in history, and even the humanities more generally, has since the late 1990s been in a process of reformulating how to study culture. There is a feeling of being at a juncture in which many analysts share a general unease 'with a definition of culture as entirely systematic, symbolic, or linguistic' (Bonnell and Hunt 1999: 26). Amongst other things his unease has manifested itself in an increasing interest in materiality born out of for example dissatisfaction with deconstruction, constructivism, and narrativism, which has led to a call for a return to things and to 'reality', however difficult it is to agree upon what these things and this reality might be (see Domanska 2006, Daston 2004). The notion that constructivism has taken us too far away from the reality of things in the world participates in a greater cultural movement, the outlines of which are as yet blurry at best.

It seems as if the countless retellings of the historicized body no longer provide helpful or existentially meaningful answers to questions that we face today. In fact, as Frank Ankersmit has argued, the lingualism of the postmodern historiography 'has become by now an obstacle to, rather than a promoter of, useful and fruitful insights. The mantras of this now so oppressive and suffocating lingualism have become a serious threat to the intellectual health of our discipline' (Ankersmit 2006: 335). There is a new set of metaphors being generated within the humanities to describe the body. Emphasis is placed on the senses, on presence, on spatial relations and on the irreducibility of experience (see Massumi 2002, Sedgwick 2003, Gumbrecht 2004, Runia 2006, Thrift 2007).

Conclusion

Evelyn Fox Keller noted in a study of the informational metaphor in the life sciences during the twentieth century that 'the notion of genetical information that Watson and Crick invoked was not literal but metaphorical. But it was extremely powerful' (Keller 2000: 19). One might even suggest that its power lay exactly in being non-literal – this allowed it to be transposed to other fields of study and be used as a generator of thoughts and ideas, just as the term itself had been imported from mathematics to genetics. Metaphors have loose moorings and drift easily from their original contexts, and perhaps part of their grip on us stems from this capacity to drift and change shape. The amorphous nature of metaphors is their strength, and what allows new ideas to spring forth and energy and capital to be generated under their sway. But they are also tied to their circumstances, and susceptible to the forces of culture, society and biology. Metaphors are apt to implode when they become stretched too far. As Lily E. Kay asks, the question is

> which differences are to be subsumed under one verbal umbrella? How much
> imprecision is constructive? When does it become useful to exchange one lexicon,
> one order of signs, for another? And finally, how is scientific understanding (or
> meaning) itself transformed by such lexical shifts? (Kay 2000: 141)

At certain points it seems as if a specific lexicon is no longer capable of asking the questions that need asking (and answering). Within the life sciences, the informational model proved to be unable to account for the variety that occurs in translation/instantiation – the forces of circumstance and spatiality transformed the code to such a degree that the letters stopped making sense. Instead, the gaze of the life sciences has fallen on the protein, which carries with it a different set of ideas, tools, viewpoints and metaphors. New problems require languages with which to ask new questions. Similarly, one might argue that the linguistic paradigm, and more specifically the new cultural history of the body, has been made to carry more than any one explanatory model can carry. Language, as important as it is, simply does not structure the entirety of our engagements and responses to the world around us. We understand, react to, interpret and deal with the world in many ways that transgress the boundaries of representationality.

It might be a bit premature to suggest a gestalt switch of the magnitude that the linguistic/informational model had, but it seems as if the informational model no longer provides adequate answers to the questions we are posing, be it in molecular biology or the history of the body. Bruno Latour noted on the linguistic paradigm that no one anymore needs to be told that the world is complex and that language is opaque – political, cultural and technological developments in the past decade has made that an abundantly clear commonplace, both inside and outside academia (Latour 2004). Thus the inherent meaningfulness and necessity in the linguistic paradigm is no longer as clearly in place – in some ways, the need to refine our conceptual tools for engaging with representations (be they positive of negative tools) is no longer nearly as poignant as the need for developing conceptual tools that allow us to engage with the non-representational. Similarly, the notion of language as the 'program' that loads the material stuff with data and information for action is slowly being transformed into a system in which the body provides its own set of influences, functioning both as instructions and as data, as command and executor. The interactions between body and material world is not primarily seen as going one way (from language to world), but is a much more complex system in which the mind is equally determined by bodily processes (Slingerland 2008, Gottschall 2008, Johnson 2008).

What do these two parallel contestations tell us? Primarily that what we think is in the grip of metaphors – it is shaped by models, suggestive themes, seemingly fresh ways of seeing the world. But these metaphors do not exist in a realm of their own, rather they are bound to the moment, to place and space and are shaped by them as much as they shape them. We must attend to the words and categories that shape our practices – gene, protein, information, proteome, discourse, historicized, body, materiality, affect, whatever they may be – and ask why exactly we choose those words and what in their formulation draws us in.

References

Adams, D. 1991. Metaphors for mankind: the development of Hans Blumenberg's anthropological metaphorology. *Journal of the History of Ideas*, 52, 152–166.

Ankersmit, F. and Kellner, H. 1995. *A New Philosophy of History*. Chicago: University of Chicago Press.

Ankersmit, F. 2006. 'Presence' and myth. *History and Theory*, 45, 328–336.

Bencard, A. 2008. *History in the Flesh* Unpublished PhD-thesis, Department of Health Sciences, University of Copenhagen.

Bentley, M. 2006. Past and 'presence': revisiting historical ontology. *History and Theory*, 45, 349–361.

Berkhofer, R. 1995. *Beyond the Great Story*. Cambridge: Harvard University Press.

Blumenberg, H. 1997. *Shipwreck with Spectator: Paradigm of a Metaphor for Existence*. Cambridge: MIT Press.

Bonnell, V. and Hunt, L. 1999. *Beyond the Cultural Turn*. Berkeley: University of California Press.

Brandt, C. 2005. Genetic code, text, and scripture: metaphors and narration in German molecular biology. *Science in Context*, 18, 629–648.

Burke, P. 1995. *New Perspectives on Historical Writing*. Cambridge: Polity Press.

Bynum, C. 1995. Why all the fuss about the body: a medievalist's perspective. *Critical Enquiry*, 22, 1–33.

Cooter, R. and Pickstone, J. 2000. *Medicine in the Twentieth Century*. Amsterdam: Harwood Academic Publishers.

Cooter, R. 2004. Framing the end of the social history of medicine, in *Locating Medical History: The Stories and Their Meanings*, edited by F. Huisman and J.H. Warner. Baltimore: Johns Hopkins University Press.

Daston, L. 2004. *Things That Talk: Object Lessons From Art and Science*. New York: Zone Books.

DeLanda, M. 2002. *Intensive Science and Virtual Philosophy*. London: Continuum Books.

Domanska, E. 2006. The material presence of the past. *History and Theory*, 45, 337–348.

Doyle, R. 1997. *On Beyond Living: Rhetorical Transformations of the Life Sciences* (Stanford: Stanford University Press).

Feher M., Naddaff, R., Tazi, N. 1989. *Fragments for a History of the Human Body Vol. 1*. New York: Zone Books. 11.

Fissell, M.E. 2004. Making meaning from the margins: the new cultural history of medicine, in *Locating Medical History – The Stories and Their Meanings*, edited by F. Huisman and J.H. Warner. Baltimore: The John Hopkins University Press.

Foucault, M. 1994. *The Birth of the Clinic: An Archaeology of Medical Perception*. New York: Pantheon.

Frank, A.W. 1990. Bringing bodies back in: a decade review. *Theory, Culture, Society*, 7, 131–162.

Franke, W. 2000. Metaphor and the Making of Sense: The Contemporary Metaphor Renaissance. *Philosophy and Rhetoric*, 33, 137–153.

Friedländer, S. 1992. *Probing the Limits of Representation: Nazism and the "Final Solution"*. Harvard: Harvard University Press.

Gottschall, J. 2008. *Literature, Science, and a New Humanities*. London: Palgrave.

Gumbrecht, H.U. 2004. *Production of Presence: What Meaning Cannot Convey.* Stanford: Stanford University Press.

Gumbrecht, H.U. 2008. Shall we continue to write histories of literature. *New Literary History*, 39, 519–532.

Haraway, D. 1997. *Modest_Witness@Second_Millennium.FemaleMan!_Meets_ OncoMouse": Feminism and Technoscience.* New York: Routledge.

Huisman, F. and Warner, J.H. 2004, *Locating Medical History: The Stories and Their Meanings.* Baltimore: Johns Hopkins University Press.

Ingold, T. 2007. Materials against materiality. *Archaeological Dialogues*, 14, 1–16.

Jenkins, K. (ed.). 1997. *The Postmodern History Reader.* London: Routledge.

Jenner, M. and Taithe, B. 2000. The historiographical body, in *Medicine in the Twentieth Century*, edited by R. Cooter and J. Pickstone.

Johnson, M. 2008. *The Meaning of the Body: Aesthetics of Human Understanding.* Chicago: University of Chicago Press.

Kay, L.E. 1993. *The Molecular Vision of Life: Caltech, The Rockefeller Foundation, and the Rise of the New Biology.* New York: Oxford University Press.

Kay, L.E. 2000. *Who Wrote the Book of Life? A History of the Genetic Code.* Stanford: Stanford University Press.

Keller, E.F. 1995. *Refiguring Life: Metaphors of Twentieth Century Biology.* Columbia: Columbia University Press.

Keller, E.F. 2000, *The Century of the Gene.* Harvard: Harvard University Press.

Latour, B. 2004. Why Has Critique Run out of Steam? From Matters of Fact to Matters of Concern. *Critical Inquiry*, 30, 225–248.

Law, J. 1973. The Development of Specialties in Science: The Case of X-ray Protein Crystallography. *Science Studies*, 3, 275–303.

Lock, M., Young, A. and Cambrosio, A. 2000. *Living and Working with the New Medical Technologies.* Cambridge: Cambridge University Press.

Massumi, B. 2002. *Parables for the Virtual: Movement, Affect, Sensation.* Durham: Duke University Press.

Massumi, B. 2004, The Radical in Academia. Interview with Brian Massumi. *Columbia Journal of Literary Criticism*, 2, 59–69.

Myers, N. 2008. Molecular Embodiments and the Body-work of Modelling in Protein Crystallography. *Social Studies of Science*, 38, 163–199.

Nerlich, B. et. al. 2002. The book of life – how the completion of the Human Genome Project was revealed to the public. *Health*, 6, 445–469.

Olsen, B. 2003. Material Culture After Text: Re-membering Things. *Norwegian Archeological Review*, 36, 87–104.

Outram, D. 1993. Body and paradox. *Isis*, 84, 347–352.

Pappas, G. 2006. A new literary metaphor for the genome or proteome. *Biochemistry and Molecular Biology Education*, 33, 15.

Partner, N. 1995. Historicity in the age of reality-fictions, in, *A New Philosophy of History*, edited by F. Ankersmit and H. Kellner, 21–39.

Pearson, H. 2008. Biologists initiate plan to map human proteome. *Nature*, 452: 920–21.

Porter, R. 1999. History of the body reconsidered, in *New Perspectives on Historical Writing*, edited by P. Burke, University Park: Pennsylvania State University Press.

Pred, R. 2005. *Onflow – Dynamics of Consciousness Explained*. Cambridge: MIT Press.

Rheinberger, H-J. 2000. Beyond nature and culture: modes of reasoning in the age of molecular biology and medicine, in *Living and working with the new medical technologies*, edited by M. Lock et al. New York: Cambridge University Press, 19–30

Roper, L. 1994. *Oedipus and the Devil: Witchcraft, Sexuality and Religion in Early Modern Europe*. London, Routledge.

Rose, N. 2007. *The Politics of Life Itself*. Princeton: Princeton University Press.

Runia, E. 2006. Presence, *History and Theory* 45, 1–29.

Sandia National Laboratories. 1995. Super-Fast Computer Program Helps to Predict Protein Structure. *News Release*.

Schiebinger, L. 2004. *Nature's Body: Gender in the Making of Modern Science*. New Brunswick: Rutgers University Press.

Sedgwick, E.K. 2003. *Touching Feeling: Affect, Pedagogy, Performativity*. Durham: Duke University Press.

Slingerland, E. 2008, *What Science Offers the Humanities – Integrating Body and Culture*. Cambridge: Cambridge University Press.

Stewart, K. 2007. *Ordinary Affects*. Durham: Duke University Press.

Tanford, C. and Reynolds, J. 2001, *Nature's Robots: A History of Proteins*. Oxford: Oxford University Press.

Thrift, Nigel. 2007. *Non-representational Theory: Space, Theory, Affect*. London: Routledge.

Tyers, M. and Mann, M. 2003. From genomics to proteomics. *Nature*, 422, 193–197.

White, H. 1992. Historical emplotment and the problem of truth, in Friedländer, S. (ed.), *Probing the Limits of Representation: Nazism and the 'Final Solution'*.

Wilson, N. 1999. *History in Crisis? Recent Directions in Historiography*. Upper Saddle River: Prentice Hall.

Wolynes, P.G. 2001. Landscapes, funnels, glasses, and folding: from metaphor to software, *Proceedings of the American Philosophical Society*, 145(4), 555–563.

Chapter 8

The Place and Space of Research Work: Studying Control in a Bioscience Laboratory

Amrita Mishra

Introduction

Robert Kohler's description of laboratory 'weediness' links the mobility of credible knowledge to the interchangeability of the places of scientific work (Kohler 2002: 191–92).[1] Similarly, Marc Augé speaks of the 'non-spaces' of modernity (Augé 1995). He believes that certain areas such as airports, underground train tubes, apartment complexes, and supermarkets are remarkable for their break from cultural interdictions on membership and access to their spaces. Mary Poovey describes 'isotropic' spaces that permit the standardized repetition of actions. These spaces are dominated by maps, plans, diagrams that enable the mastery and reproduction of these spaces and the actions performed within them (Poovey 1995: 29).

The ideas of placelessness, non-space or place isotropy are certainly useful in describing the spread of rationalized loci of modernity. Nevertheless, they present problems. The use of these terms may promote an assumption that material locations can be *purely physical places* because they spread so easily and seem so readily interchangeable. To accept that laboratories are placeless is to avoid asking why the detailing of apparatus, chemicals, and procedures in research reports do not mention physical location. The seeming interchangeability of laboratories is co-productive with the demand that experimental results be mobile and testable across interested laboratories. The assumption is that uncontaminated, controlled

---

1 'Placelessness also enables laboratory practices to disperse rapidly and widely, as weedy species are designed to disperse and occupy disturbed environments quickly. This spatial mobility makes modern laboratory science an exceptionally weedy culture. Its practitioners credit beliefs and practices that travel fast and assimilate anywhere, becoming what everyone does and thinks. Practices and beliefs that stay local must have something wrong with them, we think. It is just what weeds would think. How we have come so universally to judge the value of knowledge by its power to disperse is a problem that historians have yet to solve, but one reason certainly is that modern commercial society is an exceptionally weedy culture. One thinks of airports and autobahns, markets and malls, TV and cyberspace—the placeless places of a weedy, market capitalism. Labs and lab science are very much part of culture and are no doubt partly responsible for its present global dominance.'

test environments can be readily constituted anywhere on the planet. The point obscured by conventions of science reportage is that the attempts at reproduction are made in specific laboratories that are part of a shared field of knowledge-production. The naïve use of a term like 'placelessness' diverts attention from the fact that any location is, first of all, *local,* with a stubborn specificity deriving from a relation to specific cultural spaces. Physical appurtenances and coordinates are culturally weighted in their social use and existence. Thus ostensibly physical arrangements must be examined with a keen eye on their sociality.

I will see the laboratory as a physical place that is co-productive with an epistemic space. By epistemic space I mean the field of interests and disciplinary agendas that is linked to, includes, and depends on concrete scientific loci, on laboratories. They have a reliance on physical bounding and material enactment, a specific locale with specific bounding.[2] At the same time, this relationship is attached to cultural interpretations that define scientific placelessness, that create effective denials of specific material moorings, of local interests and interested actions. Such denial deflects the contestability that STS literature has shown to be part of scientific work. If the laboratory exists in any coherent sense over a period of time, as a material locus of intellectual production, it is because of the making and mainenance of boundaries around it. These boundaries make and keep a specific location, marked by contested and embattled interests, by powerplay and parochiality. Therefore, I will not consider the laboratory either as a purely physical place or as a place without any physical mooring.

All laboratories are bounded, but each laboratory is bounded in its own way and also in a way similar to other laboratories with which it shares a certain epistemic space. The laboratory is a locale with distinctness and specificity, physically specific and placed, located in and invoking certain epistemic spaces. Its appearance of credible placelessness is possible only through its close affinity with

---

2   The colloquial term 'neighbourhood' captures the 'place' character of the laboratory. I agree with Arjun Appadurai that this term connotes the qualities of 'sociality, immediacy and reproducibility' that mark the lived experience of 'locales' (Appadurai 1997: 204). Each laboratory may be thought of as a 'locale.' The use of the term neighbourhood accommodates the related connotations of localities and locality. The localities are particular and singular instances of locality, that is, a widely found dimension of bounded sociality. Each laboratory is local, with its enactment and sense of boundedness, but it is recognizable as a laboratory because it bears resemblance to other laboratories. Each is a neighbourhood that enacts locality, in ways that are individually unique but also comparable across neighbourhoods. Each laboratory is located within a disciplinary matrix that has its own aspects of locality. Within each of these localities, considered at each level, there are social techniques, rites of passage whose practitioners reproduce themselves through these practices that bind them. In the process they also reproduce those practices. Seminars, meetings, publication rituals, thesis examinations, the training of novices, the vigilance over sanitation and the movements of individuals are all instances of these practices. So also are the regulations of place, the strictures imposed on physical movements. These strictures and what they direct should be understood as profoundly social, *spatial*, and not just as the abstract constellation of geometrical loci.

other 'participant locales' also located in and invoking a particular epistemic space. The idea of placelessness thus depends on the interrelationships made possible by a shared invocation of distinct and bounded epistemic spaces, cultural spaces. What is called 'placelessness' or 'isotropy' is a function of the interchangeability of like places, of likenesses that are recognizable as such only by their common reference to certain epistemic and cultural spaces.

The seeming isotropy of laboratories, the possibility of replicating actions, products, behaviours, and activities across them, should not persuade us to forget that laboratories are part of distinct epistemic spaces. These sites are culturally and epistemically *spatialized* and distinct. They are thereby *localized* as distinct places. Culture, people and laboratories evade isotropy. There are no people or cultures in the overly neat ideas of isotropy and placelessness. The idea of place, in its materially grounded, localized and enacted sense, should be understood as a particular enacted phrasing of a generalized and overarching sociocultural space.[3]

The making of scientific things and places by their participants is a constant, hectic activity. It is work that can never stop. It is part of the work that we call research. Research could not occur without the constant making and stabilization of the places where research is made. Object identities – in scientific work and elsewhere – exist only through 'ontological politics'[4] that make them the contested and constantly manipulated foci of imagination and work (Mol 1999: 74–89). It is part of such politics – intrinsic to science – that objects are invested with a peculiar binarity. Scientists use object definitions both as the weapons and prizes of their jousts over 'reality.' The notion of reproducibility of research across interchangeable 'placeless' places ignores troublesome questions: what is the definition of what is to be reproduced and how? What is the specific warrant of reproducibility? What is the epistemic space that guarantees and certifies something as a valid reproduction? Is the laboratory a physical location, or also a set of resources, an enactment of a certain 'logic' or practice of credibility? Is it a site with varying degrees and types of material embodiment and enactment of forms of truthmaking? The relationship between knowledge production and the localized materiality of this production cannot be ignored. It is my aim to raise this relationship to visible relief in my depiction of a bioscience laboratory in India.

The field study that provides ethnographic data for this chapter was conducted over 6 months (January through June 2004) in a bioscience laboratory. It is part of

---

3   Douglas and Isherwood observe of physical space: 'Harnessed to the cultural process, its divisions are heavy with meaning: housing, size, the side of the street, distance from other centres, special limits, all shore up conceptual categories.' (Douglas and Isherwood 1996: 44)

4   Mol says that what we construe as reality does not precede the practices through which we think and perform it. It is shaped within these practices, which are never divorced from the political. When one takes the step of thinking of reality and the agentially cut boundaries that make the real in terms of work, one abandons notions of reality as characterized by presymbolic and apolitical serenity and stability. Reality and ideas of reality are made and marked by power, locality, and interest.

a research centre (hereafter called the Institute) located in the Southwest of India. The Institute is a highly regarded centre of research in investigative areas with a biological accent. The laboratory is conducting research in intersecting areas of oncology and virology. It is under the supervision of a professor (Sridhar hereafter) who is a published authority in cell biology. Although young, he has acquired a reputation as an expert in the molecular analysis of cervical tumour formation. The population of the laboratory included PhD candidates, postdoctoral fellows (Postdocs hereafter), and research fellows who doubled as technical assistants. In addition, there were MSc students and undergraduate summer interns from other institutes, completing research projects or acquiring some laboratory exposure. The stated mission of the laboratory of fieldwork is the study of 'the molecular pathogenesis of cervical tumours.' Therefore, I shall refer to the laboratory as CCL, or Cervical Cancer Laboratory. I will refer to the laboratory director, Sridhar (alias) as the Principal Investigator, or PI. This is also the formal designation for other laboratory directors at the Institute that houses CCL. Prior to the main fieldwork I undertook pilot studies at two Delhi laboratories. One of these is engaged in research in molecular cardiology and the other in molecular medicine. The duration of each pilot was about two months, and the studies were conducted between July 2003 and November 2003. The observations from the pilots will serve as 'controls'. I shall be using them to occasionally complement and clarify the data from the main fieldwork. The pilot studies showed that different laboratories may exhibit local differences. Thus one sees differing supervisory styles of the PIs, differing modes of restriction of laboratory space and working hours, and differing forms of social activity. However, the similarities are far more striking than the differences.

Restriction and the laboratory

Researchers have an interest in maintaining the *restricted* stability of the boundaries and contents of a scientific place.[5] These contents are the interests, activities, and

---

5　The idea of restriction is adapted from the work of Pantin (1968). He draws a distinction between the 'hard' restricted natural sciences such as physics and the softer 'unrestricted' sciences such as biology. In today's research scenarios, this distinction has more or less broken down. In choosing a bioscience laboratory as the source of insights about the making of credible knowledge, I do not aim to impose a field-specific view on all of science. There may be a blurring of margins between research specialities, between orientations to subject matter, between principal fields such as physics or chemistry or biology. Therefore, my study may identify features in one area that may be identified, in varying degrees of conspicuity, elsewhere. I would also qualify the term 'biological' because in many areas of research such as biophysics or neurochemistry or *Drosophila* genetics, the work can only very roughly be dubbed 'biological'. In their work, they use proteins or extracts of an animal origin or breed fruitflies. However, I would say that the bench-preparation of these materials, the advanced research tools and conceptual schemes

apparatus of research. These interests are co-productive with the socio-cultural spaces of science, what I call epistemic spaces. The epistemic spaces are connected to material places. In these places actors re-animate these material-non-material connections and the very possibility of these connections constantly through mundane enactments. The firm enforcement of operational norms minimizes risk, uncertainty, and excessive conceptual fluidity. These restrictions are intimately connected to the making of a specialty area, that is, possessing definition and integrity of procedure and interests. Disciplinary conformity means the ascendancy of a certain scheme of thought (for instance, signalling, information transfers, and gene action) and of specific modes of action in a research area, which is also found in each specialty in that research area. The work of each laboratory is primarily intended for a system of restricted scientific production. These conceptual goods are primarily, but not exclusively, intended for use by other producers of that same class of goods; they are all working on closely related research themes and specialties. The conceptual goods produced by a laboratory gain the greatest value when they reach these related audiences. The research output, once in a paper, must be cited, used and carried forward by other practitioners, or at least till obsolescence threatens. Thus, the work of CCL was influenced by earlier work on the implication of Notch and the determination of cell fate signalling. The continued use of Notch-related data attests to its continued usefulness and also adds to that usefulness.

Restriction has various aspects. These concern the cognitive and physical demands of work performance in the laboratory. There are spatial and temporal constraints on the pursuit of work at these sites. The experimental method is in reciprocity with the structured regularity of its research objects. This affinity is based on stringent restriction of the choices, methodic protocols, instruments, actions and products of research – the overall control of the laboratory space and contents, and what comes in and goes out of it.

Some specific aspects of restriction in the Notch laboratory are outlined here. *First*, research interests are circumscribed, around the mechanism and effects of the disregulation of one protein's activity or around the activity of proteins closely related in the pathogenic pathways of that particular disease. Thus, although the perspective of the cell as integrated circuitry implies a huge amount of 'cross-talk' between pathways, there is a sort of 'structured forgetting' of the 'cross-talk.' This is implicit in the chosen focus on a particular pathway or on the relationships between 'closer' pathways.

---

subsequently brought to bear on them, and in sum, the positioning and perspective of the work in these areas situates them sufficiently close to or right within the camps of physics and chemistry. The contemporary 'biological sciences' are extremely physico-chemical. On the surface, CCL looks no different from the biophysics or the membrane-ion-channel laboratory at the Institute. I saw machinery and procedures to subject 'living substances' to physico-chemical transformations and analyses. However, Pantin's basic idea is still useful to understand how stringent regulation makes a place of research viable as a site for producing credible and accredited knowledge.

Venturing into new areas, with different material requirements and not always predictable success, means a high-risk, unknown-dividend gamble on existing resources. One may only speak of variable chances of success, dependent on the variable chances of procuring symbolic and financial profits from research. This unpredictability motivates the PI to protect and reinforce the boundaries that mark 'his' area of expertise, 'his' intellectual property, and to ensure that research in 'his' laboratory engages in a limited quest for novelty. Thus research at CCL has been on thematic variations within the area of Notch signaling, ensuring its 'Notch-centric' reputation at the Institute and even in the Delhi laboratories. CCL and other laboratories with related research specializations are clustered around certain ordering principles that are largely agreed upon. In this situation, disputes and divergences are rarely such as to threaten central concepts and disciplinary frames. Disagreements are 'not so much between rival definitions of the disciplines and concepts of science, as between interpretations of the main view and its application to research problems and approaches' (Whitley 1976: 480). Thus, Sumitra, a PhD student at the Delhi molecular cardiology laboratory informed me 'Sridhar is known as a Notch diva.' At CCL, Smita, a Postdoc said, 'Is Boss [an epithet for Sridhar, also used for PIs at the Delhi laboratories] trying to move away from Notch? Tina [a new postdoc] has been working on *smad* [another protein implicated in cancer].' Arpita, a research trainee at CCL, said, 'It's not likely he would try to move away from Notch, would he? This is a Notchocentric lab after all.'

Second, the techniques used to study this closely related set of research themes are restricted in number, conducted according to the local interpretations, 'standardizations', of highly specific protocols – modes of using reagents in experiments – in molecular biology. These techniques must be mastered to the extent that they are performed as routine, without constant reference to instruction material.[6] These local interpretations are in no way a proof that 'anything goes' in the matter of actually doing benchwork in the laboratory. Every interpretation of protocol is noted in data-and-method registers. These registers are very literally

---

6 I was limited by my lack of technical expertise in the use of laboratory equipment and technical procedures, such as the preparation of reagents, or of techniques to capture protein bands and to develop these photographically. Further, there was no question of a non-scientist, a non-member being taught the techniques, and making mistakes, possibly wasting expensive reagents or mishandling the machinery such as the gel shakers or ultracentrifuges. With severe time and financial constraints involved in the generation of experimental data, the PI and the other associates saw such training investments as cumbrous and infructuous in my case. Consequently, my participation was permitted in non-technical activities. These included helping to check lists of products (such as DNA primers, i.e., abbreviated chains of DNA, ATTGCC, CAATTG, etc., needed for the Polymerase Chain Reaction process to generate genetic material in bulk for experimental use) to be ordered from firms supplying these to the laboratory. On some occasions, I edited spelling and grammar on texts intended for seminar presentation. I also fetched and carried equipment, trays of tubes etc., when assistance was needed.

account books because what is written in them eventually makes its way to a rigorously scrutinized account of methodology given in seminars, conferences and journals, the scrutiny increasing as the work makes its way to the domain of black-and-white inscription.

Third, the novice must master standard terms of usage in order to participate adequately in research processes. There is a tacit understanding of terms such as HeLa, CaSki, W12 Rafts, HaCaT (cell lines, of varied provenance and use, employed in experimental work), RT-PCR (Reverse Transcriptase Polymerase Chain Reaction), microarray analysis, and so on. A fluent command of English is essential for mastering the technical terminology of the larger field and the laboratory patois. This is true for both the laboratory worker and the ethnographer who wishes to least partially participate in the life of the site. [7]

Fourth, the research-labour force of the Institute is differentiated and stratified. The permanent supervisory group, the PIs, is far outnumbered by the impermanent labour force. This includes the Postdocs, the PhD candidates, Research Trainees of other institutes, Junior Research Fellows, Summer Interns, and Short-term Visitors. The first two categories, PhDs and Postdocs, are relatively more stable presences in the laboratory population, as they are at the Institute, in a laboratory, for a period of 2–3 years in the case of Postdocs and 5–6 years in the case of PhDs. The others stay for variable periods, ranging from 5 months (Short-term visitors, as I was) to about two years (JRFs). The ratio of PI to researchers was 1:7 in CCL, by discounting the more transient members such as the Research Trainees and Summer Interns, and the writer. The inclusion of all members places it as 1:13. This is a representative figure per laboratory across the Institute.

---

7   In an effort to make myself visibly of some use to the work in the laboratory, I compiled a cache of specialized research papers and review articles pertinent to the laboratory's field of research. A reading of these articles had served as a quick orientation for me, in the initial stages of observation, familiarizing me with the laboratory's area of research. This cache later became a useful quick reference for fresh entrants. The more senior laboratory members also used it on occasion. In the process of reading the articles and papers, I also gained an adequate grasp of the specialized terminology of the intellectual field of the laboratory. The primary benefit of this activity was that I was able to converse with the laboratory members with a greater fluency in their own 'language', using specialized terms with greater frequency and without appearing to require detailed explanations constantly. As a result, I became aware that it became easier over time to initiate conversations with them, as they were less wary of me, seeing me as less of an 'outsider.' My performance of fieldwork required me to gain a working familiarity with these concepts, with the lexicon, and the way of thinking about these research problems. Without a familiarity with the 'language of the tribe', I would not have been able to adequately converse with the laboratory members. The development of interpersonal rapport and trust depended on my familiarity with their language. The terms and usages of that language pepper their daily conversation, both in and outside the laboratory. The divide between the public and the private worlds of the laboratory scientists is tenuous. The language of the laboratory is in considerable measure the language of their everyday lifeworld.

The research-labour force was stratified on the basis of official rank, possession or non-possession of institutional academic certification, and relative involvement or non-involvement in research for data meant for publication. The PhDs and the Postdocs ranked high on all these counts and were broadly considered to be the core, or senior, research personnel. Thus, at CCL, the work of the PhDs and the Postdocs, unlike that of the JRFs, Research Trainees, and Summer Interns, was seen as crucial for the laboratory's reputation and continued existence, specifically intended for publication. In the words of Sridhar, 'this laboratory has been built on the work of the PhDs. It is a PhD driven lab, as are most of the other labs here. We insist on the PhDs, and to a lesser extent, the Postdocs, travelling...' When asked why, the response was 'It builds confidence, the exposure is good for them, and they really are the face of the lab.'

The paper discusses the significance of restrictive actions and technologies in the boundary work that is co-productive with the life of the laboratory. Restriction makes every laboratory a bounded, cohesive entity. This cohesion presents a contrast to the rhythms and patterns of what lies 'outside' the laboratory. Restriction has the overall effect of constituting differences between the laboratory and its wider setting. These differences are between the arrangements of the laboratory and those of everyday life, and between laboratory arrangements across time and space. I seek to understand how these technologies are enacted as part of the projects of spatio-temporal regulation towards the making of credible knowledge.

I will describe how in the laboratory, physical and electronic space (the 'proper' use of the internet and e-mail) and work and leisure time-rhythms are subject to restrictions. In the description, my explicit aim is to map and track my own movements into, through and out of CCL and the Institute. In this paper I present myself as a case or an example of what it means to acquire spatial orientations at a research site. It means constant work, incessant performances. Restrictions on place have the attendant practices of collegiate and self-surveillance. I had to constantly learn these restrictions and impose them on myself; I also learnt to evade and contend with these restrictions. This is par for the course, given the ambiguous and anomalous position of a sociological observer in a laboratory.

Accessing the laboratory

The first-time visitor must pass through several levels of access before entering any laboratory at the Institute. On my first day of fieldwork at the Institute, I had no formal certification, except for the letters of reference and the ID card from the Jawaharlal Nehru University. On entering the Institute grounds, the guards at the main gate asked me to submit proof of identity and to enter in a register details such as the person to see, purpose of visit, time in, time out etc. The gate security placed a call to the Institute Reception. On entering the Institute building, the security guard and the receptionist asked me to resubmit identifying information. The reception point is an obligatory point of access and passage, where all entries and exits are accounted for in meticulous registers. It is also an enclave, a point of suspension of transitions, laden with the ambivalence caused by the entry of strangers. Like the seminar rooms for presentations by visitors, and the work spaces set aside for visiting academics, it is a site for exchanges with travellers, containing their strangeness while also reinforcing their identification as strangers, by situating them in a zone where their incongruity is quickly identifiable. At the Institute, control on movements is designed into the entire locale. Furniture, courtyards, cafeterias, library, laboratories, equipment rooms and corridors are all designed in a way that discourages encroachment, anything resembling indolence or 'loitering.' The *Handbook of Guidelines for Graduate Students* at the Institute instructs, 'If you see suspicious persons lurking around, please report to security.'

At the Institute, the security placed a telephone call to the laboratory. The PI, Sridhar, came out to meet me and to escort me inside. I had to persuade the PI to permit me an observer's position in the laboratory. I had to explain that I would not write a sensationalistic 'scoop' on his laboratory. Further, I would not divulge or cite unpublished research material. Finally he allowed me to take position in the laboratory space, with the proviso that I could stay on after a month only if the other members did not object. On Sridhar's recommendation, I was assigned the formal designation of a short-term visitor. This was a catchall term to describe all individuals who visited the Institute but were not attached in any way to the research process as such. It describes no research responsibilities. However, the Short-term Visitor can receive this designation only on the word of a PI and is regarded as attached, however ambiguously, to that PI's laboratory. Short-term visitors generally come to the Institute to use the library facilities or for consultation with a PI or to make a presentation at a seminar. Ambiguous as this tag may seem, it reduced the ambiguity of my presence in the laboratory. Everyone in the laboratory space must be identifiable, and any official tag provides a classificatory answer for the puzzle of the stranger's presence.[8] After receiving formal identification as a Short Term Visitor, I was able to enter the Institute and the laboratory without successive clearance. I could straightaway enter the grounds and go to the laboratory. I could enter the library and freely access their material, although I was not allowed to borrow books. Further, I was not issued an electronic key that allowed the PIs, PhDs and Postdocs access to the library before 9.00 am and after 6.00 pm on weekdays and on Saturdays and Sundays.

The formal permission from the PI and the Institute to enter the laboratory did not gain me easy or untroubled access to the social space of the laboratory – to the quotidian social and working lives of CCL's researchers. The members were initially baffled by my activity and presence, which seemed to be entirely

---

8   Zygmunt Bauman argues that the 'gardening cultures' of modernity are inherently inimical to the stranger, who is both outside and inside, and also neither. In this Simmel-inspired understanding, *persistent* strangerhood presents an irresoluble anomaly and these strangers inherently defy classification. They are seen to fundamentally disturb the ordering of time, place, space, and history. (Bauman 1989, 1991 and 1995)

extraneous to the laboratory.[9] The presence of 'non-scientists' is frequently seen as somehow anomalous, a potential disruption in the daily work of the laboratory. Some of CCL's members, who had not been consulted when the PI made his decision, found my presence highly unwelcome and suspect, although no one vocally challenged his decision. On several occasions, I was asked 'What does sociology have to do with molecular biology?' The question was rhetorical, a challenge. They were suspicious that I might write a lurid exposé-style journalistic tale of the laboratory and the Institute. They feared that I would report negatively on their professional conduct to the PI. Moreover, they strongly disliked the prospect that *they* would be under observation. At that stage, it promised to be an unpleasantly novel experience for people conversant and comfortable with the experience of primarily being observers. As an ethnographer, I found myself in an 'alienness' somewhat similar to that in which the novice-laboratory researcher finds herself. The challenge of gaining entry to the highly restricted zone of the laboratory is followed by the challenge of spatio-temporal orientation within it. In the next section, I will describe the particularly non-private physical layout of the laboratory. This was another reason why I had to try and merge into the wallpaper. It also made such self-erasure spectacularly difficult.[10]

---

9   The control process of scientific professionalism involves 'generation and institutionalization of relatively autonomous subuniverses of meaning highly impenetrable to non-professionals by virtue of their being constituted through the active sharing of specialized stocks of knowledge.' (Jagtenberg 1983: 43)

10   I had to publicly underplay the observer role in which I had entered the laboratory. This was necessary to minimize the discomfort of some laboratory members who at first felt that they had been placed under surveillance and would accordingly behave awkwardly, circumspectly, tailoring their body language and speech according to what they thought would be most appropriate for me to see and note. At first, I sat in a corner of the laboratory, writing field notes, and consciously attempting not to be caught looking at people. I wrote down observations as they came to me constantly. I also committed to text all conversations, both overheard and in which I participated, as soon as possible after their conclusion. The need to win the trust and comfort of the laboratory members precluded the use of tape-recorders. In fact, when I was introduced to two members, they asked, only half-joking, 'Do you have a bug in that purse?' I was jocosely introduced as 'a spy' in a laboratory meeting. Later, I started reading protocol manuals, dictionaries and textbooks of cell biology, papers by people working in Notch signalling. I made sure that they saw me doing this; perhaps they would think that I was more interested in procedures and instruments rather than people, something they would perhaps understand. The next step was to stroll around when the laboratory was unoccupied, looking at equipment and asking questions about its working. It was only to the end of two months in the laboratory that the conversations started up with ease and frequency, and I could start them without being very worried about the setting, tone, opening lines, etc.

Negotiating laboratory space

Laboratory and institute architecture serves to make visible – necessary for the economy of credibility – and also to exclude or conceal. The sheer visibility of all elements across the institute makes it possible to identify someone as insider or outsider. The physical architecture (one-level floor plan and high-wattage fluorescent ceiling lights) of the laboratory ensures the high visibility of everything and everyone in it. The laboratory lights are kept on unless a photosensitive reagent is being prepared at a workbench. The last person to leave the laboratory switches the lights off.

Modes of spatial ordering and restriction are tacitly understood and carefully enacted. Researchers learn these modes interactionally in laboratory life. In CCL, and in other laboratories, the researchers maintain daily logs of activity, method and data registers that also serve as registers of performative discipline. The work and leisure spaces of the laboratory are tightly ordered. Perhaps because of the paucity

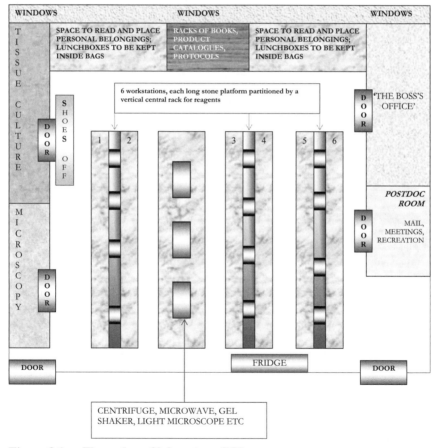

Figure 8.1   Floor plan of laboratory CCL

of written, official and formal prescriptions and proscriptions, there is a largely tacit and diffused awareness of the restrictions that order the laboratory space. People generally enacted their awareness of these requirements, which can be seen as unwritten rules of civility, maintained through a tacit agreement. Underlying this is the awareness of eventual accountability to the 'Boss', as the laboratory members dub the PI. The PI was particularly insistent on spatial proprieties, and takes pains to ensure that the subordinates enact and enforce certain local ideas of dirt and hygiene. The PI has a driving interest and command position in directing the production of uncontaminated results on time. His interests and commands profoundly marked the orderings of matter in the laboratory.

Restrictions on space included prohibitions on carrying experimental materials into the Postdoc room, wearing shoes in the tissue culture room, carrying food from the Postdoc room into the laboratory space or else excessive time spent netsurfing. (The Postdoc room was a small room adjoining the experimentation area and PI's office. It was officially meant for Postdoc use only, but it was accepted practice to use it for many other purposes. It contained three computers always logged onto the central server of the Institute. These computers were used to prepare documents, to check mail, and to download and read scientific papers.) I saw handwritten, stickers over workstations, saying, 'do not TOUCH these tubes…grrr…,' or 'flies in medium', or 'do not switch on the light, buffer solution in stock here', or 'do not touch, trespassers will be shot.' These were put up and removed depending on need and timing of work. The laboratory members obeyed these seemingly informal instructions to the letter. Such obedience was as much as if the stickers had really been official injunctions to do or to avoid doing something.

In CCL the tissue culture room, the microscopy room, the PI's office, and the Postdoc room were never sequestered from each other. Doors were open from as early as 6.00 am till midnight or even later. The senior researchers could enter the laboratory at any time because they were entrusted with keys. The ancillary research personnel did not receive these keys. The PI Sridhar's office was within the laboratory space adjoining the experimentation area, but separated from it by a glass and aluminium door which was always open. He could see through it if anyone entered or left the laboratory space. The researchers were always aware of his presence and of his eventual presence even if they could not see him.

The CCL members had a shared tacit awareness of when laboratory space and space elsewhere was frontstage or backstage (Goffman 1959). It is possible to say that no place in the laboratory was backstage for very long. The PI's office was always treated as frontstage regardless of his presence or absence. When Sridhar or a visitor from another research institute was in the laboratory, all of CCL became frontstage. This was the case even when Sridhar was not in the workspace or the Postdoc room, but in his office room. Even when Sridhar was physically absent, no one spent more than an hour away from work or work-related matters, unless so compelled. In a certain sense, Sridhar was never really absent from the laboratory, because his social presence ensured the ordering of work, recreation, space, and time spent on work and recreation, just as if he were physically present.

The laboratory is not a place where physical solitude is possible. Absolute privacy is precluded by the high degree of self- and collegiate inspection of work performances.[11] Although researchers are careful to avoid disturbing each other during busy spells, they must and do constantly call on each other to clarify doubts over concepts and over the interpretation and implementation of protocols.

The Postdoc room was used for the weekly laboratory discussions of work progress, and also for 'the journal club', which was a weekly event in the laboratory during which recently published work would be critically examined. These are overtly frontstage activities. The room was also a site for recreational activities, for relaxation between spells of work, for checking mail and netsurfing, but it became frontstage the moment Sridhar entered it. Further, when Sridhar was in his office room, which was separated from the Postdoc room by a large glass-aluminium partition, researchers very much acted as if the Postdoc room was frontstage too. They did not idly surf the net or read a novel or take a nap or talk loudly.

Architectural arrangement marks differences of rank between the members of the laboratory population. It also makes visible and enables the practices that realize the division of labour in the laboratory. Within the laboratory for instance, there is a separate office for the Postdocs (the rather versatile Postdoc room) and another single room for the PI, as opposed to the wall-mounted desks for the PhD candidates and the other short-term researchers. It is possible to compare this with the greater visibility-at-work of the shop floor worker in an industrial unit as opposed to senior management with their partially enclosed cubicles. There is a clear difference of power between those who are compelled to be seen at all times as opposed to those who are authorized to see and are only sometimes to be seen.

---

11   As long as I was inside the laboratory, I had no backstage. Further, frontstage impression management was important. It means altering and controlling vocal inflections, accent, speed of speech and movement, emotional states and facial expressions. I kept writing notes in my field diary, and strove to keep my smiling personal front and manner. Mercifully no one complained of anything to the PI, and I generally kept a good face on even when irked by remarks like 'Who on earth would want to fund research like yours?' or, 'Don't see what good it does us, you being here, its a small lab, y'know' or 'you should have kids before your chromosomes start getting really sticky – you ARE 31, after all.' Self-mockery was a partial solution. It loosened up the members. I started rounds of questioning with requests like 'I just don't understand this *Cancer* paper. Can you tell me what this transcription factor does in this pathway?' or 'Are *myc* and *jun* proto-oncogenes, or tumour suppressors?' Usually responses to such timid science-related questions were immediate. This sort of conversational opening created a setting in which technical questions could be subtly followed up with other questions related to, for instance, 'Did you have help in tackling all this information when you started doing this?' 'How did you learn to operate those machines? They look so difficult to me.' Self-deprecation went a long way in making them talk.

Ordering things

In the laboratory, self- and other-directed vigilance ensured that matter moved as little out of place as possible. Shoes were scrupulously removed outside the tissue culture room. Food stayed inside the satchels and was never consumed in the workspace. Things were not moved from other researchers' workstations. Equipment was not shifted around arbitrarily. In this regard, Mary Douglas' understanding of purity-concerns is relevant (Douglas 2002). Douglas says that taboos reduce disorder. The preservation of taboos, of order, requires a 'community-wide complicity' about keeping clean things clean and 'dirty' things away. She asserts that there is no such thing as dirt. Things are dirty only when they do not fit in a scheme of classification. Thus the lunchbox could be ignored only as long as it is safely inside the satchel or perhaps opened in the corridor. For instance, at the Delhi molecular medicine laboratory, I observed that the researchers were very careful to keep their aluminium-foil wrapped lunches within their bags and to go to a cafeteria to eat these. When I asked why this was so, a PhD student responded, 'Boss will blow a fuse if he even sees me put my apple on the bench.' At a later date the same student rebuked her junior for eating wafers within the laboratory.

To open food packets at a workstation invites horror and anger, not only from the PI but also from the other benchworkers who would see this as a flagrant, irrational disregard of the collective, rational need to keep the work area sterile. At CCL, once, I saw Sridhar rinsing his coffee mug at the laboratory sink. Seeing my quizzical expression perhaps, he smiled and said, 'Boss's privileges.' It was a strict rule that no benchworker could have any food, beverage, or condiment within the entire laboratory bench space. It was acceptable to eat in the Postdoc room. Often, in that room, all members shared chocolates brought by a researcher from a trip abroad. When someone completed a stay in the laboratory, the practice was to give a small going-away party in that room, as I did. The usual purity/ impurity distinctions were suspended in the Postdoc room. This was most visible during the levity that followed the ritual solemnity of a procedure such as a journal paper discussion (weekly event), a presentation of minutes from conferences, or a departure talk, such as I gave on completion of fieldwork.

Through practice, the awareness of spatial proprieties acquires normative strength and becomes embodied in manifest and meaningful actions. New entrants to the laboratory acquire this awareness by communicated instruction from older hands. Peers or superiors verbally check behaviour seen as inappropriate such as violations of what is supposed to be the space ordering of CCL. As I saw in the laboratory meetings I attended, senior researchers are quick to rectify the smallest verbal slips of the junior researchers presenting their findings. Such corrections extend to the following of 'proper' etiquette in the laboratory space. For instance, once I observed that the summer intern, Shilpa, walked into the Postdoc room, abutting the experimental space, wearing her sterile gloves and holding a test tube. This was promptly reprimanded by Vandana who had been paired with her in experimental work: 'Shilpa, please do not ever again bring those gloves or tubes in here and better not let Boss see you doing it.'

These practices are rooted as much in the collective local customary practices of each laboratory as they are in unspecified and variable notions of laboratory hygiene. For instance, in the molecular cardiology laboratory at Delhi, researchers drank tea and ate snacks at workstations although they were careful to keep some minimal distance between the food and the experimental set-up at the workstation. Researchers and others did not remove their shoes when entering the tissue culture room. In this laboratory, I was not allowed to enter the tissue culture room, whereas I was allowed to do so in CCL so long as I had removed my shoes like everyone else.[12] In the Delhi molecular medicine laboratory, everyone removed their shoes before entering the tissue culture room. I was not allowed to enter the tissue culture room with or without shoes. In this laboratory, the PI strictly discouraged consumption of food and drink or even taking out food from bags within the laboratory space; the researchers not only obeyed but also actively enforced the observance of this 'rule.'

A consideration of these details yields the view that all three laboratories had an awareness of the possibility of 'contamination' and the effects thereof. However, there were different local interpretations of the modes of contamination. There were different notions about the permitted size of zones of pollution and of sterility (purity). There were also different notions about who could or could not enter certain highly restricted zones of purity. A powerful vernacular of scientific civility, spoken *sotto voce,* guides the specific modes of association and conduct of the laboratory. In speaking this vernacular, the members of the association recognize an obligation to comply with it and follow procedures for enacting and interpreting it. In mastering this speech, the scientist learns also to take position in the structures of authority, first in his local context and later beyond it.

---

12   Even at CCL, I could enter the tissue-culture room only if one of the senior researchers had been informed. This raises the question: to what extent does identification as an insider or as an outsider order physical movement *inside* the laboratory area? Within the laboratory, local practices establish and alter the lines and definitions that constitute permitted-forbidden zones. Perhaps I was seen as less of a stranger, an anomalous outsider in CCL and much more so in the Delhi laboratories. The reason for the greater ease of movement at CCL was perhaps that I was relatively more integrated into a structure of membership and thereby into the networks of recognition between associates. It is also the fact that the degree of this integration at CCL was far less in my case as compared to the regulars, owing to my relatively ambiguous identification and also to my lack of recognizable function in the context of hands-on research work. Boundary work, physical and symbolic, constantly occurs within the laboratory's physical limits to create and alter boundaries within the ostensibly fixed but equally variable physical limits of the laboratory.

Time points and schedules

Time points are the specific times, over a period of time, at which actions have to be taken in the course of an experiment. The researchers and assistants keep track of time points with digital alarm-timers found at each workstation. The rhythms of the benchworkers' lives are strongly determined by the temporal demands of the experiment.[13] A significant part of the researcher's day – 12 hours on an average – is spent in the laboratory. This figure can stretch up to round-the-clock during crucial experimental runs or when preparatory work is being done on a research paper. At the Institute, there were rooms to sleep in and showers had been installed in the bathrooms for people unable to go home for stretches of time.

At the Delhi molecular medicine and molecular cardiology laboratories, researchers went back to their residence halls to eat and then returned promptly. The workday was on an average from 9 am till 9 pm. I observed in the residence

---

13   Knorr-Cetina describes the laboratory's life as marked by innumerable schedules. In the laboratory, schedules pace, phrase and state the work, allocating turns within which certain points must be made or else the points and the turns may be lost. For someone to take and hold their turn in the collective life of the laboratory, it is important that the pace of the activities that constitute this life such as a study, a check, a calculation be conducive to turn taking (Knorr-Cetina 2003). I realized soon that respondents met my queries with wariness, irritation, or outright rebuffs if I did not set them properly in time and space. In the early stages it was frequently difficult to judge when there was a lull in activity so that I could ask questions or even make a request to ask questions. Entering the temporal flow came from observing the pattern how, on some occasions, I was ignored or requested to wait and on others my questions were answered promptly, leisurely, hurriedly etc. The effort to get information meant I had to 'build ease' with as many of the group as possible. I couched questions in casual interaction so that it would appear that I was satisfying a positive interest in the laboratory's work instead of passing adverse judgement on it. Over time, I learnt to time my questions and to situate, tone and phrase them in conversation so that the 'interviewing' aspect was diminished. Eventually, my queries were not treated with irritation as a waste of time, or viewed with suspicion as muckraking. I inserted queries in the course of general conversations. For my purposes, these were unstructured interviews. However, my purposes were served only because the queries were in a 'non-interview setting'. These settings included coffee breaks, mealtimes, late in the evening when the pace of activity in the laboratory slowed perceptibly, the occasional lengthy gaps in work when one experimental procedure had been completed but the material was not yet ready for the next stage. Queries received lengthy responses only when they were posed in verbal, spatial and temporal contexts seen as appropriate, i.e., non-intrusive, non-interrogatory, casual and friendly. On some occasions, I needed immediate information which meant initiating what was obviously an interview. When I started a barrage of questions, the respondents were wary, monosyllabic, and hesitant to reply. This meant that they would answer at length only if they did not feel 'quizzed.' I could camouflage interviews as conversations, and insinuate questions about work and work relations into conversations without sounding inquisitorial. I avoided words like power, authority, inequality, coercion, etc., in my conversations when I was asked about my work.

and was informed that researchers would regularly wake around 2–3 am and rush to the laboratory in order to lyse cells-in-culture, as these cells would have matured by that time and had to be lysed at that time and no later.

Bench researchers see themselves as either in the laboratory or away from it. Being at home primarily means being away from the laboratory. An outing for a picnic, or a shopping expedition, or a film, or any leisure activity is decided by the degree of need to attend to work. 'Public time' takes over private time and renders it similar to itself. The researchers' sleep and wakefulness is decided by the needs of the experiment. To adapt an idea from Michel Foucault, researchers' bodies are rendered docile and plastic in the service of the experiment. Experiments are marked by 'plasticity' (Gooding 1989). Their identity is never fixed. The plasticity of the experiment means that the flow of the experiment is akin to the flow of premises and settlements in an argument. Until a settlement is reached, the researcher must render his 'personal' schedules as plastic as those of the experiment itself. Settlements on experimental planning, trajectory and outcome are contingent upon the discretion of the PI or of a senior researcher delegated by the PI to supervise a junior. Authority and power relations are thus quite woven into the experimental process. They influence both the plasticity of experiment and the experimenter. Experimental performances, their protagonists, and the visible places of these dramaturgies of the real are situated within an invisible space of power relations. This space is the configuration of differentially empowered players. Their mutually oriented material actions, performed in a materially visible place, animate and embody that relational space.

Foucault suggests that 'power is articulated directly onto time; it assures its control and guarantees its use' (Foucault 1979: 160). The temporal demands made on the researcher are the expression of power. This power is productive because it is not an occasional intervention in the life of the researcher. It is not periodical or intermittent. The physical resources for doing research are primarily, though not completely, found in the single physical location of the laboratory and these are not portable *en masse*. Thus, the presence of the researcher in the laboratory becomes both the cause and the effect of the exercise of power over the researcher's body and time, so much so that these can hardly be said to be the possession of the researcher. Nor would it be accurate to say that time and body are at the researcher's disposal. To say this would be to assume that the temporal demands made on the researcher are substantively regulated by his choice. On the contrary, the researcher's time and body are at the disposal of and under the power inhering in the eponymous association between the PI and the laboratory considered as a set of quasi-owned epistemic resources and products. This power organizes the processes of production and its penetration of actions and schedules are such as to greatly curtail the discretion of the researcher. The rhythms of laboratory life become the encompassing quotidian rhythms of the researcher's life. Through this enveloping and annexation of 'private' time, the power exercised over the researcher becomes both constant and ubiquitous. Power over the researcher is unified and consolidated through the usurpation of private time by public time.[14] In this regard, the progression of calendrical time, crucial to the governance of laboratory life, is intercut with the consideration of 'social time.'

Consider the PI's caution to choose a certain time for submission, at which point calendrical time submits to 'social time.' In other words, the PI decides that the time is right or not to submit a paper to a journal, whether the work is ahead of competitors, that enough research has been done, or that the research and the researcher be suitably controlled for the generation of more satisfactory data. The management of time-points is of great importance in the quotidian government of the laboratory and in its benchwork. But time-points assume a particularly rigid non-negotiability in the matter of journal submission and even more in the matter of resubmission, as I observed in CCL. The reviewers for papers submitted to journals may outright reject it or else send it back with the proviso that certain doubts be clarified (by re-experimentation if necessary) and textual imperfections be rectified before the paper is resubmitted. The resubmission must be completed within a very rigid timeframe. This is currently done online so as to meet deadlines. If the paper is not resubmitted by a specific time of a specific date, an electronic gate shuts off access to the electronic portal for submission. The rigid timeframe also contributes to the difficulty of contesting the reviewer's decision. Loss of time on debate would prevent timely resubmission, thus making it necessary to submit the paper as an entirely fresh entry. According to Sridhar, the CCL PI, this means a further delay of at least 4–6 months. This delay is regarded as something to be avoided at any cost. A loss of time is regarded as a large threat of loss of priority. There is a consciousness of an ever-present possibility that someone else would publish something similar first. The loss of priority is a loss of competitive advantage in the economy of credibility.

---

14   At the Institute, while constant temporal and spatial linkage of the researchers to the laboratories may be seen as a practical necessity, it has its attendant problems. The PhD Divya of CCL said that claustrophobia and angry outbursts are all too frequent in her hostel. Prateek and Divya said that they often 'get sick' of seeing the same people through the day at the same place, everyday, year-round. The Institute authorities have floated the idea of a gym as 'a de-stressing facility'. Such facilities, similar to the gyms and yoga classes of corporate campuses, are means to optimizing productivity by keeping people mentally and physically fit to keep performing work. Recreation and so-called leisure activities are not separated from work. They are a means to keep the workforce in working condition. Leisure is private time that defers and apologizes to public time while also refurbishing the worker in preparation for his return to the rhythms of public time. Leisure is a means of repair, just as public time is a means of production. They are integrated into a powerful form of discipline. For instance, in conversations with junior researchers during the pilot studies at Delhi, I was told that closeness to the laboratory is 'practical' for the efficient and timely execution of work. Divya at CCL said that she spends Saturdays and Sundays in the laboratory, even when she does not really have work. She said that this is because there is really nothing much else to do around her room, and she finds it nicer to work on weekends and after hours when she has the laboratory space all to herself. This indicates the 'inertia of work' induced by the conflation of leisure and work.

Virtualization of laboratory space

At the Institute, the Web mail service creates a non-physical, electronic space, which contributes to the high publicity and corporate solidarity of life in each laboratory and throughout the Institute. Any mail sent to one person or to more is open to surveillance, because it goes through the central server. Content of mails is subject to checks based on sensitive keywords so as to detect and curtail spam and abuse. The Handbook of Guidelines for Graduate Students contains explicit and detailed instructions on electronic etiquette, advising against sending unnecessary e-mail, reconfiguring software, sending angry e-mails and so on. Collective mails are sent out to all with a mail ID at the Institute. Within the laboratory they are sent out to the dedicated laboratory-group ID.

The Institute mails are either formal or informal in content. Formal mails are notices of work seminars, colloquia, workshops, and conferences. These mails may invite the submission of abstracts for conferences, workshops and seminars. They may also notify the entire Institute about the time, venue, speaker, and topic of a slated seminar or colloquium. Other mails may notify researchers of the shifting of rooms or the shifting, use, malfunction and repair of equipment. The Library staff sends out mails notifying everyone about new books and journal subscriptions (electronic and in hard copy). The presence or absence of the staff of the Infirmary of the Institute is also mailed out to everyone. The informal mails may concern 'unofficial' matters such as a fruit sale near the Institute, a musical concert, a film screening, or a cricket match. They even inform all people about engagements, marriages and the birth of children to staff either presently working at the Institute or relocated elsewhere.

Formal institute mails for seminars:

1.   Thesis seminar

---------- Forwarded message ----------*[FROM EVENT CONVENOR]*
Date: Fri, 17 Sep 2004 17:23:40 +0530 (IST)[15]
From: N. S— <s—@mailsvr.inst.res.in>
To: all@mailsvr.inst.res.in
Subject: THESIS SEMINAR BY A—
[Institute's postal address]
Date: Wednesday, September 22, 2004
Time: 10:15 a.m.
Speaker: A— B—

---

15   Although my fieldwork was between January–June 2004, my Institute mail ID is still functional. I was in the city of fieldwork in September 2004, and was able to attend this thesis seminar and other talks at the Institute, in addition to holding further conversations with the PI.

Title: Genome-wide survey of Protein superfamilies and calculation of diversity
measures : In-depth study of Protein Phosphatases
Venue: Ground Floor Lecture Hall (LH1)

ABSTRACT
Successful genome sequencing projects unveiled a wealth of information
regarding the proteome of an organism. However, a dearth in gene annotation
resulted in a significant gap between characterized and unannotated sequences.
Previous studies on available protein sequences and structural information
display a strong convergence implying many proteins share similar folds. [...]
The current study enunciates immense diversity among phosphatases within and
across genomes. [...]
ALL ARE WELCOME
N.N. S—
[Institute's postal address]
Telephone : 2******2(direct), 2******1/429 Fax : ***-23******
E-mail: s—@ mailsvr.inst.res.in

2.   Annual work seminar

Date: Mon, 5 Apr 2004 14:05:35 +0530 (IST)
From: P— <p—@mailsvr.inst.res.in>
To: all@mailsvr.inst.res.in
Subject: AWS *[Annual Work Seminar]*
Dear all,
My seminar is scheduled for tomorrow at 10.15AM. Abstract is attached:
Role of Epidermal Growth Factor Receptors in cervical cancer progression:
Notch signaling is involved in cervical cancer progression and localization
of Notch in the nucleus is observed in carcinomas [...] We find that EGFR is
phosphorylated at a unique Tyrosine residue in both tumors and Caski cells [...]
Further, preliminary results from the laboratory link Notch to ERBB2 rather
than EGFR in activating the PI3kinase PKB/Akt pathway.
Please be there
Regards P. –
PRATEEK. N. PhD Post Doctoral Fellow
[INSTITUTE'S POSTAL ADDRESS]

The mails sent out within the laboratory can also be classified as formal or
informal. The formal mails outnumber the informal mails. A person who is to
give a journal review, a report from a conference, or an introductory or farewell
seminar sends out an invitation-style mail the day before to notify all people in
the laboratory. This mail contains the time, place, and abstract of the seminar. The
informal mails may be to pass on a message such as 'X has got chocolates and
everyone can grab a bite in the Postdoc room.' The formal and informal mails are

similar in that they are appeals to and reinforcements of the corporate solidarity of the laboratory.

There are constant mail notifications across the Institute about the equipment rooms. The common equipment rooms are sites where people from various laboratories must coordinate their requirements and schedules. These are sites of considerable interactional density (Orr 1996). They are transitional points where quotidian tasks from different locales are brought into conjunction. As such they carry the potential for conflict of schedules and requirements. This is no small matter considering the importance of temporal management in research. Mailing is an instance of the management of activities at these transitional places.

Mail across the institute: equipment use

---------------------------- Original Message
Subject: Re: confocal facility and EMBO workshop
From: j@inst.res.in>
Date: Fri, September 10, 2004 7:02 pm
To: hk@inst.res.in
     academic@mailsvr.inst.res.in

Dear Confocal Users,
Due to set up and testing of experiments for the EMBO functional Imaging workshop, I have a very specific request to make (I can already listen to the groans and moans...as I make this request). From today's attempt to set up life time imaging on the Multi-Photon set up, it is clear to me that we may need the system for the next five days (at least till Wednesday) at the drop of a hat.

While I could simply say is that the system is unavailable till next Friday, instead I say that (in the interests of those of you who have planned most urgent experiments for the use of this set-up) go ahead with your experiments, but please be prepared for interruptions at any random time. I am sorry that we did not anticipate this before, but now there is no way that we can hold up the course.

Please let us know also if there are slots that you can postpone till after Friday. I know this will inconvienience [*sic* – in original text] some of you some what but please bear with us. If your work does not require the multiphoton set up please feel free to use the BioRad set up for which experiments are not being planned on such a exploratory fashion....The schedule for this set up has already been circulated by Krishna.
Best wishes,
J-

At 02:14 PM 9/8/2004 +0530, H.K.- wrote:
Dear Confocal Users,
Starting from 13th to 17th of Sept, both the confocal micrscopes [*sic* – in original text] in Lab 27 will be used for the EMBO functional imaging workshop.

However, the microscopes are free to use (for the CERTIFIED USERS ONLY) during the pre-lunch session on all the above said days. For new users, there will be NO training sessions on these days. We strongly recommend you to do routine expts [*experiments*] and NOT try anything new to avoid break down of machines on these days!
Thanks
H. K—
>*[Institute's postal address]*
Telephone : 2******2(direct), 2******1/429 Fax : ***-23******
E-mail: k—@mailsvr.inst.res.in

The 'Webmail' establishes a continuity between public and private space-time. Modem points are installed throughout the Institute, including the hostel rooms, the corridors, the library, and in every laboratory. Whether physically in or out of the laboratory the researcher can rarely plead paucity of information as an excuse for negligence of some task in the laboratory. The Internet and Intranet permit the centralization of activities even in their dispersion and fragmentation. Even while working at home the researcher remains 'embedded within a social structure increasingly subject to the centralizing and managerial tendencies' emerging from virtualization (Robins and Webster 1988: 44–75). The rhythms and space of the researcher's leisure and work are more effectively colonized. Everyday life is mobilized into the service of laboratory life.[16]

The Internet has virtualized CCL laboratory space. Informational technologies strongly condition the work and leisure spaces of the laboratory. The 'virtualization' tends to sharpen the researchers' awareness of the competitive demands of the field and the possibilities of collaboration and parochial adaptation. The Internet is a subsidiary hub of work, providing information, working from remote locations, and enabling transactions with companies that provide chemicals and apparatus to the laboratory. Virtualization works in tandem with multiple visible, spatial and material means of control and surveillance over the researchers and the boundaries that define them and their work.

---

16   At the Institute, the availability of crèches for children of the researchers, the residential proximity of most of the researchers, and the arrangement of meals, snacks and beverages at the single cafeteria, and the tendency of laboratory associates to commensality and socializing with each other indicate that professional and non-professional roles and temporal rhythms are integrated rather than segmented. The demarcation of home and work is blurred and home is integrated into and subsumed under work. Within CCL, the associates tend to visit the nearby temple together between sessions of work. They also keep pictures of family, of the marriages and parties of associates, and religious icons tacked to the workbenches. There are no prohibitions on conversing about personal matters during working hours. It is also quite usual for cricket, politics, and films to be discussed and argued over volubly both in the main experimental area and in the postdoc room.

Conclusions: Placing the laboratory

Each laboratory is characterized by a strong parochiality in its projects and interests. This is sustained through the making and maintenance of boundaries. The laboratory associates can be described as colleagues in projects of territorialization that constitute distinct epistemic spaces. These projects involve 'marking out a territory in thought and inscribing it in the real, topographizing it, investing it with powers, bounding it by exclusions, and defining who or what can rightfully enter' (Rose 1999: 34). The research laboratory is a site built upon distinction from other laboratories, consisting of competitors and collaborators and from the 'non-scientists.' The associates in each laboratory together work for the safety of enclosure, preventing the entry of objects and individuals perceived as contaminants and interlopers in laboratory space. However, boundary work also seeks to ensure a limited porosity around the laboratory. At certain moments, such as during visits or seminars by acknowledged disciplinary peers, the vigilance over boundaries permits the entry of these real or potential affiliates who are recognizable and identifiable as useful, credible, trustworthy, and relatively unthreatening.

In the laboratory, the PI is always interested in curbing the entry and initiation of new and alien people, events and actions that would disrupt the production processes of laboratory life. According to Norbert Elias scientific establishments are groups of people who collectively produce and exercise monopolistic control over knowledge-resources needed by others (Elias 1982: 3–69). This implies that they place controls on administration and transmission of a fund of knowledge and on the skills needed for developing it. It also means that they restrict membership and deny or limit non-members access to the resources they produce. Thus, they are establishments only insofar as there are groups who need the resources produced by them. Members of organizations have a commonality of interest, physical proximity and values. As such they have an advantage over and a level of suspicion towards outsiders who are not conversant with aspirations, problems, and situations of the 'insiders.' Identity, membership, autonomy, and a power surplus – there is coherence and a possibility of concomitant variation between these elements. A reduction in one implies a reduction in another element, and risk to the establishment.

In the forms of control over the research groups, one sees the highly productive surveillance potential of information technologies and architectural modalities as new panoptical tools of control, which simultaneously individualize and gather together the activities of researchers. These technologies particularly enable the observation and scrutiny of individuals. The databases, mail systems and so on place each individual within a giant, even a global grid formed of integrated micro-networks. Within each Institute and at the level of the giant databases such as PubMed researchers are within monitoring reach of other researchers within and across research areas. Sequestration is impossible in this scenario. The electronic grid encourages and is sustained by increasingly hectic movements between the many parochial, local nodes in the networks of science. This also encourages practices of incessant gathering of information which is an important stake in the contests between those who have information and those who desire it.

Secrecy and publicity are in mutual tension once the discourse of envy and scarcity has defined and enveloped information as a commodity. The PI and the researchers incessantly gather information from and about their competitors/collaborators. Where information is given in return, the reciprocation is calculated and hesitant because it is seen as inherently risky. When secrecy and publicity confront each other, they are co-productive with laboratory boundaries. To give too much information is seen to be risky for the laboratory because the perception is that it might endanger chances in the race for priority. To give too little is to risk isolation from laboratories working in the same or similar areas. The perception is that isolation and paucity of information might lead to loss of reputation through duplication of research, the wastage of resources, and the risk of accusation of plagiarism. Thus, the boundaries of the laboratory and the negotiation of the economies of information and credibility are co-productive.

The authority of the doctor partly draws its surcharged legitimacy from its credible enactment in the closely monitored and calculated rational-legal setting of the hospital or clinic. Similarly, the credibility of the scientist is related to its exercise in settings that can be scrutinized by teams of others who are similarly qualified to exercise professional judgement. Research attracts estimations of 'dignity' from the location of research-performance in a cordoned-off space into which only specialists or approved visitors have regular access. The publicity of research communications is defined through the procedures of scrutiny wherein communications are meant for the specialists who would knowledgeably read and rate the communicated research.

Place is always informed by power, interest, locality; place is a function of space. The separation of one laboratory from another is itself a mark of the separation of research interests and personnel. These separations, made visible, also guide the movements of those who are the members of a laboratory and those who are not. They are integral to the disciplinary practices of research work. These practices include also the making of demarcations of *scientific disciplines*. The interdictions on the entry of unauthorized outsiders into the laboratory space maintain the distinction between the non-linearity of benchwork and the neatness of a research seminar or presentation.[17] The fluidity of a research experiment, the element of

---

17   François Jacob observes that scientific writing transforms and formalizes research: 'It substitutes an orderly train of concepts and experiments for a jumble of disordered efforts...In short, writing a paper is to substitute order for the disorder and agitation that animate life in the laboratory' (Jacob 1988). This is comparable to the writing of anthropological reports. Akhil Gupta and James Ferguson say that the performance and writing of anthropological fieldwork are linked to a spatio-temporal separation of 'home' and 'field.' Data is gathered in the field and the ethnographic analysis is written up elsewhere. Spatio-temporal distancing, a form of boundary work, is also achieved through the sort of writing in the analysis, as compared to the field notes. The notes are 'close to experience, textually fragmentary, consisting of detailed "raw" documentation of interviews and observations as well as spontaneous subjective reactions. The monograph and ethnographic paper, done "at home", is reflective, polished, theoretical, intertextual, a textual whole.' (Gupta and Ferguson 1997: 12)

unpredictability, the local improvizations on protocol recipes are smoothed away in the write-ups, and the fact that there is a screen between the front and the back of the laboratory facilitates the smoothening. The material effects of spatial ordering must be considered along with the ordering of the dispositions that inform the material actions, the visible hard work of ordering space. Through the formation and stabilization of these dispositions, the participants in social ordering become associates in projects of mutual stabilization. They become actors and subjects who are mutually recognizable and reliable to the extent that they co-produce a reliable and recognizable locale.

Acknowledgements

I am profoundly indebted to Professor Dipankar Gupta for his invaluable advice towards the research for this paper. I am also grateful to him for a clarified perspective on the relationship of space to culture and on how to apply this idea in my research.

References

Appadurai, A. 1997. *Modernity at Large: The Cultural Dimensions of Globalization*, New Delhi: Oxford University Press.

Augé, M. 1995. *Non-places: Introduction to an Anthropology of Supermodernity*, London: Verso.

Bauman, Z. 1989. *Modernity and the Holocaust*, Oxford: Polity Press.

Bauman, Z. 1991. *Modernity and Ambivalence*, Oxford: Polity Press.

Bauman, Z. 1995. *Life in Fragments: Essays in Postmodern Morality*, Oxford: Polity Press.

Callon, M. 1986. The sociology of an actor-network, in *Mapping the Dynamics of Science and Technology*, edited by M. Callon, J. Law and A. Rip. London: Macmillan, 19–34.

Charlesworth, M., Farrall, L., Stokes, T., and Turnbull, D. 1989. *Life Among the Scientists: An Anthropological Study of an Australian Scientific Community*, Melbourne: Oxford University Press.

Douglas, M. and Isherwood, B. 1996. *The World of Goods: Towards an Anthropology of Consumption*, London: Routledge.

Douglas, M. 2002. *Purity and Danger: An Analysis of Conceptions of Pollution And Taboo*, London: Routledge Classics.

Douglas, M. 2004. *Natural Symbols*, Chennai: Routledge.

Elias, N. 1982. Scientific Establishments, in *Scientific Establishments and Hierarchies: Sociology of the Sciences Yearbook*, edited by N. Elias, H. Martins and R. Whitley. Volume 6, Dordrecht: D. Reidel.

Foucault, M. 1960. *Discipline and Punish: The Birth of the Prison*, Harmondsworth: Penguin.

Goffman, E. 1959. *The Presentation of Self in Everyday Life*, New York: Doubleday Anchor.

Gooding, D. 1989. History in the laboratory: Can we tell what really went on?, in *The Development of the Laboratory*, edited by F. A.J.L. James. New York: American Institute of Physics.

Gupta, A. and Ferguson, J. 1997. Discipline and practice: "the field" as site, method and location in anthropology *Anthropological Locations*, edited by A. Gupta and J. Ferguson. Berkeley: University of California Press.

Gupta, D. 2000. *Culture, Space and the Nation-State: From Sentiment to Structure*, New Delhi: Sage.

Jacob, F. 1988. *The Statue Within*, New York: Basic Books.

Jagtenberg, T. 1983. *The Social Construction of Science*, Dordrecht: D. Reidel.

Knorr-Cetina, K. 2003. *Epistemic Cultures: How the Sciences Make Knowledge*, Cambridge, Massachusetts: Harvard University Press.

Kohler, R.E. 2002. Place and practice in field biology', *History of Science*, l: 190–210.

Latour, B. and Woolgar, S. 1979. *Laboratory Life*, London: Sage.

Mol, A. 1999. Ontological politics: a word and some questions, in *The Political Economy of Information*, edited by V. Mosco and J. Wasko. Madison: University of Wisconsin Press.

Orr, J. 1996. *Talking About Machines: An Ethnography of a Modern Job*, New York: ILR Press.

Pantin, C.F.A. 1968. *On Relations Between the Sciences*, Cambridge: Cambridge University Press.

Poovey, M. 1995. *Making a Social Body*, Chicago: University of Chicago Press.

Robins, K and Webster, F. 1988. Cybernetic capitalism, in *The Political Economy of Information*, edited by V. Mosco and J. Wasko. Madison: University of Wisconsin Press.

Rose, N. 1999. *Powers of Freedom: Reframing Political Thought*, Cambridge, UK: Cambridge University Press.

Whitley, R. 1976. Umbrella and polytheistic scientific disciplines and their elites, *Social Studies of Science*, 6, 471–497.

Chapter 9

Almost Human:
Scientific and Popular Strategies for Making Sense of 'Missing Links'

Murray Goulden and Andrew S. Balmer

Within western culture there exists a rigid distinction between animal and human, a distinction sustained by the Judeo-Christian tradition (Thomas 1996: 17–25) and by eminent philosophers including Aristotle and Descartes. 'Man', created in the image of God and possessor of a soul, language, and culture, stands clearly distinct from all other animals, senseless and soulless as they are. Such a binary continues to dominate the popular taxonomy, despite the emergence and development of radical evidence to the contrary from the life sciences. One such example is palaeoanthropology, which has troubled this polarization of life, through the introduction of multiple species to the imagined point of humanity's departure from animals. Our principle concern is with 'missing links', those figures deemed to fall somewhere between the categories animal and human. It is these fossils that should undermine the dichotomy but that have somehow, within the popular conception, been made to serve it. Two famous examples will be drawn upon, Piltdown Man and *Homo floresiensis*, as we study how these liminal figures are reconciled with the dichotomous model that popular culture holds, and what shapes their journey from science to the public.

This book's focus is life sciences, which may ordinarily be thought to exclude a science far removed from popular images of the cutting edge laboratory work seen in fields like genomics. However, palaeoanthropology, the scientific study of early humans through fossil evidence, is just as concerned with life as any biological laboratory-based investigation. In fact, it is the very origins of human life, the question of how we came to be the way we are, to which palaeoanthropologists apply themselves. More specifically this book examines life science categories with regard to science-culture interactions. In this respect palaeoanthropology is a field much overlooked by the social sciences, which is regrettable given the huge media attention its discoveries can receive. In the case of *Homo floresiensis*:

> When the discovery was announced all hell broke loose, as the world's media e-mailed and phoned our offices and homes – about 200 inquiries a day for the first week, with Peter doing 100 interviews in the first three days. The interest was

overwhelming: we were featured in about 98,000 websites and were headlined in about 7,000 newspapers. (Morwood and van Oosterzee 2007: 186)

Introducing Piltdown man and Homo floresiensis

The discovery of Piltdown Man was announced in 1912 by a team led by prominent British scientist A.S. Woodward and amateur geologist Charles Dawson. It has the dubious honour of being perhaps the greatest hoax in scientific history and the identity of the perpetrator(s) remains disputed. Like other "missing links" Piltdown awoke in a purgatory somewhere between animal and human. It embodied both with its large human-like skull and ape-like jaw but fit solely in neither one. It was not until four decades later, in 1953, that the creature was found to be a fake: no more than the juxtaposition of a modern human skull and a modern orangutan jaw. The constituent parts had been stained to feign age and the teeth filed to appear human. That the creature was found to be a hoax is of little concern to us here however, since it is its original reception as a missing link that provides our focus.

Homo Floresiensis was discovered on Flores – one of the larger islands of the chain that makes up Indonesia – in 2003. The site from which the type specimen was removed, known as Liang Bua, gave the figure its name – LB1. The specimen was most remarkable for its short stature and small brain, and was announced to the world at joint conferences in London and Sydney on the 27th October 2004. The events were hosted by the journal *Nature,* which carried two papers on the find in its issue released the following day. The discovery received huge attention from the world's media, as the quote in our introduction attests.

The purpose of this chapter is to study the means by which scientifically categorized knowledge is made sense of within the public realm. We chart this process through the use of two concepts that originate in Serge Moscovici's study on the adoption of psychoanalysis in France (Moscovici 1961). Moscovici identified the processes by which unfamiliar knowledge becomes familiar through 'social representations'. His exposition on this process as regards scientific knowledge is particularly prescient for our present concern:

> One often hears that a good science should begin by proposing clear and carefully defined concepts. Actually, no science, not even the most exact, proceeds in this way. It begins by assembling, ordering, and distinguishing phenomena which surprise everyone, because they are disturbing, or exotic, or create a scandal.

The ordering of the ontologically disturbing and geo-temporally exotic phenomena of missing links occurs via the strategies of 'anchoring' and 'objectifying', which Lievrouw (1990: 5) explicates thus:

> Representations [of scientific knowledge claims] are generated by a dual process
> of *anchoring* (classifying an unfamiliar phenomenon into a set of categories) and
> *objectifying* (converting the unfamiliar and abstract phenomenon into a familiar
> and concrete phenomenon by developing an image of it).

The translation of these objects, or categories in our present parlance, involves the movement from one realm to another and requires a reconfiguration of their categorization, as they have to be made sense of by a different audience with a very different conceptual framework. For Piltdown and LB1 this takes the form of a journey from '*Homo*' to 'human'. In the present study anchoring refers to the process by which missing links are made to fit within the animal – human binary of popular culture. We shall see that this primarily involved declaring these finds, despite their contradictory features, 'human'. Here, objectifying concerns the creation around the figures of narratives that act to cement their conceptually unstable status. This, we shall see, took the form of stories demonstrating these figures' humanness. It is *why* these figures became human, and *how* they were made human, that will reveal the interactions that take place between science and non-science culture when scientists investigate life.

Becoming Homo

Before exploring these processes empirically it is instructive to consider the scientific category '*Homo*', as it is demonstrative of the self-interested role we *Homo sapiens* play in the process of creating order from nature's disorder which rests at the heart of this chapter. Indeed it lies at the heart of modernity itself, for it is only our strict division of nature and culture conceptually which allows the two to be mixed so readily in practice (Latour 1993).

The genus *Homo* was created by the father of scientific taxonomy, Carl Linnaeus, and meant 'man', whilst the species name *sapiens* meant 'wise'. In a forerunner of later uncertainty we, as *Homo sapiens*, were not alone in this genus, but joined by *Homo troglodytes* ('cave-dweller'), which comprised anthropomorphic apes of which Linnaeus had received reports (Marks 2003: 21). Now known as chimpanzees, these animals have long since been removed from *Homo* to their own genus, *Pan*, but the source of Linnaeus' confusion – the combination of similarity and difference that marks our ontological relationship with both extant non-human primates and extinct missing links – remains all too evident. The personal stake we hold in this relationship leads Haraway to state 'western primatology has been about the construction of the self from the raw material of the other, the appropriation of nature in the production of culture' (1989: 11). Whilst most evident in our dealings with our closet ancestors, it does in fact extend to all animal life (Daston and Mitman (eds) 2005, Franklin 1999).

These problems are not unique to *Homo sapiens* and their phylogenetic relatives, since all attempts to categorize nature, as scientific taxonomy does, face the problem of a disjuncture between the ruler-straight demarcations of classification, and the ebbs and flows of the natural world. Species are not biological 'natural kinds', as the units of evolution are individuals, not groups. It is for this reason that Dupre argues against

> the picture of evolutionary change flowing down sharply defined channels, branching at well-defined nodes... A more realistic picture would be a river estuary at low tide. We find large streams of water and many side streams, some petering out, others rejoining a main channel or crossing into a different channel, and a few maintaining their integrity to the ocean; there are islands around which streams flow and then rejoin; eddies and vortices; and so on (2001: 207).

Despite what is implied to the uninitiated by the clean lines of taxonomic charts, there is no missing *link* between any two species, but rather enumerable missing *links*. The act of taxonomy, however, shrinks all these links down to the width of a single line. In the face of similarity and difference, the decision as to what goes on which side of the line often relies as much on value judgments as it does on empirical evidence.

Even those tangible divisions that separate contemporaneous, analogous species such as reproductive incompatibility, disappear once viewed from the perspective of evolutionary history, a perspective which the missing link demands. Here all species are interconnected through an unbroken chain of progenitor and descendant. When you add in to this mix the self-interested role that modern *Homo sapiens* hold when drawing lines separating or joining ourselves and our evolutionary relatives, it is unsurprising that the categorization of missing links as *Homo*, human, or neither, can become highly contested.

Anchoring missing links

Piltdown Man was received as a sensation in the English scientific media and press, both of which quickly proclaimed him to be an English find to match those of imperial rivals Germany (*Homo neanderthalensis*) and France (*Dryopithecus fontani*)[1]. The discrepancy between the skull and jaw size went – almost without exception – unchallenged in the UK, which is telling of the national pride that came to influence Piltdown's human character.

Notably, Piltdown's categorization as human by English scientists is in evidence right from the beginning. The presentation of the find on the 18th December 1912 at a meeting of the Geological Society was made under a title proclaiming: 'On the Discovery of a Paleolithic *Human* Skull and Mandible in Flint-Bearing Gravel Overlying the Wealden (Hastings Beds) at Piltdown, Fletching (Sussex)'

---

1   Remains of *Dryopithecus fontani and Homo Neanderthalensis* were discovered in France and Germany respectively in 1856, and as such were the first recognized hominan discoveries.

(Dawson and Woodward 1913, authors' italics). Dawson refers to an 'unusually thick human parietal bone' (ibid: 117) and 'the right half of a human mandible' (ibid: 121), assertions of humanness that are also made by Woodward (ibid: 124). The ambiguity of the find is raised though it doesn't appear to challenge the humanness of the specimen in any significant fashion: 'The great width of the temporal insertion, the situation of the mylohyoid groove behind rather than in line with the dental foramen… are all characters of the mandible in apes, not in man' (ibid: 131). Woodward goes so far as to place the find in an entirely new genus – *Eoanthropus* ('Dawn Man') – in recognition of the unusual character of the jaw (ibid: 135). It was given the species name *Dawsoni* in honour of its discoverer. The result is that humanness is applied outside our own genus *Homo*. Despite its contradictions which they acknowledge in its scientific classification, Dawson and Woodward use their considerable authority as scientists to categorize this missing link as human. Why, if this creature's physical remains were so contradictory, was it claimed as human by scientists, rather than 'ape'? Why, indeed, did scientists use 'human' at all when it would be safer to stick to scientific categorizations?

The answer is twofold. Firstly, anthropocentricism meant that Piltdown the 'backwards human' was far more salacious a story than Piltdown the 'forward ape' (*Express* 12.08.13: 1). The desire among scientists to grab the news media's – and hence the public's – attention was as important as any scientific evidence in the decision to declare Piltdown human. This same pressure encouraged the use of human rather than sticking to a more esoteric, but defensible, scientific categorization.

The English press repeat the process of forcing Piltdown to fit into the human side of the binary, even whilst acknowledging its contradictions:

> a new race of men, in points strongly resembling the apes, but still unquestionably 'man', although devoid of the power of speech. (*Express* 20.12.12: 1)

> the oldest human remains yet discovered in Europe… a being that is partly ape, partly man. (*Times* 11.08.13: 3)

Secondly, driving Piltdown toward humanness was a strong nationalistic desire to proclaim the find significant enough to rival those made already in mainland Europe. The original *Guardian* report states the find is 'quite as early as anything that has been found in Europe' (21.11.12: 8) and later declares 'it is extremely satisfactory to English scientists that this find should have been made here and that it should have been made by two well-known English geologists' (20.12.12: 16). Following this theme, the *Illustrated London News* refers to 'this Ancient Briton' (28.12.12: 958) and Woodward's own memoir of Piltdown, published only five years before the hoax was unmasked, is entitled *The Earliest Englishman* (1948). In the discussion section of a follow-up paper, a tool found with the remains is referred to as being that most quintessential of the English gentleman's trappings: a 'cricket-bat' (Dawson and Woodward 1915: 148). Whilst the find was overwhelmingly supported as human in the UK, the reception in Europe and America was far more mixed. American palaeoanthropologists Miller (1915, 1918), MacCurdy (1916) and Hrdlicka (1922) all doubted that the find was a single individual (Goulden 2009).

It is clear then that anthropocentricism and nationalism both influenced the manner in which Piltdown was anchored in relation to the human–animal binary within the public realm. The influence of anthropocentricism is similarly visible, almost a century later, in the case of *Homo floresiensis,* to which we now turn.

One of the principle scientists in the Flores find, Mike Morwood, shows his clear awareness of problems brought by blurring scientific and popular categories during anchoring: in his account of the discovery, he states 'The definition of genus *Homo* has always been difficult because it is closely tied to the concept of "being human"' (Morwood and van Oosterzee 2007:97). The conflating of *Homo* and human only makes the task of categorizing the former even more difficult than taxonomy is ordinarily. The former is a scientific category, clearly (though, as we shall see, flexibly) defined, separated from common language not only by its history and usage but also by its capitalization and italicization. 'Human' has no such isolating elements however. As a word and as a concept it is very much a part of both popular culture and of individual's self-perception. As a result it often finds itself tied to other concepts relating to the Self, hence the prominent influence of racism in Piltdown man's journey towards humanness which we discuss below. Additionally, using *Homo* and human interchangeably means that as many as seven other species[2], all now extinct, were human too. Popular culture, however, has only ever applied 'human' to one living species – ourselves – and it is what we are (however that is formulated) which determines its properties. One must question then whether the extension of humanness to other species is semantically coherent. Morwood cites *floresiensis'* ability to use fire and basic stone tools as reason for its declared humanity, but at the same time acknowledges that it lacked several key human characteristics:

> [not] the least hint of symbolic behaviour, such as pigments, art, adornments or formal disposal of the dead, which are core characteristics of all modern human cultures. (2007: 114)

Morwood's keenness to label LB1 human returns us to the anthropocentrism which makes discoveries of 'backwards humans' bigger news than discoveries of 'forward apes'. This attitude encourages both scientists and journalists alike to categorize a find not just as '*Homo*', but also the more emotive, the more personal, 'human'. It quite literally gives a discovery more 'human interest'. Piltdown as a

---

2   As this chapter implies, there is no clear scientific consensus on the number of species within the genus *Homo*, but some list as many as eight – *H. ergaster, H. erectus, H. habilis, H. heidelbergensis, H. neanderthalensis, H. rudolfensis, H. sapiens* (Woods and Collard 1999), plus newly discovered *H. floresiensis*.

human fits well with 'media news values such as meaningfulness and relevance to daily life' (Cassidy 2005: 136). The recollections of Australian science journalist Deborah Smith, who won a Eureka Science Prize for her coverage of *Homo floresiensis*, hints at this too with her usage of the label 'person':

> I can remember the look on my editors face when I went up and said 'now I've got a very good front page story here, its about *a little person*, they hunted pygmy elephants, giant rats, they lived on Australia's doorstep until 12,000 years ago, they fended off Komodo dragons, they've been found by Australian's, and we got all this fantastic graphic material', and she just looked at me and said 'Deborah, *this story has everything*' (2007, authors' italics).

The mixing of the categories of *Homo* and human not only intensifies our self-interest in who, or what, *Homo* includes and excludes, but also leaves scientists attempting to find physical evidence of an intangible concept – what makes a human human? In their original submission to *Nature*, the team which discovered LB1 placed her within a new genus, *Sundanthropus* (meaning 'man from the Sunda region'). Morwood was desperate to label the find *Homo*, stating that:

> Selecting the right name for the species was important scientifically and politically, to ensure that LB1 was not regarded as just some Southeast Asian oddity of little relevance to the understanding of hominid evolution and dispersal generally (Morwood and van Oosterzee 2007: 100–101).

However, fellow scientist and team member Peter Brown refused on the grounds that its skull capacity, at 380 cc, was significantly below the 'Cerebral Rubicon' of 600 c.c., considered mandatory for inclusion in the genus *Homo* (Woods and Collard 1999). The 'Cerebral Rubicon' is demonstrative of the difficulties scientists face in attempting to attribute humanness on the basis of limited physical evidence – it requires a reifying of humanness. Prominent Piltdown scientist Sir Arthur Keith had set this at 750 c.c. (1949), whilst Franz Weidenreich declared it to be 700 c.c. (1943), at least in part because this ensured his discovery, *Pithecanthropus*, was on the human side (Krantz 1961: 86). In the 1960s, the discovery of the smaller brained *Homo habilis* by Louis Leakey (1964) led him to lower the bar further, down to 600 c.c. This is the figure that Wood and Collard cite in their influential[3] (pre-Flores) paper, which Brown used to justify LB1's status outside *Homo*. Morwood's response to this highlights the flaw in the idea that we can determine humanness on the basis of a specific brain capacity:

> But should size matter? I thought. Surely, it is more a question of cognitive capabilities – and there was abundant evidence that the Liang Bua hominids

---

3   Woods and Collard's paper is recorded by the Web of Knowledge (http://wok. mimas.ac.uk/) to have been cited by 164 articles in the last eight years.

were smart. While they did not make adornments, paint, or bury their dead, they made use of fire, and were handy with scrapers, anvils, points and assorted stone implements (Morwood & van Oosterzee 2007:110).

The referees of the *Nature* papers agreed with Morwood, and in the published draft the creature was labelled *Homo floresiensis*. Where this leaves the Cerebral Rubicon, given that chimpanzees (approx. 400 c.c.) now qualify for human status, is a matter for palaeoanthropologists, but here it serves the purpose of demonstrating that there is no hard, empirically-valid point at which the non-human becomes human. This is true not just for brain size, but any other feature one might wish to use:

> In reality, many of these features evolved gradually, and at different rates, and it could not be expected that they evolved suddenly as a 'package'. Thus recognizing the first 'humans' is likely to remain a matter of great controversy, as it was for most of the last century (Stringer and Andrews 2005: 131).

Despite the fact that linking *Homo* and human makes palaeoanthropologists' jobs all the more difficult, the evidence from the case studies shows that they themselves have led the process. Although Morwood rues the difficulties brought by this conjoining, he uses *Homo* and human interchangeably in his discussion of LB1 (2007). He also cites Wood and Collard's paper '*The Human Genus*' (1999), which sets out to clarify several explicit criteria upon which palaeoanthropologists might determine a potential *Homo*'s inclusion or exclusion. Despite drawing attention to the complexities of categorizing a figure as *Homo*, they notably use 'human' as interchangeable with '*Homo*', as their title suggests. In the two papers that announced the discovery (Morwood et al. 2004, Brown et al. 2004), neither claims her as human, settling instead for *Homo*. However, the *Nature* press release for the discovery, which introduced journalists to the find, begins with the sentence

> The discovery of a new species of human living on the Indonesian island of Flores as recently as 18,000 years ago demonstrates that human diversity in the recent past was much greater than expected (2004: 1).

All the press coverage followed this lead and was universal in labelling the find a human, as these opening lines from two newspapers demonstrate:

> SCIENTISTS have discovered a previously unknown species of HUMANS who lived in a lost world stalked by giant rats and mutant elephants (*The Sun* 28.10.04).

When Indonesian and Australian archaeologists started to excavate a limestone cave on the Indonesian island of Flores, they weren't prepared for what they found, the skeleton of an entirely new species of human, *Homo floresiensis*, that lived as recently as 18,000 years ago (*Guardian* 28.10.04).

Linking to pre-existing anchors

Though both missing links considered here were declared human by scientists and journalists, there remained inescapable elements of *otherness* to them. These included their taxonomic positioning outside our species *sapiens*, their physical appearance as given by artists' reconstructions, and their limited capabilities. How then, could these creatures' status as human, but not human *like us*, be fixed? Pre-existing cultural figures that already inhabited a conceptually ambiguous status provide the solution. This is a further element in the process of anchoring, that helps secure a category's position by tying it to others around it.

Unfortunately, the examples used to make sense of Piltdown's humanness were living indigenous tribes, or 'savages' as they were more likely to be labelled. There were two elements to this process. The first achieves its effect simply through the repeated comparison of Piltdown's primitive features with non-whites. In Woodward's (1913: 126) paper, he states that Piltdown's intermediate brain size 'equals that of some of the lowest skulls of the existing Australians'.

Similar claims pepper the news coverage. On the subject of Piltdown's canines (only uncovered later), the *Illustrated London News* states that they would have 'an ape-like character met with in savage races to-day' (28.12.12: 958). On the same page it offers up for comparison photos of three jaws, labeled 'Kaffir', 'Chimpanzee' and 'Indian' respectively. Below it another picture compares three more with 'Chimpanzee' and 'European' either side of a suggested intermediary: 'Torres Strait Islander'. Also in this article, a metaphor regarding the Piltdown eoliths with the same implicit message: 'they speak as surely as did the footprints found by Robinson Crusoe'. The footprints in question were of course those of the black savage, who Robinson called 'Man Friday'. In this way another link is made between Piltdown and non-whites. Of the brain, the *Express* says: 'as large as that of the lowest type of savage – the Australian aboriginal or the Tasmanians' (23.12.12: 1) and similarly, from the *Times*, 'the skull of *Eoanthropus*, though typically human, was as low in brain capacity as that of the lowest existing savages' (17.09.13: 10). The *Guardian* quotes Keith as claiming, 'in size of brain it is human – at least equal to the brains of many individuals in living races' (20.12.12: 16).

The second element is more subtle but just as effective. Throughout the debate there is a continual conflation of the terms 'species' and 'race' such that they become indistinguishable. Stocking's (1994) work shows how 'race' as a concept in the early 20th century was often blurred with others such as 'nation'. The effect achieved in the Piltdown case is that species becomes weakened as a divider and race becomes strengthened. The *Express* describes Piltdown as 'a race of men who could not talk' (20.12.12: 1) and mentions 'the monkey race' (23.12.12: 1). From the *Illustrated London News* we have this theme rendered explicitly in a suggestion that Piltdown is no more different from modern *Homo sapiens* than we are from each other:

> these fragments of man from the Sussex gravel tell us that already at this early period the human race had begun to split up into different peoples (28.12.12: 958).

The use of indigenous tribes in this way allows Piltdown's ape jaw and human skull to travel from the 'doubtful borderland between recognisable man and indubitable ape' (*Guardian* 19.12.12: 16) to become a human no more or less remote from white Europeans than an Aborigine. The fact that this process simultaneously moves non-whites away from us at the same time that it moves Piltdown nearer, presumably only heightened its appeal amongst racist English scientists and journalists of the time.

In the Flores case, occurring almost a century after Piltdown, there was no such living human figure available – to try and claim any living *Homo sapiens* as examples of semi-humanness would be politically unacceptable. Instead, a figure was needed that existed outside the protections of our culturally and ethnically sensitive times. The answer: a fictional creation – the 'hobbit'. It provokes no political sensitivities and performs the role of the 'savage' perfectly – its anthropomorphic form brings it close to us, whilst its diminutive dimensions and hirsuteness keep it distant.

Appearing originally in the fictional work of J.R.R. Tolkien, the hobbits were a diminutive sub-species of human. Despite the enduring popularity of Tolkien's work, it was Peter Jackson's *Lord of the Rings* films that cemented the Hobbit character widely within the contemporary consciousness. An often overlooked element of Tolkien's fantasy is its setting on our own Earth, deep within pre-history:

> he did indeed create a new 'mythology' (or at least mythical mode of thinking) not just suitable but deeply appealing for our time. (Thomas 2006: 83)

It is a pleasing reminder of how popular science blends fact and fiction then that his work – creating an origins story suitable for contemporary interests – should be used to tell the tale of a missing link.

It certainly was used extensively – all seven of the UK newspapers included in our study adopted the hobbit label. Whilst it might be tempting to put the label's usage down to journalistic distortions of science, the reality is that the original connection was made by the scientists who discovered LB1. Peter Brown was against its use, but Morwood and the rest of the team had no such qualms:

As it transpired, the matter was out of Peter's hands; my younger Indonesian colleagues liked the name 'Hobbit' and had begun to use it affectionately for LB1. 'Hobbit' stuck (Morwood and van Oosterzee 2007: 153).

This whole process of anchoring via affiliation is necessary because of the discrepancy between the flexible, multi-category scientific system of taxonomy, and the rigid, binary model of human-animal in popular culture. In this way both missing links were anchored in the category 'human'. Yet whilst each of these structures, taxonomy and binary, differed in positioning of the anchor, each utilized a procedure of comparison to some pre-existing, ambiguous figure. The process of categorizing the unfamiliar, of producing a social representation, whether within science or the media, was not as dissimilar as scientists might wish to be so. These exemplars of quasi-humanity, the savage and the Hobbit, enabled the rapid integration of the foreign physiognomic features of Piltdown and *floresiensis* whilst retaining some of their peregrinate nature. Both realms were prominently shaped by anthropocentricism and nationalism, the former directing the placement they were given, the latter some of the particular connections they made. The product was something like us, but not so much so as to be indistinguishable; related, but not familial; human, but not quite.

We now continue forward by discussing the process of objectifying our missing links, using as examples two narratives that emerged from the case studies.

Objectifying missing links

Whilst the scientific presentation of Piltdown proclaimed it human it did little to justify that decision and rather concerned itself with proxies of humanness such as brain size and speech capabilities. Scientists were happy to explicate Piltdown's humanness in the public realm however, where they provided some of the most sensationalist material, either directly, or in interview with journalists. This material relied far more upon preconceived folk knowledge than it did upon empirical, 'scientific' evidence. It is a similar conclusion that leads Haraway to state, 'Scientific practice is above all a story-telling practice in the sense of historically specific practices of interpretation and testimony' (1989: 4). The first coverage in the *Guardian*, a month prior to the official announcement, not only renders Piltdown a human, but creates a hunter narrative to put flesh on its bones:

It was the age when the cave bear, the woolly-haired rhinoceros, and the mammoth roamed over Europe, and man maintained a strenuous struggle for existence... Palaeolithic man was a river-draft hunter, and the Sussex skull was found in an old river bed. It is open to surmise that he met with his death while following his prey (*Guardian* 21.11.12: 8).

Similar images appeared in coverage elsewhere:

Through the dark forests of our land there roamed, many hundreds of thousands of years ago, a strange, hairy ape-like creature, a female member[4] of a curious race, from whom all other animals shrank. She was a new type, possessing a new cunning, and an amazing power over the other denizens of the forest, for she could do what they could not – use implements, and clothe herself in skins... When she hunted she used no dogs to help her track her prey; she and her companions followed their quarry and killed it with a stone spear or hatchet (*Express* 23.12.12: 1).

now a word or two as to his probable appearance and mode of life, and the creatures which he chased, and was occasionally, in turn, chased by. ... Elephants and rhinoceros of species long since extinct roamed in herds all round him. These and the hippopotamus no doubt he killed for food, and, besides, he must have hunted a species of horse long since extinct, while the lion, bear, and sabre-tooth tiger afforded him plenty of opportunities for hairbreadth escapes. He had probably inherited the use of fire from his forbears, and this useful ally served to harden the ends of his wooden spears, and perhaps to cook his food (*Illustrated London News* 28.12.12: 958).

It might be argued that this is a media driven process to make the find human-relevant, however Woodward himself is quoted in an *Express* article as being the source for a similar claim. It is clear this hunting narrative is not a journalistic distortion of the scientists' research, but rather a feature that is used by scientists and journalists alike to cement Piltdown's humanity. Woodward claims:

The thickness of the skull suggests outdoor life, and the teeth are ground down in a way that human teeth are not usually ground; they indicate a root and vegetable diet, mixed with dust and sand, accidentally introduced. The stone implements found by the skull were rude in design, and were employed in preparing skins, also in cutting wood. It is pretty certain that this was a race of wandering hunters. They had no domestic animals, for no bones of any have been found (in the *Express* 23.12.12: 1).

Tellingly, Woodward presents the hunting narrative despite empirical evidence that seems quite contrary: 'they indicate a root and vegetable diet'. Similarly, in the *Guardian* article (21.11.12: 8) Man 'the river-draft hunter' is so because his skull is found in the river, and no consideration is given to other interpretations

---

4   The 'female' reference follows a suggestion made by Woodward that Piltdown Man was actually Piltdown Woman. The other newspapers ignore this claim, but the *Express* makes great play of it, labelling the find 'The New Woman' – a barely veiled reference to the Suffragette movement that was demanding emancipation for women. The *Express* was highly critical of the Suffragettes, and sought to mock them by drawing parallels. See (Goulden 2007).

– perhaps Piltdown was a particularly poor swimmer? In the *Illustrated London News* (28.12.12: 958) Piltdown 'must' have hunted a species of horse, and 'no doubt' killed hippopotamus for food. This presupposition of a hunting lifestyle, "Man the Hunter", colours the scenery in which man lives with a blood red hue.

Donna Haraway (1989) ascribes this Man the Hunter discourse, most popular in palaeoanthropology during the middle of the 20th century, but present much earlier, to Western Cold-War scientists who created these proto-humans in their own image:

> What it meant to be universal man and to be human generically turns out to look very much like what it meant to be western scientific men, especially in the United States, in the 1950s... Man the Hunter embodied a socially positioned code for deciphering what it meant to be human – in the western sense of unmarked, universal, species being – after World War II (186–187).

Pre-historical figures like Piltdown are receptive to such abstractions, and so are open to being shaped by cultural discourses, such as that of the heroic, technologically-enhanced hunter.

The Man the Hunter trope returns as a prominent repertoire with which Flores' human status is supported within popular culture. However, differences in the actual realization of the Hunter template compared to the Piltdown case demonstrates clearly how it is flexible and open to adaptation, depending on the cultural mood of the time (Cartmill 1993). The imaginings of the creature's life resonate closely with those given of Piltdown some ninety-eight years earlier, with elements of hunting, technology, and terrifying beasts present once again:

> On the island of Flores in the Malay Archipelago, scientists have found remains of a race of three-foot high humans who hunted pony-sized elephants and rats as big as dogs and who battled dragons with saliva laced with deadly bacteria (*Observer* 31.10.04: 21).

> a previously unknown species of HUMANS who lived in a lost world stalked by giant rats and mutant elephants (*The Sun* 28.10.04).

> they used fire, made sophisticated stone tools, and hunted stegodon – a primitive type of elephant – and giant rats (*Daily Telegraph* 28.10.04: 01).

Just as Piltdown's life was narrated as a struggle against monsters given a semi-mythic quality by their absence from our contemporary world, Flores' existence is repeatedly built around bizarre adversaries – huge rats, tiny elephants, and "dragons" – i.e. large lizards related to the Komodo dragon. Despite these constants, there are deviations from the Man the Hunter template. These contemporary twists have at least two sources. The first of these is simply the particular physical characteristics of the discovery – Flores' diminutive stature provided a paradoxically vertiginous hurdle to clear for any scientist or journalist hoping to present the figure in the Mighty Hunter mould. Creating a three foot high fearsome warrior would be no mean feat. The mass media turns this challenge into an advantage however, and makes great play of contrasting Flores' stature with the fellow occupants of its island:

> THE remains of a diminutive cousin of modern Man ..... Also known affectionately as "Flo", it hunted pygmy elephants the size of ponies and giant rats as large as golden retrievers, while trying to avoid huge Komodo dragons and other predatory lizards that are extinct. (*Times* 28.10.04: 6).

> A story of tiny Hobbit-like creatures battling giant, slavering dragons, of forest folk living in a tropical lost world, hunting miniature elephants and rats the size of retrievers (*Daily Mail* 28:10: 04: 24).

Other labels attached to the figure include 'mini-men' (*ibid.*), 'the height of a three-year-old child' (*Daily Telegraph* 28:10:04: 1), 'toddler-sized human' (*ibid.* 03.05.04: 22), and 'no bigger than a dwarf' (*The Express* 28:10:04: 17). The *Times* described the tools found in situ as 'toy-size' (28.10.04: 6). The image created then is more 'Cute Hunter' than Mighty Hunter, perhaps demonstrated best by Australian artist Peter Schouten's iconic image of the creature shown below. Originally commissioned jointly by *National Geographic* and Morwood and Brown's team for the former's initial coverage, the image was widely reproduced in the mass media. Notably, although it features a weapon-wielding figure engaged in hunting – as in Forestier's Piltdown image (*Illustrated London News* 28.12.12: iv,v) – the creature itself is markedly less imposing and is drawn post-hunt in a relatively relaxed state.

The grim determination on the face of Forestier's figure is replaced in Schouten's by a somewhat beatific grin. The sizeable spear carried by Piltdown dwarfs the small club held by Flores. Interestingly, although Brown et al's paper – like that of Dawson and Woodward's – declares the skeleton to be most likely female, Schouten's Hunter – like that of Forestier's – is a male. This repetition also flags up a note of difference, one that purely reflects changing cultural tastes – although both figures appear naked, Piltdown Man's modesty is maintained by a strategically extended thigh. Flores Man apparently has no such qualms, and appears 'full-frontal'. However, in keeping with the character's welcoming charm, the phallus itself is rather non-confrontational in appearance.

The second deviation from the Hunter template is more profound, and more telling of how reimaginings of these figures are structured by their particular socio-political context. In the twenty-first century version of the Hunter template, as expounded in the discourses around the Flores find, the killer has become us. The inspiration for this is the current of misanthropy within post-modernism that Franklin (1999) identifies in our changing relationship with animals. He states:

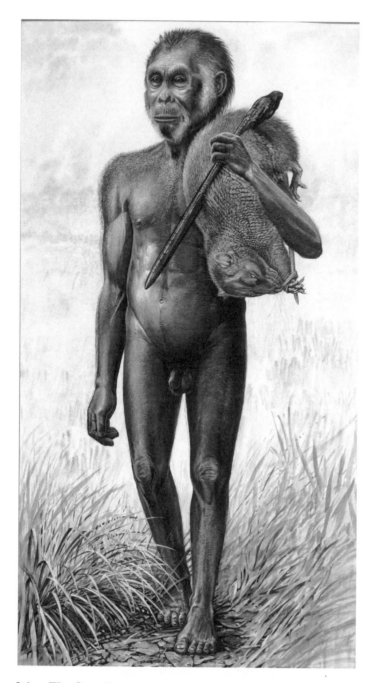

Figure 9.1   The Cute Hunter

Source: The Artwork "Homo floresiensis" by Peter Schouten is reproduced with kind permission by the artist.

Figure 9.2   The Mighty Hunter

Source: The Illustrated London News; 16 August 1913, front cover. © Illustrated London News/Mary Evans Picture Library.

In the late twentieth century a generalized misanthropy has set in: according to this view humans are a destructive, pestilent species, mad and out of control. By contrast, animals are essentially good, balanced and sane (Franklin 1999: 3).

Thus in LB1's media coverage, the Hunter is modern humans:

Many of these [species of hominin] may have been exterminated by Homo sapiens, which is also suspected of genocide in the demise of Homo erectus and Neanderthal Man (*Times* 28.10.04: 6).

And elsewhere:

[The division of human body lice into two species] could only have happened through some act of primal genocide when Homo erectus met Homo sapiens somewhere in eastern Siberia... the lice must have come from very fresh corpses and it is hard to suppose that they had died peacefully just before the intruders turned up (*Guardian.co.uk* 01.11.04).

This theme is further developed by imagining LB1's habitat as a tranquil paradise protecting its inhabitants from the threat of modern humans:

Their Eden remained undisturbed while modern humans colonized the world (*Mirror* 28.10.04:24).

We swept all before us. There was probably no deliberate conquest, just a steady outgunning by spear and arrow of precious resources from rival breeds.... safe in their lost world, the Hobbits lived on, undisturbed by the rise and rise of Homo sapiens (*Daily Mail* 28.10.04: 25).

Prominent in objectifying both figures were hunting narratives. These narratives connected with particular cultural mores specific to the figures' respective periods. Scientists themselves were highly active in this process, and in the case of Piltdown Man at least, they essentially created proto-man in their own image. For objectifying LB1 the hunter narrative remained, but was applied in a manner appropriate to the time. LB1 was not recreated as a Mighty Hunter, but a Cute Hunter. The feared killer became us, modern *Homo* sapiens, and not in a tone that was celebratory. In this way, both creatures were made meaningful for the societies receiving them.

Conclusion

We set out in this chapter to analyse how the categorization of missing links – hybrids of human and nonhuman animal – change as they move from within science outwards into the public realm. During this process the creatures are transferred from the box marked '*Homo*' to the box marked 'human'. The reason for this recategorization was predominantly pragmatic. *Homo* is a category of science, and as such has far less meaning, whether emotional or intellectual, for the general public than does the category human. It was in the interest of scientists and journalists alike to declare both finds human, as this ensured a greater public readership than would otherwise be the case. With public interest comes financial security, for both professions. The fact that the reconfiguration of missing links coincides with their transition from the science media to the news media may appear to implicate journalists alone. In considering the origins of particular claims we demonstrated that scientists themselves were heavily involved in the popularization of Piltdown and LB1.

We charted the processes by which recategorization is achieved through the utility of Moscovici's production of social representations via 'anchoring' and 'objectifying' knowledge. When the discoveries were moved into the popular realm their positional options were reduced to just two categories – human or animal. Scientific taxonomy has, built in to it, a considerable flexibility that popular culture's dichotomous model of human–animal lacks. We saw this with our discussion of the 'Cerebral Rubicon', the classificatory line above which type specimens become *Homo*. The regrading of this requirement, from 750 c.c. down to just 380 c.c., was not achieved without argument among scientists, but it did happen in a relatively short 50 year time span. Popular culture's dichotomous model has remained unchanged for much longer, and is not controlled by a single, broadly homogenous community, as taxonomy is. As such it is exceedingly resistant to reconfiguration. *Homo*'s flexibility means that it can formally incorporate chimeric figures that the popular human–animal binary struggles with. Scientists have the opportunity to simply create a new subcategory when they come across an ambiguous find – hence *Homo floresiensis* and *Eoanthropus dawsoni*. Within the popular binary no such strategy is available: discoveries are either human, or they're not.

Human was chosen by scientists and journalists for the pragmatic reason given above, and, in the case of Piltdown man at least, because nationalist sentiments amongst English stakeholders desired an ancient ancestor to which they could lay claim for the glory of the nation. Scientists and journalists anchored the figures by forcing them into the class human, even whilst acknowledging characteristics that seemed to preclude their entry. The instability of this positioning was fixed more firmly by linking to pre-existing figures who already occupied a tenuous position somewhere close to human, but not quite. Hence 'savages' and hobbits came to play a role in the process.

The fact that such ambiguous figures already exist raises the question of whether there really is a human–animal dichotomy within popular culture, as does their presence not invalidate such a claim? We suggest that there is in fact another category, somewhere between human and animal, but one that only exists unconsciously. Bauman (1991) too describes these 'third categories', claiming they are an inevitable outcome of the non-fit between the contiguous natural world and the dichotomizing human mind that seeks to understand it. When a case appears that does not concur with popular binaries the result is a third category that straddles the division. However, for Bauman, these third categories are a threat to the status quo, as they reveal the dichotomy for the sham it is:

> They are waste, as they defy classification and explode the tidiness of the grid. They are the disallowed mixture of categories that must not mix. They earned their death-sentence by resisting separation. (Bauman 1991: 15)

In our own work, this middle category, somewhere in the no man's land between human and animal, acts to protect the dichotomy by subsuming ambiguous figures. It is for this reason that Goulden labels these middle categories 'trinaries', a concept discussed in more detail elsewhere (Goulden 2007).

The second part of this process of making the unfamiliar familiar, objectifying, consists of scientists and journalists creating a recognizable set of narratives around missing links, as a way of bringing meaning to their newly claimed humanness. 'Man the Hunter' discourses were present in the repertoires built around both Piltdown man and LB1, although the different meanings invested in this trope reflect the fact that such stories are more a mirror of contemporary ideas than a window to the past. Regardless of specific meanings, why Man the Hunter featured in both cases is an interesting question. It may be that the discourse appeals to patriarchal western culture not only because of the militaristic/technological elements that Haraway (1989) identifies, but also because Man the Hunter echoes 'natural man', a man existing without culture. Marks (2003: 166) notes the prominent role that such a figure played in the hugely influential works of Hobbes, Locke and Rosseau. Such figures offer a vision of life stripped bare of the complexities of modernity: existence at its most honest and brutal. Cartmill's analysis of hunting emphasizes how the act is fundamentally an exploration of the boundary:

> hunting takes place at the boundary between the human domain and the wilderness, the hunter stands with one foot on each side of the boundary, and swears no perpetual allegiance to either side. He is a liminal and ambiguous figure, who can be seen either as a fighter against wildness or as a half-animal participant in it (1996: 31).

Perhaps then it is fitting that this repertoire should be used to bring to life missing links, since they too inhabit this borderland, swearing no perpetual allegiance to either side. And, in a more limited sense, it resembles the act of scientific categorization itself, in which scientists occupy a liminal and ambiguous position between science and non-science culture, whilst struggling to impose order on disorder.

References

Bauman, Z. 1991. *Modernity and Ambivalence*. Oxford: Polity Press.

Brown et al. 2004. A new small-bodied hominin from the Late Pleistocene of Flores, Indonesia. *Nature,* 431, 1055–1061.

Cassidy, A. 2005. Popular evolutionary psychology in the UK: An unusual case of science in the media? *Public Understandings of Science,* 14, 115–141.

Cartmill, M. 1993. *A View to a Death in the Morning*. USA: Harvard University Press.

Dart, R. 1926. Taung and its significance. *Natural History*, 26, 315–327.

Dart, R. 1957. The Osteodontokeratic culture of Australopithecus Prometheus. *Transvaal Museum Memoirs*, 10, 1–105.

Dart, R. and Craig, D. 1959. *Adventures with the Missing Link*. New York: Harper.

Daston, L. and Mitman, G. (eds) 2005. *Thinking with Animals: New Perspectives on Anthropomorphism*. USA: Columbia University Press.

Dawson, C. and Woodward, A.S. 1913. On the discovery of a Paleolithic human skull and mandible in a flint-bearing gravel overlying the Wealden (Hastings Beds) at Piltdown, Fletching (Sussex). *Quarterly Journal of the Geological Society of London*, 69, 117–151.

Dupre, J. 2001. In defence of classification. *Studies in History and Philosophy of the Biological and Biomedical Sciences*, 32(2), 203–219.

Franklin, A. 1999. *Animals and Modern Culture*. Trowbridge: SAGE Publications.

The Guardian: http://www.guardian.co.uk/news/2004/nov/01/wormseyeview.wrap [accessed: 1 November 2004].

Goulden, M. 2009. Boundary-work and the human-animal boundary: Piltdown Man, science and the media, *Public Understandings of Science*, 18(3), 275–291.

Goulden, M. 2007. Bringing bones to life: how science made Piltdown Man human, *Science as Culture*, 16(4), 333–357.

Haraway, D. 1989. *Primate Visions: Gender, Race, and Nature in the World of Modern Science*. USA: Routledge.

Hrdlicka, A. 1922. The Piltdown Jaw. *American Journal of Physical Anthropology*, 5, 327–347.

Keith, A., Sir. 1949. *A New Theory of Human Evolution*. New York: Philosophical Library.

Krantz, G.S. 1961. Pithecanthropine brain size and its cultural consequences. *Man* 102 (May), 85–87.

Latour, B. 1993. *We Have Never Been Modern*. Hemel Hempstead: Harvester Wheatsheaf.

Leakey, L.S.B., Tobias, P.V. and Napier, J.R. 1964. A new species of the genus *Homo* from Olduvai Gorge. *Nature*, 202(4927), 7–9.

Lievrouw, L. 1990. Communication and the social representation of scientific knowledge. *Critical Studies in Mass Communication* 7(1), 1–10.

MacCurdy, G.G. 1916. The revision of Eoanthropus Dawsoni. *Science* 43, 228–231.

Marks, J. 2003 *What it Means to be 98% Chimpanzee*. USA: University of California Press.

Miller, G.S. 1915. The jaw of Piltdown Man. *Smithsonian Miscellaneous Collection*, 65, 1–31.

Miller, G.S. 1918, The Piltdown Jaw. *American Journal of Physical Anthropology*, 1, 25–52.

Morwood et al. 2004. Archaeology and age of a New Hominin from Flores in Eastern Indonesia. *Nature*, 431, 1087–1091.

Morwood, M.J. and van Oosterzee, P. 2007. *The Discovery of the Hobbit: The Scientific Breakthrough that Changed the Face of Human History*. Sydney: Random House.

Moscovici, S. 1961. *La psychanalyse, son image et son public*, Paris: Presses Universitaires de France.

Moscovici, S. 1998. The history and actuality of social representations, in *The Psychology of the Social Cambridge*, edited by Uwe Flick. Cambridge University Press, 209–248.

Stringer, C. and Andrews, P. 2005. *The Complete World of Human Evolution*. Thames & Hudson Ltd: China.

Stocking, G.W. 1994. The turn-of-the-century concept of race. *Modernism/ Modernity* 1(1), 4–16.

Thomas, K. 1996. *Man and the Natural World*. Oxford: Oxford University Press.

Thomas, P.E. 2006 Scholarship in honor of Richard E. Blackwelder, in *The Lord of the Rings 1954–2004*, edited by Hammon, W.G. and Scull, C. Marquette University Press: USA.

Weidenreich, F. 1943. The skull of *Sinanthropus pekinensis*: a comparative study of a primitive hominid skull. *Palaeontologica*. Sinica New Series D. no. 10 Whole Series no. 127, 1–162.

Wood, B and Collard, M. 1999. The human genus. *Science*, 284(2), 65–71.

Index